Recipes for

"The book is EXCELLENT! I'm ve
very proud to have my name associ

"I was amazed at how many good dishes they were able to create even with the limitations of the earlier phases of the diet."

Scott Forsgren, www.betterhealthguy.com

"Finally, a cookbook I can give to my clients with food sensitivities without hesitation!"

Kelly Lang, Certified Health Coach

"Coupled with gorgeous photographs, the recipes should appeal to anyone seeking wholesome food. No sense of deprivation here. And no need for the cook to be preparing two different menus for people with a different health status."

Dorothy Kupcha Leland, book review on LymeDisease.Org's Touched by Lyme blog

"**If I could give this 6 stars, I would.** I want to sing this book's praises. ... Lost 20 pounds. Feel even better. ... please give this a try. It's been better than any of the medications I've been on."

★★★★★ *Sleepy Dad, Amazon.com reviewer*

"**BEST recipe book I have EVER bought.** Both my husband and I have Lyme disease and it has been such a challenge to cook for this, until this cookbook! My husband says I have never made better food and it makes having to restrict what we eat a pleasure rather than a pain."

★★★★★ *Rachelle, Amazon.com reviewer*

"**A healthy, delicious way to eat for just about anyone.** After following the diet for a week, my joint pain has decreased by 75%. Meanwhile, I have lost 8 pounds without cutting back on calories and feeling hungry. The recipes are easy to follow and the results are phenomenal."

★★★★★ *Kathryn, Amazon.com reviewer*

"This book is a great way to start and maintain your elimination diet. It is easy and has really great tasting recipes and tips. I actually hate to cook, but this book has been a great success in our household. It has also made me feel better!"

★★★★★ *TiffT, Amazon.com reviewer*

Updated and Expanded Second Edition

Recipes for Repair

A 10-Week Program to Combat Chronic Inflammation and Identify Food Sensitivities

By Gail Piazza and Laura Piazza

Foreword by Kenneth B. Singleton, MD, MPH
Author of *The Lyme Disease Solution* and the
Lyme Inflammation Diet® featured in this book

PECONIC
PUBLISHING, LLC

Recipes for Repair: A 10-Week Program to Combat
Chronic Inflammation and Identify Food Sensitivities

Copyright © 2016 Gail Piazza and Laura Piazza
Foreword copyright © 2016 by Kenneth B. Singleton, MD, MPH

All rights reserved. No part of this publication may be reproduced or transmitted in any form or by any means, mechanical or electronic, including photocopy, recording, or any other information storage and retrieval system, without written permission from the publisher.

Book design and photography by Laura Piazza
Recipe development and food styling by Gail Piazza
Copy editing by Elizabeth Urello

The text relevant to the Lyme Inflammation Diet® and chronic inflammation (pages 14-31) was adapted from *The Lyme Disease Solution*, with permission from Kenneth B. Singleton, MD, MPH.

Library of Congress Cataloging-in-Publication Data
Piazza, Gail; Piazza, Laura
Recipes for Repair: A 10-Week Program to Combat
Chronic Inflammation and Identify Food Sensitivities

Published by
Peconic Publishing, LLC, PO Box 265, Sunapee, NH 03782

Orders can be placed at www.recipesforrepair.com

ISBN-13: 978-0-9830977-4-7
ISBN: 0-9830977-4-7
LCCN: 2016940607

1 2 3 4 5 6 7 8 9 10

Printed and manufactured in the United States of America
Second Edition

Disclaimer: This book provides healthy and nutritious recipes and all information provided is for educational purposes only. All matters regarding your health, including changes in your diet, should be discussed with a health practitioner. Those who might be at risk from the effects of salmonella poisoning should consult with their doctor before consuming raw eggs. Neither the authors nor the publisher assume any responsibility or liability for any possible adverse effects resulting from the use of information contained within this book.

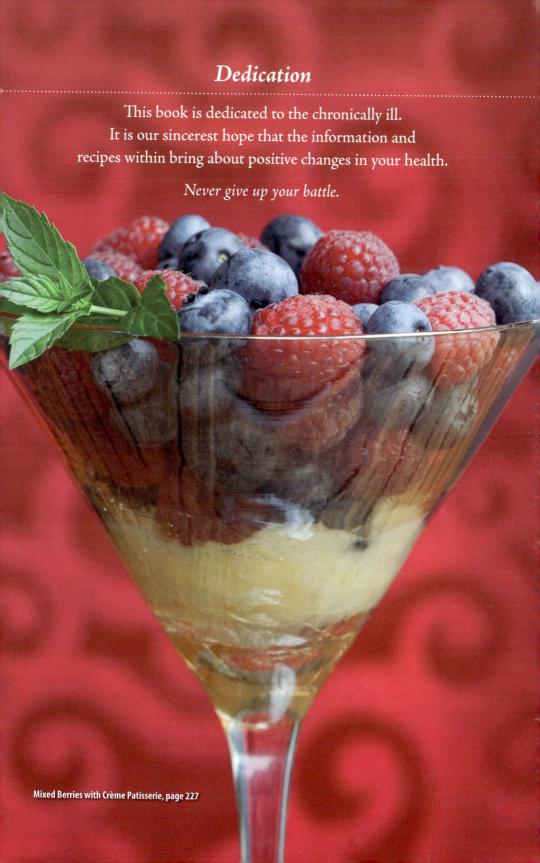

Dedication

This book is dedicated to the chronically ill.
It is our sincerest hope that the information and
recipes within bring about positive changes in your health.

Never give up your battle.

Mixed Berries with Crème Patisserie, page 227

Table of Contents

Dedication 3
Foreword 6
Introduction 10

Part I: Understanding Chronic Inflammation 13-22
    The Mechanisms of Chronic Inflammation. 14
    The Causes of Chronic Inflammation 15
    Chronic Inflammation and Lyme Disease 16
    Ed's Success Story: Lyme Disease 19
    Assessing Your Risk for Chronic Inflammation 19
    Dr. Singleton's Chronic Inflammation Self-Assessment Tool. . . 20
    Toxins and Enzymes 22
    The Need for Detoxification 22
    Enzymes and Their Role 22

Part II: The Lyme Inflammation Diet 23-51
    Phases of the Diet 24
    Chrissy's Success Story: Aches and Pains, Allergies,
        Brain Fog, PMS, Fatigue and a Thyroid Condition 25
    Complete List of Allowable Foods. 26
    General Food Guidelines 28
    Dealing with Sugar Cravings 29
    Food Choices for Detoxification 29
    Dr. Singleton's Special Dietary
        Considerations for Problem Headaches. 31
    Using the Symptom Journal with the Diet 32
    Emily's Success Story: IBS and Hashimoto's Disease 33
    Lyme Inflammation Diet Food Glossary 34
    Nuts and Seeds 39
    Beans, Peas and Lentils 40
    Whole Grains 42
    Fats 43
    Refined Foods: Progress or Setback? 44
    Organic Versus Conventional 45
    How to Read "Nutrition Facts" Food Labels 48
    How to Save 50

Part III: Getting Started 53-289
   "Week Zero"—Preparing for the Diet 54
   Snack Ideas and Easy Meal Suggestions 56
   Packaged Foods That Comply with the Diet 57
   Adding Cultured Foods to Your Diet 57
   Dr. Singleton's Tips on Probiotics with the Use of Antibiotics . . 58
   Using Recipes as a Template 59
   Introductory Cooking Terms for Beginners 59
   Before You Cook, Remember.... 63
   Explanation of the Recipes 64

   Phase 1 Contents 66
   Phase 1: The Induction Phase 67
   Modifying Fruit Consumption While Using Antibiotics 67
   Foods Allowed During Phase 1 68
   Food Sensitivities and Testing 69
   Why Eggs are Included in Phase 1. 69
   Phase 1 Meal Plan. 70
   Phase 1 Recipes 72-117

   Phase 2 Contents 118
   Phase 2: The Early Reentry Phase. 119
   Foods Allowed During Phase 2 120
   Phase 2 Recipes 121-163

   Phase 3 Contents 164
   Phase 3: The Late Reentry Phase 165
   Foods Allowed During Phase 3 166
   Gluten-Free Baking Tips 167
   Phase 3 Recipes 168-233

   Phase 4 Contents 234
   A Note About Gluten. 234
   Phase 4: The Maintenance Phase 235
   Foods Allowed During Phase 4 235
   Phase 4 Recipes 236-255

   Pantry Contents. 256
   Pantry Recipes. 258-268

   Sauces & Condiments Contents 269
   Sauces & Condiments Recipes. 270-289

   Resources 290-292
   Acknowledgements 293
   Index 294-308
   About the Authors 309

Foreword

What if I were to tell you that one simple thing can improve your energy and reduce your pain within hours, help you lose unwanted weight within days, and improve your mood within minutes? You might call it a miracle. Or maybe you'd call it a wonder drug.

And what if I were to tell you that this simple thing does not come from the medical field or the scientific community, is affordable to everyone and can be exceptionally pleasing to all five senses: taste, smell, sight, touch and even sound? You might say it was beyond miraculous.

Hippocrates said "Let food be your medicine, and let medicine be your food." How interesting that the father of Western medicine knew some 2,400 years ago that food is not only meant for basic sustenance, but also as medicine to cure disease and promote health.

Food is indeed very powerful medicine. Healthy food, tastily and pleasantly prepared, is especially powerful, because it heals both the body and the soul. This book is a guide to help you discover the healing power of healthy and tasty foods.

Today, an epidemic of chronic inflammation confronts us. After nearly forty five years of practice as medical doctor (MD), I can say with great confidence that this outbreak is out of control. The list of serious disorders linked to chronic inflammation is extremely long, and it grows longer every day, with no solution or end in sight. Medicine does not yet have the right kinds of drugs to treat or prevent this scourge, nor does medicine have a good idea for how to prevent it.

Hippocrates knew the answer: food!

Fortunately, healthcare science is beginning to recognize the vital importance of nutrition. More and more published articles explain how foods can heal, and it is increasingly recognized and scientifically documented that food is a powerful influencer of health and disease.

As a board-certified specialist in Internal Medicine, I have worked a long time in the field of chronic disease care (the focus of over 85% of all healthcare spending in the United States). About seventeen years ago, I discovered that I had Lyme disease. Since my recovery, which included gaining total control of all inflammatory symptoms, I have devoted much of my practice to helping other people with Lyme and similar tick-borne diseases regain their health by using the principles I learned through research and experience.

In treating patients with chronic Lyme and similar diseases, I have learned that proper nutrition is a critical factor in healing and recovery. Moreover, I discovered that an integrative approach – combining conventional medicine, including antibiotics, with natural, holistic therapies – is the only way to fully reclaim your health.

Yes, regaining vitality and health is possible, and you should never give up hope. Remember that it's always too soon to quit. The odds of recovery are greatly increased once a patient takes responsibility for his or her own health, and makes a good approach to lifestyle – especially nutrition – a fundamental component of his or her recovery plan.

As a result of what I learned in my personal Lyme disease journey, combined with what my patients taught me over the years, I decided to write a book that would help others understand basic principles of Lyme recovery. That book is *The Lyme Disease Solution*, published in 2008. It is the first physician-authored, Lyme-oriented book to include at its core a truly comprehensive and integrative approach to Lyme disease recovery. Reflecting the impact of diet and food on Lyme-related chronic inflammation, I included a major chapter on diet and nutrition in the book.

That chapter, Chapter Five, recognizes the crucial role of nutrition in the healing process and integrates that information into a total program for recovery of health. The chapter introduces the Lyme Inflammation Diet® (LID), which provides a wide-ranging nutritional program to reduce inflammation. It describes a multi-phase program to eliminate unhealthy foods and promote healthy, detoxifying foods, followed by slow reintroduction of additional healthy foods.

Thousands of patients with inflammation from a variety of inflammatory or autoimmune conditions have tried the LID approach to nutrition with excellent results overall. In fact, according to patient response and feedback, the LID chapter has been perhaps the most helpful section in my entire book.

Several of my colleagues direct their patients to "read Chapter Five of Dr. Singleton's book" for a detailed approach to their nutrition needs. Patients, in turn, often say that it changed their lives. While there is no such thing as "one size fits all" when it comes to diet or therapy, about 75% of my patients say that the nutrition program made a positive difference for them.

Anthony is one example of the effectiveness of the LID nutrition program. He didn't really believe that diet could make much difference in his joint inflammation pain. Then he tried the LID, and was shocked by how eliminating two simple food types (gluten-containing grains and casein-containing dairy) dramatically reduced his joint symptoms. Incidentally, his gut symptoms also got much better. He said to me: "Gee, doc. I had no idea how much the bread and dairy were contributing to my symptoms. As much as I love pizza, I guess for now I'll have to let it go." He is right when he says "for now." Many patients are later able to reintroduce some foods to which they are sensitive, but only in a planned, phased-in manner over time.

As delighted as people were with the LID chapter, it mainly provided an overview of healthy, anti-inflammatory dietary principles. While the chapter did include several helpful and delicious recipes, it was not a "how to" recipe book. Overwhelmingly, people wanted more recipes, and they also wanted more LID-friendly food choices. Based on the feedback I received, it was also clear that people wanted recipes that were easy to follow that their families would also enjoy.

Thus, a recipe-based companion book to the LID was needed, with additional food options added to the program. Fortunately, as so often happens, the time must have been right. In 2009, soon after my wife and I began discussing the need for a new book to deal with these issues, I received a letter from Laura Piazza proposing a book that would meet that need. *Recipes for Repair* was the result.

In this book, Gail and Laura Piazza did a masterful job of developing dozens of delicious and beautifully presented recipes based on the principles of the Lyme Inflammation Diet. The wonderful flavors and appearance of these tasty recipes are such that the entire family (not just the patient) will enjoy them.

Anna would agree. She was diagnosed with Lyme disease, chronic fatigue syndrome, seizure disorder, and arthritis. Although not a patient of my medical practice, she was so excited by her success on the LID program, and specifically *Recipes for Repair*, she reached out to Laura and Gail to share her experience. Within the first few weeks of starting the diet, she started to see profound improvements in her symptoms. She began to notice major reductions in joint inflammation, in bowel issues such as chronic constipation, and in "sugar crashes" from blood sugar fluctuations.

Additionally, she discovered that having *Recipes for Repair* was essential for proper implementation of the diet for a very important reason. She realized that using the recipes in the book assured her that she would be ingesting only the ingredients she was supposed to be eating on the diet. In other words, she didn't have to figure out whether the food components were the right ones or not. If they were in the recipe, they were the right ingredients! The recipes made compliance so much simpler for her.

Not only did she thoroughly enjoy all the recipes, but she also said that she never felt deprived. Her girlfriend, who was also following the diet initially in order to support her, was especially pleased to find that she too loved all the recipes. Truly, this is a testament to Gail's superior culinary talents! She created the recipes in this book the way she would for any of her clients – with taste and ease in mind. When recipes didn't meet her high standards they did not make it out of her test kitchen.

Keep in mind that the practical, affordable, expertly designed recipes are for the repair and healing of chronic inflammation from *any* cause. In addition, this new edition contains a much-expanded food list based on my consultation with the authors, as well as updated information about the LID program itself and I have also shared my thoughts on food sensitivity testing (page 69).

Now, please allow me to briefly introduce the authors and my friends, Gail and Laura. Gail Piazza is a home economist with a Master's degree in Food and Nutrition from New York University. A highly experienced food expert, she has been developing delicious recipes and styling food for over 40 years for high profile clients such as Emerilware, Dr. Andrew Weil, All-Clad, Lennox and Farberware. Along with expert recipe development, she has styled food in thousands of attractive images and her work is seen in print ads, packaging, commercials and movies. Her considerable talents are obvious in this cookbook.

Gail's daughter, Laura Piazza, is a graphic designer and professional photographer with nearly 20 years of experience. She has designed this book to present both health and food information in a simple, engaging manner, and has used her unique artistic skills to capture recipes in gorgeous color photographs. Incidentally, Laura is also a Lyme patient who has herself struggled with chronic inflammation, just like most chronic Lyme patients. After experiencing positive results with the diet, she has remained in the maintenance Phase of the diet since she first implemented it in 2009.

Food-based healing is possible, and *Recipes for Repair* is a wonderful resource to help you accomplish your healing goals in a way that's highly satisfying to all of your senses. Gail and Laura have created a book that is not only healthful, but also beautiful and easy to put into practice. Regardless of your likes and dislikes, you will find appetizing recipe solutions here. Try them, and I promise you won't be sorry. Monitor your progress, and it won't be long before you see the difference that these recipes will make in your life and in the lives of your family members.

Please enjoy this wonderful book, and taste the difference health can make!

Kenneth B. Singleton, MD, MPH
Author, *The Lyme Disease Solution*

Introduction

After years of misdiagnoses, in 2009 I was finally properly diagnosed with, and began treatment for, Lyme disease and two other tick-borne diseases.

As I would quickly discover, there was and continues to be a lack of understanding surrounding Lyme disease and other tick-borne illnesses, not just among the general population, but also in the medical community. I began a quest to learn as much as I could about these illnesses.

One book that I found to be most encouraging was *The Lyme Disease Solution*, by Kenneth B. Singleton, MD, MPH. Not only is Dr. Singleton a Lyme-literate medical doctor, but he actually had a misdiagnosed case of Lyme disease himself and is now recovered. What inspired me most was his view on nutrition and its relationship to healing, which was new to me and prompted me to make major, permanent dietary changes.

Chapter 5 in his book was all about nutrition and outlined the Lyme Inflammation Diet (LID), a multi-phase nutritional plan that he developed to help patients learn how to eat a diet rich in nourishing foods with known anti-inflammatory properties and to help them discover unidentified food sensitivities.

At first glance, I was hesitant: the initial week-long Phase is quite restrictive, because it is designed to jumpstart the body's detoxification process. The foods I was accustomed were not permitted until Phase 3, making me wonder if I could survive the first four weeks.

I decided to call my mother, Gail, who has been professionally developing recipes for over 40 years and is the most creative and accomplished cook I've ever known. She asked me to email her the list of allowable foods in Phase 1. Shortly after receiving the list, she called to say that there was PLENTY I could eat, and she would come up with some recipes for me. By the end of the day, I had received several delicious-looking recipes. I started to think following the diet was not going to be nearly as challenging as I had feared.

After following the diet for only a few days, I had an epiphany. My mom, besides being a talented cook and recipe developer, has spent her career styling food for books, ads and product packaging. And I make my living as a graphic designer and photographer. Together, I determined, we could use our skills to create a cookbook filled with delicious and nutritious meals specific to Dr. Singleton's diet. I wrote to him to see if he had ever considered publishing a cookbook specific to his diet.

A few weeks later, he called and said that he and his wife, who is a nutritionist, had been considering the same idea. The eventual outcome was *Recipes for Repair: A Lyme Disease Cookbook* (the first edition of this book).

Since its first publication in 2010, we have learned that the diet has helped readers with a variety of inflammatory and autoimmune conditions, not just Lyme disease. This doesn't come as a great surprise, however, because as we are learning, inflammation is a major contributor to most, if not all, chronic conditions. At its core, the diet is an anti-inflammatory diet, so it makes sense that people with other inflammatory conditions would succeed with it.

Lyme Inflammation Diet Versus the Paleo Diet

Several years ago I developed a yeast overgrowth (a side effect from Lyme treatment) and so had to make further modifications to my diet in that I discovered I needed to remove all grains, legumes and starches. In essence, I was on the Paleo diet. While the further dietary restrictions did help with my new condition, I also found that it severely zapped my energy. Once I was feeling better I slowly reintroduced some grains, legumes and starches and with this my energy level greatly improved.

This experience gave me an even greater appreciation for the Lyme Inflammation Diet, because when you work your way through the 10-week elimination portion of the diet (Phases 1-4), the end result is a truly customized plan that is the perfect plan for you. I find that this approach results in a more inclusive diet, allowing a larger variety of healthy and nourishing foods. It seems a shame to eliminate high-quality foods that your body can tolerate (or even thrives on) and the important nutrients those foods have.

We believe that implementing the Lyme Inflammation Diet and discovering unrecognized food sensitivities can have a profound impact on your health.

We also understand that making such a change may pose quite a challenge, especially if you are not used to cooking from scratch, rely on the convenience of packaged foods, and/or not feeling well. After years of living the diet and receiving feedback from readers, we've worked hard to provide a resource that will help you more easily make important changes to your diet, so you can reap the benefits the way that I have.

The New Edition

We've divided the book into three parts. Part I features information about chronic inflammation adapted from Dr. Singleton's *The Lyme Disease Solution*. Here you will gain an understanding of contributors to chronic inflammation and how they impact your health. You can also use Dr. Singleton's self-assessment tool to determine if you are at a high risk for chronic inflammation.

Part II introduces you to the Lyme Inflammation Diet. You will learn about the four Phases of the diet, allowable foods, food guidelines, about the importance of eating organic foods, how to read nutrition labels and more.

Part III covers both preparation for and implementation of the diet. It also teaches you how best to transition your way to a new and healthier way of eating. We want to make this process easy, so we've devised a diet preparation planning period called "week zero." Here, we give you pointers on how to best prepare. We've also created a meal plan for Phase 1, which is the most restricted week of the diet. We have divided the last part of the book into sections based on the four Phases of the diet and have included a contents page of the recipes for each. Here the recipe titles have symbols indicating whether a recipe is egg-free, dairy-free, vegetarian and/or Paleo (for those who do find that they do best on a diet free of grains, starches, dairy and legumes). We no longer indicate if a recipe is gluten-free because every recipe in this new edition is now gluten-free!

In all, there are over 180 recipes—25 of which have been revised and 52 that are brand new to this edition. The recipes are created from all-natural, whole foods, without refined ingredients, cane sugar or artificial ingredients.

As I implemented the diet all those years ago, I benefited from my mother's extraordinary culinary talents. I envisioned a book that would help others benefit from and succeed at the diet the way I did, all while enjoying my mother's delicious meals. My vision has come to fruition in ways I could have never expected and we have been delighted to hear all the reader success stories over the years.

We've had such positive feedback from readers who tell us they never feel deprived because of the delicious recipes and that they are thrilled that they can serve them to friends and family without disclaimer.

It is our hope that the information and recipes in this book will help you realize that changing your eating habits is an achievable goal—one that can be filled with many wonderful family meals.

Laura Piazza, co-author
Recipes for Repair

Part I
Understanding Chronic Inflammation

Inflammation is a natural part of your immune system's healing process. Marked by increased blood flow, swelling, redness and warmth, inflammation helps contain harmful irritants or isolate an injury, while also rushing healing agents to the afflicted area.

At times, however, inflammation gets out of control – your immune system thinks your body is under continuous attack – and this can lead to an abnormal, long-lasting state called *chronic inflammation*.

Chronic inflammation is a cause of many symptoms associated with autoimmune and inflammatory conditions, including tick-borne illnesses. You may experience symptoms like joint and muscle pain, swelling, stiffness, indigestion, congestion, diarrhea, breathing difficulties, weight gain, insomnia, headaches, to name a few. Many health conditions and environmental factors can cause chronic inflammation. The Standard American Diet (known, too appropriately, as SAD) is notorious for causing and exacerbating inflammation.

No matter what the cause of your inflammatory symptoms, you may find it helpful to learn about the mechanisms and causes of chronic inflammation, the problems they can cause and how nutrition can help.

Below, we look at how chronic inflammation works and the factors that cause it, in preparation for understanding how improving your diet can be an effective anti-inflammation strategy.

The Mechanisms of Chronic Inflammation
Inflammation is a normal bodily process triggered by your immune system in response to injury, infection, allergens, temporary stress or other damaging factors. In healthy people, the inflammation process is *acute*: short-lived, and ending when the original problem is resolved. When inflammation becomes chronic, however, a wide range of health problems can eventually arise.

To better understand why chronic inflammation is so hazardous, let's look at what happens inside your body when inflammation becomes chronic.

At the beginning of an acute inflammation response, your immune system rapidly releases specific hormones, proteins and other chemicals that act in unison to dilate your blood vessels. This increases blood flow and swells tissue in the area the immune system is attempting to heal. The immune system then unleashes a second wave of chemicals – cytokines, eosinophils, prostaglandins, leukotrines and interleukins – that continue the inflammation process, resulting in further tissue swelling, redness and possibly sensations of heat and pain.

The body then makes proteins called *antibodies* that seek out and attach to the invaders, which are called antigens. When the antibodies and the antigens come together in battle, they form what are called *circulating immune complexes* (CICs).

Good CICs occur when there are enough antibodies to exceed and overwhelm the antigens. This type of CIC causes a chemical reaction that enables the white blood cells to eat (or phagocytize) the foreigners. The CICs are then cleared away in the bloodstream, and inflammation is kept to a minimum.

Bad CICs occur when there aren't enough antibodies to overwhelm the invaders, and the CICs contain more antigen than antibody. When this happens, the CICs become deposited in tissue instead of being cleared by the white blood cells, resulting in inflammation.

Chronic inflammation can be caused by an unresolved acute inflammatory response like the one just described, or it may develop on its own (encouraged by several factors described below). In either case, the immune system believes the body is still under attack, and tries to continue its healing functions. This action is appropriate in the case of an infection as the body *is* still under attack! But in other cases, the perception of attack by the immune system is faulty.

The result is that the immune system literally starts to attack the wrong parts of the body, such as joints, organs and other tissues. This inappropriate activity on the part of the immune system is known as *autoimmune dysfunction*, an increasingly common cause of chronic inflammation in many people today.

The Causes of Chronic Inflammation
Medical science recognizes several specific potential causes of inflammation. Most of these are rooted in or exacerbated by poor diet, and the Lyme Inflammation Diet can help you avoid or overcome them.

Below are some of the potential causes:

- **Infectious Microorganisms.** Bacteria, mold, fungi, parasites and viruses all initiate an inflammation response that can become chronic if the offenders can't be eliminated. Some organisms even disrupt the body's normal inflammation control mechanisms for their own protection.

> **Chronic Inflammation and Lyme Disease**
>
> This book was previously published under the name *Recipes for Repair: A Lyme Disease Cookbook*. In it, we focused more heavily on Lyme disease but have since discovered that the diet developed by Dr. Singleton targets any chronic inflammatory condition. If you do have Lyme disease, however, and would like to learn more about chronic inflammation and Lyme disease, this box of information is for you.
>
> Lyme disease and chronic inflammation are a terrible combination, and the degree to which chronic low-grade inflammation exists in the body is directly related to the severity of symptoms that Lyme patients experience.
>
> Lyme disease itself can trigger chronic inflammation, and any inflammation that exists before infection impairs the immune system's ability to fight off the invading bacteria. The cycle of infection and increasing inflammation gives the bacteria an ever-stronger foothold in the body, causing increasingly severe health symptoms. This relationship between chronic inflammation and Lyme disease explains why the severity of symptoms for people with widespread Lyme disease can vary so greatly, with some people nearly incapacitated and others only mildly affected.
>
> Fortunately, following the diet should, over time, produce powerful anti-inflammatory effects. The reduction in inflammation will in turn reduce the burden on your body's immune system and other organ systems, so that it can more effectively target and eliminate the bacteria from Lyme and/or other tick-borne co-infections.

- **Allergies and Sensitivities.** Though the terms are often used interchangeably, allergy and sensitivity are actually caused by quite different immune mechanisms. An example of a food allergy is peanut allergy, which causes an immediate, severe, often life-threatening reaction. An example of a food sensitivity is celiac disease, in which a non-allergic immune reaction occurs in response to gluten, resulting in chronic inflammation as long as the person keeps eating foods containing gluten. Most chronic inflammation triggers are sensitivities rather than allergies: because exposure to the sensitizing substance is persistent, the immune system doesn't shut down the normal inflammation process. The first 10 or so weeks of the diet will help you to determine if you are sensitive to any foods that you are eating (page 24).

- **Environmental Toxins and Pollutants.** When toxins and pollutants become lodged in the body, the immune system struggles to eliminate them, resulting in chronic inflammation. Toxic environmental chemicals can cause a variety of additional health problems, including cancer, that also throw off the immune system. .

- **Cigarette Smoking.** Smoking is a significant cause of chronic inflammation and reduced immune function. If you smoke, seek help in quitting.

- **Free Radical Damage.** Free radicals are unstable atom groups that occur naturally as part of the body's oxidation process. They are normally balanced by the presence of antioxidants, which act to neutralize them. When this process fails, the unchecked free radicals circulate throughout the body, damage cells, and lead to chronic inflammation. An unbalanced diet low in foods containing antioxidants (fruits and vegetables) and high in foods that contribute to excessive oxidation (processed and fried foods) is a major contributor to chronic inflammation.
- **Fatigue and Lack of Sleep.** Failing to get at least seven or more hours of sleep on a regular basis can lead to persistent or chronic fatigue. This in turn causes stress and low energy levels, which can contribute to chronic inflammation. Sleep disruption may also alter the endorphin cycle and hinder proper adrenal function, both important bodily processes for controlling inflammation.
- **Lack of Regular Exercise.** Among its many health benefits, exercise helps to reduce stress. Conversely, lack of exercise can contribute to stress buildup, thereby leading to chronic inflammation. Additionally, exercise strengthens and regulates the immune system – and its ability to regulate inflammation – by increasing the body's normal production of endorphins.
- **Obesity.** Chronic inflammation is often a problem for people who are overweight because fat cells may release chemical substances (*cytokines*) that can cause inflammation. Many obese people also suffer from two other significant contributors to chronic inflammation: insulin resistance and leptin resistance.
- **Insulin Resistance.** Insulin is a hormone produced by the pancreas to help pass glucose from the bloodstream, where it circulates to the cells that need it to function. Glucose is a type of sugar that acts as the body's chief fuel; its primary source is carbohydrates in our diet. Insulin resistance occurs when the amount of insulin produced by the pancreas is too small to enable glucose to pass into the cells. Glucose then builds up in the blood, and the pancreas tries to produce even more insulin to balance the glucose level. This imbalance can result in high blood sugar (hyperglycemia) or type 2 diabetes, and can also encourage chronic inflammation. Chronic inflammation itself can also cause insulin resistance, resulting in a vicious cycle of unhealthy consequences.
- **Leptin Resistance.** Leptins belong to a special class of hormones known as *adipokines* that are produced by your body's fat cells. Leptins help the brain know how much body fat you have, helping to reduce appetite and increase metabolism so you don't become overweight. In women, leptins also help

regulate fertility and the functioning of the ovaries. Leptin resistance occurs when leptins no longer perform their job properly. The problem isn't that the leptins are malfunctioning, but that the fat cells aren't properly responding to the messages the leptins are sending them. This causes the body to produce even more leptins, which in turn can contribute to chronic inflammation. As with insulin resistance, chronic inflammation can also cause leptin resistance, setting up another vicious cycle of unhealthy conditions in the body.

- **Advanced Glycation End Products (AGEs).** These unstable, toxic compounds form when excessive simple sugars abnormally bind to proteins. The body mounts an immune attack against the resulting "foreign" AGEs, resulting in inflammation. AGEs have been associated with several diseases linked to chronic inflammation, including Alzheimer's disease, arthritis, atherosclerosis (hardening of the arteries), diabetes, high blood pressure and certain types of vision problems including cataracts and macular degeneration.

    There are two sources of AGEs. *Exogenous* AGEs are already present in food we eat, especially in poor-quality carbohydrates (such as cakes and donuts) and fried or high-temperature-cooked foods (such as barbecued meats). *Endogenous* AGEs are created in the body after we ingest certain foods, usually after the excessive use of sugar (such as sucrose and glucose) and fructose (such as high fructose corn syrup). Either way, AGEs contribute to inflammation, and their primary source is a poor diet of unhealthy carbohydrates, sugar and overcooked foods.

- **Poor Diet.** Perhaps the most widespread and serious cause of chronic inflammation is eating foods that either encourage chronic inflammation, or don't encourage a healthy body and immune system, or both. The standard diet of most people in the United States is excessive in processed fast foods and other nutrient-deficient food products, and is the number one lifestyle choice responsible for our nation's healthcare crisis. It's a primary source of free radicals, food allergens, oxidized fats (from fried foods), excessive omega-6 fatty acids (and deficient omega-3s), empty calories, sugar, AGEs and many, many other unhealthy ingredients. All of these potentially harmful products can cause or prolong chronic inflammation.

By taking responsibility for how you eat and following the guidelines of the diet as described in the upcoming pages, there is much you can do to significantly reduce and eventually, possibly, even eliminate chronic inflammation.

Ed's Success Story: Lyme Disease

Below is the story of Ed, one of Dr. Singleton's patients, as told in The Lyme Disease Solution.

Ed came to our office after suffering from severe Lyme arthritic symptoms for several years.

A hard-working man, Ed woke for work at 4:00 a.m. every morning, and stopped at the corner fast-food store for his coffee, donut or pastry, and sometimes fried tater tots. At lunch he would usually have a diet cola (extra large), along with two hot dogs on white buns smothered with pickles, mayonnaise, ketchup and mustard, and an order of French fries on the side. For dinner, his wife would prepare potatoes and steak, along with one vegetable and several dinner rolls, and ice cream for dessert. While watching TV in the evening, Ed would usually have two or three beers and nachos with cheese dip or guacamole.

As Ed described his diet, I was shocked by several things: the complete lack of fruit, the nearly complete lack of fiber, the relative lack of vegetables, the excess of sugar and fried foods and, finally, the use of coffee, colas and beer instead of water.

I told Ed he would have to make major changes in his dietary program if he wanted to get well. I explained that if he was willing to follow the Lyme Inflammation Diet, he would feel significantly better by the time of his one-month follow-up visit, and that we would begin antibiotics at that time.

Ed's wife, sitting beside him, smiled and said her husband could never follow this radical approach to diet. Ed, however, is the kind of man who loves a challenge: he said he would do it, and he did.

One month later, Ed returned with the good news that his joints were 75% better, his energy was 50% better, and his thinking processes were also 50% better. His wife added that he also wasn't as grouchy as usual. Remember, these improvements all happened before we started Ed on antibiotics. They happened because the Lyme Inflammation Diet not only greatly reduced Ed's inflammation, but also supplied the necessary antioxidants and vital nutrients his body had been craving for years.

Ed's positive experience with adopting the diet has been quite common among the many patients I have treated for Lyme disease.

Assessing Your Risk for Chronic Inflammation

A simple and inexpensive blood test, the CRP, can help your health practitioner determine whether or not you suffer from chronic inflammation, and the extent of the problem.

CRP stands for C-reactive protein, a type of protein that is present in small amounts in the blood of all people. As chronic inflammation sets in, levels of CRP in the bloodstream become elevated because the liver produces more C-reactive protein in response to the inflammation. Ask your doctor about the CRP test, which is widely available across the country.

In addition to the blood test, Dr. Singleton's Chronic Inflammation Self-Assessment Tool on the following pages can help you quickly determine your chronic inflammation risk level. If your answers indicate a high level of inflammation risk, the good news is that the diet could greatly benefit you.

Dr. Singleton's Chronic Inflammation Self-Assessment Tool

Positive (Anti-Inflammatory) Daily Dietary and Lifestyle Factors

Award yourself the indicated positive (+) number for each of the following items that are part of your average daily or weekly dietary and lifestyle routine. If the item does not apply to you, leave that particular score blank.

___ *Fruit Consumption*
   (5 points for each serving of fresh, frozen or dried organic fruit you consume per day; 3 points for each serving of unsweetened fruit juice)

___ *Vegetable Consumption*
   (5 points for each serving of raw or steamed vegetables)

___ *Daily Vitamin/Mineral/Antioxidant Supplementation*
   (5 points)

___ *Consumption of Oily Fish (e.g., Salmon) or Omega-3/Fish Oil Supplements*
   (7 points for consumption four or more times/week; 4 points for consumption 1-3 times/week)

___ *Organic or Range-Fed Meat Consumption*
   (5 points)

___ *Regular Use of Olive Oil and/or Other Healthy Oils for Cooking*
   (5 points)

___ *Regular Exercise*
   (3 points for each 10 minutes of exercise performed per day)

___ *Consumption of Pure, Filtered Water*
   (1 point for each 8-ounce glass of water; 8 points total for 8 glasses or more)

___ *Laughter*
   (2 points for each good, hearty laugh per day, up to 6 points total)

___ *Positive Attitude/Gratefulness/Giving Spirit*
   (7 points)

___ *Daily Prayer or Meditation*
   (7 points)

___ *Daily Exposure to Sunlight for 10 or More Minutes*
   (5 points)

___ *Daily Exposure to Fresh Air/Deep Breathing Exercises*
   (4 points)

___ *Healthy Relationships and Social Networks*
   (5 points for each, including church groups, therapy and so forth)

___ *Daily Giving and Receiving Hugs*
   (2 points for each hug, up to 6 points total)

☐ **Total Positive Score:** (add all the above scores)

Negative (Pro-Inflammatory) Daily Dietary and Lifestyle Factors

Give yourself the indicated negative (-) number (e.g., -5) for each of the following items that are part of your regular dietary and lifestyle routine. If the item does not apply to you, leave that particular score blank.

___ **Smoking**
(-10 points for each pack smoked)

___ **Overweight**
(-7 points if up to 50 pounds overweight; -10 points if over 50 pounds overweight)

___ **Consumption of Wheat, Dairy or other Sensitivity-Causing Foods**
(- 5 points for each food consumed daily – e.g., eating bread daily = -5))

___ **Use of Trans-Fatty Acids (margarine, hydrogenated and partially-hydrogenated oils)**
(-5 points for each time used per day)

___ **Exposure to External AGEs (fried foods, doughnuts, pastries, etc. See page 18 for details)**
(-5 points for each exposure per day)

___ **Consumption of Sugar or Artificial Sweeteners (aspartame, splenda, etc.)**
(- 5 points for each food consumed daily – e.g., eating bread daily = -5)

___ **Excess Omega-6 Fatty Acid (Arachidonic Acid) Consumption (including corn and other vegetable oils)**
(-3 points for each time consumed per day)

___ **Use of Cooking Oils Other than Olive or Other Healthy Oils**
(-5 points)

___ **Alcohol**
(-7 points for each alcoholic beverage consumed per day)

___ **Negative/Pessimistic Attitude and/or Victim Mentality**
(-7 points)

___ **Tendency Towards Unforgiveness**
(-7 points)

___ **Averaging Less Than Seven Hours of Sleep**
(-7 points)

___ **Poor Water Intake**
(-7 points for less than six 8-ounce glasses per day)

___ **Chronic Exposure to Mold in Home or at Work**
(-5 points)

___ **Less than Ten Minutes of Daily Sun Exposure**
(- 4 points)

[ ] *Total Negative Score* (add all the <u>above</u> scores)
[ ] *Combine both of your positive and negative scores to tally your NET SCORE.*

Rating

50 or above = Excellent (Very low risk of chronic inflammation)
25 to 49 = Very Good
0 to 24 = Fair
-1 to -24 = Poor
-25 to -49 = Very Bad
-50 or below = Emergency (Extremely high risk of chronic inflammation)

Toxins and Enzymes

While the primary focus of the diet is to control inflammation, it also has the related goals of detoxification and providing your body with important enzymes.

The Need for Detoxification

Our daily environment and our typically poor diet expose our bodies to an alarming amount of toxins. When the organs of detoxification, such as the liver and skin, are unable to keep up with this toxic assault, toxins become lodged in the cells.

This can result in impaired immune function, impaired metabolism, hormonal imbalances, increased inflammation, diminished cognitive function, chronic lack of energy, unhealthy weight gain and many other health problems.

Research indicates that toxins make it more difficult for the immune system to identify and target harmful bacteria, fungi and viruses, making it easier for such microorganisms to take deeper root in the body and cause more serious symptoms. Lessening the body's toxic burden is therefore vitally important in all cases of chronic infection. (See pages 29-30 for food choices for detoxification.)

Enzymes and Their Role

Systemic enzymes are one of the most fascinating natural therapies for treating chronic inflammation. An enzyme is a type of protein that facilitates a chemical reaction that in turn causes change to another substance. Digestive enzymes are one good example: when you chew, enzymes in your mouth begin breaking down carbohydrates so they can be absorbed when arriving into the intestines. Other enzymes (from the pancreas, primarily) join the mouth enzymes in the intestines to further break down carbohydrates and other food elements, such as proteins and fats. Without these enzymes, your food would never be broken into absorbable components, and malnutrition would result.

We produce hundreds of different types of enzymes in our bodies, each with specific purposes and functions. Even so, it's also essential that we ingest additional enzymes in our foods. The problem is that many of the best sources of food enzymes (such as fruits and vegetables) are typically overly processed or overcooked and so have lost significant amounts of their enzyme content. Additionally, chronic illness increases the body's requirements for enzymes. This combination of illness and typically inadequate diet can set you up for one of the worst consequences of enzyme deficiency: chronic inflammation.

Fortunately, the diet is a "high enzyme" nutrition program, which is one of the reasons for its effectiveness.

Part II
The Lyme Inflammation Diet

Salted Roasted Chickpeas, page 135

The Lyme Inflammation Diet was developed by Lyme specialist Kenneth B. Singleton, MD, MPH. After realizing the critical role good nutrition played in his own recovery from misdiagnosed Lyme disease, he began to develop a dietary protocol to share with his patients. He refined his nutrition plan based on clinical experience and patient outcomes and eventually developed the diet which became popularized in his book, *The Lyme Disease Solution*.

Though the diet was originally created for patients with Lyme disease, many reader accounts have indicated that the benefits of the diet are far-reaching and can help people with other health conditions improve or even heal their symptoms of chronic inflammation.

The basic principles of the diet are to:
- Eat foods that help minimize or eliminate symptoms caused by inflammation
- Discover food sensitivities
- Strengthen your immune system
- Help with detoxification; and
- Improve your overall health

The diet is powerfully effective tool, and following it may help to reverse chronic inflammation and boost your immune system. In addition, this nutrition program will help reduce or eliminate both insulin resistance and leptin resistance. The dietary recommendations will further help you build a foundation of wellness by supplying your body with a rich supply of nutrients, including the fiber, vitamins, minerals, antioxidants, essential fats and other vital substances that it needs in order to function optimally.

Phases of the Diet
The diet is both an elimination diet (designed to help you to discover foods that you may be sensitive to) and an anti-inflammatory diet. You begin by eliminating the most common foods that contribute to chronic inflammation. You gradually add back foods and monitor the effects to establish a broad yet healthy diet. Below is a brief overview of the four Phases of the diet. (For a more comprehensive explanation of each Phase of the diet, read pages 67, 119, 165 and 235.)

Phase 1: Induction. The goal of the first Phase is to shut down the mechanisms of chronic inflammation and begin detoxifying your body. Food is very restricted during this Phase, making it the toughest of the four Phases, but it only lasts one week. Further explanation about this Phase can be found on pages 67-68.

Phase 2: Early Reentry. The second Phase begins the process of relaxing food restrictions to see how you are affected. Phase 2 permits additional new foods (pages 119-120), which you will add back into your meals very slowly, over the course of at least three weeks. If you experience any symptoms of inflammation after any foods are reintroduced, this is a sign that you should continue to avoid them for the time being.

Phase 3: Late Reentry. During Phase 3, your goal will be to reintroduce additional foods (pages 165-166) that are normally healthy, but have a greater risk of triggering inflammation in some people. For this reason, you must proceed cautiously, once again reintroducing the new foods no sooner than every other day. Should symptoms occur as a result, quickly stop and go back to Phase 2 until you feel better.

Phase 4: Maintenance. If all has gone well, you can initiate Phase 4 just eight weeks after first starting Phase 1. Phase 4 allows you to introduce even more healthy foods (page 235) – again, slowly and with careful monitoring – and to reach a maintenance level where you have a wide variety of healthy food options and little or no symptoms of chronic inflammation. Once you have introduced all the foods from each diet Phase into your diet you will have completed the elimination portion of the diet. This takes around 10 weeks. (See the full diet on pages 26-27).

> **Chrissy's Success Story: Aches and Pains, Allergies, Brain Fog, PMS, Fatigue and a Thyroid Condition**
>
> Chrissy was experiencing allergies, general aches and pains, bloating, fatigue, brain fog and was diagnosed with a thyroid condition. She decided to try the diet to see if nutritional changes could make an impact on how she was feeling.
>
> Prior to implementing the diet she had not had any self-imposed dietary restrictions. In her estimation she was eating too much take-out and quick and easy (unhealthy) snacks and meals to save time in the kitchen. She was excited to find that within the first 30 days that she started to notice improvements with her symptoms. But the real transformation happened between 45 and 60 days.
>
> At this point she found that she could breath easier, hardly having to blow her nose at all. Her premenstrual symptoms (irritability, breast tenderness and brain fog) completely disappeared. She found that she had more energy and her bloating resolved. People would tell her that her skin was glowing. Her chronically sore feet felt fine again. Unexpectedly, like many who go on the diet, she found that she lost weight. The most significant outcome, however, was that her doctor was able to decrease her thyroid medication.
>
> Beyond the reward of seeing her symptoms improve or disappear, she found that having the recipes in the book kept her motivated because they all tasted so great. She didn't feel deprived, but rather felt very satisfied, which she says made it easier for her to stick with it.
>
> Through the elimination period of the diet (the first 10 weeks) it became clear to her that she was both dairy- and gluten-intolerant. While the changes in her diet means she now has to spend more time in the kitchen preparing, she has no desire to go back to her old eating habits because of the dramatic impact the diet has had on how she feels.

Complete List of Allowable Foods

Below is a comprehensive list of all of the allowable foods in the diet, categorized by food type so you can see the diet as a whole. For complete information on the foods in each Phase, review pages 68, 120, 166 and 235.

Beverages
Phase 1
Açai juice
Blackberry juice
Blueberry juice
Cherry juice
Cranberry juice
Pomegranate juice
Pure filtered water
Raspberry juice
Rooibos tea

Phase 2
Green tea
Black tea
Vegetable juice
Carbonated water

Phase 3
Apple juice
Citrus juice
Coffee (organic)
Orange juice

Phase 4 - N/A

Fruits
Phase 1
Açai
Avocado
Blackberries
Blueberries
Cherries
Coconut (or coconut milk)
Cranberries
Green apple
Pomegranate
Raspberry

Phase 2
Apricot
Cantaloupe
Date
Fig
Mango
Olives
Pear
Pineapple
Plum
Prune
Watermelon

Phase 3
Apple (all varieties)
Banana
Grapefruit
Lemon
Lime
Nectarine
Orange
Peach
Strawberry

Phase 4
Grapes (purple)
Kiwi
Papaya
Raisins

Nuts and Seeds
Phase 1
Almonds (or almond milk)
Chia seeds
Flaxseed
Pine nuts
Walnuts

Phase 2
Brazil nuts
Caraway seeds
Cashews
Pecans
Poppy seeds
Pumpkin seeds
Sesame seeds
Sunflower seeds

Phase 3
Peanuts
Pistachios

Phase 4
Hemp seeds

Vegetables
Phase 1
Artichoke
Arugula
Asparagus
Beets
Bok choy
Broccoli
Cauliflower
Brussels sprouts
Cabbage
Carrots
Celery
Chard
Collard greens
Cucumber
Garlic
Kale
Leeks
Mushrooms (shiitake are the best choice)
Mustard greens
Onions
Lettuce
Scallions
Spinach
Sprouts
String beans
Watercress

Phase 2
Arame
Celery root
Dulse
Fennel
Hijiki
Kelp
Kohlrabi
Kombu
Nori
Pumpkin
Squash
Sweet potato
Tapioca (cassava)
Wakame
Wasabi

Phase 3
Dill pickles
Jicama

Nightshades
Cayenne
Chili powder
Chilies
Eggplant
Green pepper
Hot pepper
Mild pepper
Paprika
Potato (white)
Red pepper
Tomato

Phase 4
All other pickles
Parsnips
Radishes
Red potatoes
Turnips
Watercress
Yams

Grains
Phase 1
Brown rice
Wild rice

Phase 2
Brown rice flour
Oat flour
Oatmeal

Phase 3
Buckwheat
Corn
Millet
Oat groats
Quinoa
Sorghum
Teff

Phase 4 - Possibility of gluten-containing grains (see page 234)

Beans and Legumes
Phase 1 – N/A

Phase 2
Black beans
Chickpeas
Kidney beans
Lentils
Navy beans
Peas
Pinto beans

Phase 3 – N/A
Phase 4 – N/A

Protein
(organic, if possible)
Phase 1
Eggs (free-range)
Haddock
Halibut
Flounder
Mackerel
Salmon
Sardines
Sole
Tilapia

Phase 2
Lamb
Venison
White meat chicken or turkey

Phase 3
Beef
Bison (free-range)
Chicken (dark meat)
Turkey (dark meat)

Phase 4
Cod
Grouper
Pork
Shellfish

Herbs and Spices
Phase 1
Basil
Bay leaf
Cardamom
Chives
Cilantro
Cinnamon
Cloves
Cumin
Curry
Ginger
Lemon grass
Mint
Mustard
Mustard powder
Mustard seed
Oregano
Parsley
Rosemary
Sage
Sea salt
Thyme

Phase 2
Black pepper

Phase 3
Cayenne
Chili powder
Paprika

Phase 4
Horseradish

Dairy
Phase 1 – N/A
Phase 2 – N/A

Phase 3
Butter (organic)
Cheeses
Milk
Cream
Yogurt

Phase 4
Feta
Unsweetened kefir

Traditional Soy Bean Products
Phase 1 – N/A
Phase 2 – N/A

Phase 3
Miso
Natto
Tamari
Tempeh
Tofu

Phase 4 – N/A

Fats
Phase 1
Extra virgin coconut oil
Extra virgin olive oil
Ghee
Virgin olive oil

Phase 2
Margarines without trans fats

Phase 3
Almond oil
Avocado oil
Grapeseed oil
Palm oil
Safflower oil
Sunflower seed oil

Phase 4
Peanut oil

Sweeteners
Phase 1
Lakanto
Raw honey
Stevia

Phase 2
Coconut palm sugar
Coconut nectar
Honey
Maple syrup
Sorbitol
Xylitol

Phase 3 – N/A
Phase 4 – N/A

Other
Phase 1
Almond extract
Baking soda
Coconut aminos
Coconut extract
Cream of tartar
Mint extract
Raw apple cider
Vinegar
Vanilla extract

Phase 2
Coconut kefir
Psyllium husk powder

Phase 3
Air-popped popcorn
Arrowroot
Baking powder
Guar gum
Nutritional yeast
Mustard
Other vinegars
Xanthan gum

Phase 4
Chocolate
Gelatin
Yeast

Note: If you notice that a food is missing from this list, it is possible that it may have inadvertently been left off the diet. If you feel like the food in question has anti-inflammatory properties and nutritional value, use your judgment and add it into the Phase that you feel would be most appropriate. During all diet Phases, you should avoid eating foods you know you are allergic or sensitive to, even if they are on the list of allowable foods. As your inflammation lessens and you are feeling better, however, you may try to introduce some of the foods you were sensitive to as a test to see if you can now tolerate them. You may also decide to try gluten-containing grains, which are discussed on page 234.

General Food Guidelines

Follow these guidelines during all four Phases of the diet to maintain the health benefits you will achieve.

- Generally, the foods you eat each day should consist of a wide array of fresh vegetables (preferably organic), high-quality protein foods, whole grains and quality fats. All should be eaten as close to their natural state as possible, which means no fast foods or processed and refined foods. Please note that while this is not a calorie-restricted diet, most do find that as an added bonus, they lose weight while going through the Phases of the diet.
- Enjoy sources of good fats, including coconut and extra virgin olive oil, avocado, nuts and seeds, sesame oil, organic butter (especially from pasture-fed cows), organic raw milk cheese and other cheeses from pasture-fed cows.
- For cooking purposes, use extra virgin olive oil (or olive combined with sesame oil) in general, and unrefined extra virgin coconut oil for high-temperature cooking.
- Be sure to have a healthy breakfast. Many health experts consider breakfast the most important meal of the day, so don't skip it!
- While there are recipes for sweets and baked goods included, it's best to have them as a treat, on an occasional basis.
- Eat fresh fruits rather than canned, and limit your intake of fruits that are high in natural sugar content, such as bananas, grapes and raisins.
- Avoid all foods to which you are sensitive or allergic.
- Avoid sodas and all commercial beverages, including carbonated beverages that contain sugar or artificial sweeteners, sports drinks, commercial fruit and vegetable juices and any beverage that contains sweeteners and/or other chemical additives and preservatives.
- Avoid all commercially-packaged foods and all fried foods.
- Avoid the use of all refined carbohydrates, including white pasta, white rice, white flour and white flour products.
- Avoid sugary desserts, especially cakes, donuts, pastries and other cooked high-sugar products that are high in exogenous AGEs (page 18).
- Avoid honey-glazed meats, barbecued meats cooked over direct flame (see page 151 for proper grilling technique) and processed commercial meat products. This includes bacon, bologna, hot dogs, salami, as well as all fast-food fish, meats and poultry.
- Avoid all farm-raised fish and non-organic beef, chicken, lamb and turkey. Eat shellfish or pork only occasionally.

- Avoid all trans-fatty acids and hydrogenated and partially hydrogenated oils. Avoid vegetable oils, such as corn and cottonseed oil.
- Avoid the use of table salt (Celtic and Himalayan sea salt are permissible).
- Avoid all food additives, especially aspartame, MSG, nitrates and sulfites.
- For those on antibiotics, it's best to avoid alcohol completely for at least three to six months after you stop taking antibiotics. While it's best that you abstain permanently, if you do choose to drink alcohol, limit yourself to one to two glasses of wine (or one to two beers) per day, after you complete the three to six month abstinence period.

As you become more conscious of the relationship between healthy eating and good health, pay attention to how the foods you eat make you feel. You'll notice a big difference between the physical and emotional satisfaction derived from high-quality, nutrient-dense foods, and the addictive "quick fix" feelings that come from eating unhealthy foods. By tuning into how you feel as you eat, you'll develop an unerring instinct for what foods are most appropriate for you, and when you should eat them.

Dealing with Sugar Cravings

Discontinuing all use of sugar is essential for recovery from chronic inflammation. It's difficult, though, because sugar is addictive. Dr. Singleton suggests the following strategies for dealing with the inevitable cravings.

- Plan on feeling poorly for about three days while your body adjusts to the sudden lack of sugar.
- Eat multiple small meals each day, making sure to include a source of protein and quality fat at each meal. Almonds are a good snack; they contain healthy protein and fat.
- Take a good quality multi-vitamin that contains B-complex and chromium.
- If your healthcare provider approves them for you, three supplements that might help are glutamine, alpha lipoic acid and 5-hydroxytryptophan. Always consult a physician before adding supplements as they may interfere or have adverse effects in combination with any prescriptions you are taking.

Your cravings for sugar should be greatly reduced by about one month after quitting it. Sugar will then seem extremely sweet, and you'll feel lousy when you eat it (especially on an empty stomach). You'll also notice increased energy and weight loss, and your gastrointestinal system will work better.

Food Choices for Detoxification

Your food choices can support your liver in its role of cleansing the body of toxins. To assist in this process, the following guidelines can be extremely helpful:

- Concentrate your food choices on "brain foods," including water, egg yolks, raw organic nuts, liver, meat, fish, cruciferous vegetables, beans, turkey, milk, potatoes, whole grains, antioxidant fruits, avocado and other healthy omega-3 and -6 foods and green vegetables.

- Make foods high in omega-3 oils a regular part of your diet. Sardines and wild-caught salmon are excellent food choices for this purpose.

- Eat plenty of raw foods, especially fresh fruits and vegetables. Plant-based foods (except for beans, potatoes and tomatoes) help the processes of liver detoxification more when consumed raw or juiced, rather than cooked. Artichokes and dandelion leaves are two notable liver-helpful vegetables, and these fruits and vegetables are also particularly helpful: apples, blueberries, cherries, grapes, lemons, pineapple, beet greens, celery, garlic, green leafy vegetables and onions.

- Eat only organic foods, if possible. Non-organic foods contain herbicides, pesticides and other substances that add to the burden of liver detoxification. Organic foods, by contrast, help to reduce the toxin burden placed on the liver (page 45-47).

- Glutathione is considered a "superstar" when it comes to detoxification and antioxidant properties. Foods with sulphur-rich amino acids can increase your Glutathione level; such foods include asparagus, broccoli, avocado, spinach, raw eggs, garlic and fresh unprocessed meats. The Indian spice curcumin (turmeric) has been found to help by increasing the expression of glutathione S-transferase and protecting neurons exposed to oxidant-stressing brain cells called astrocytes.

- Vitamin C aids in the overall process of detoxification and provides many other health benefits, including improved immunity. Vitamin C and niacin (vitamin B3) both help fat cells and tissues expel toxins (but may cause severe flushing).

- Garlic aids detoxification and also has antimicrobial characteristics.

- Cilantro is another powerful herb; it acts as a natural detoxifying "magnet" that pulls toxins from the body (including heavy metals). If you enjoy the flavor of cilantro, add it to your meals to aid in detoxification, especially in the early Phases of the diet.

- Make nuts a regular part of your diet, as they assist both liver and gallbladder function. They are an excellent source of healthy oils and quality protein, and thus make an ideal snack food between meals.

- Drink plenty of pure, filtered water every day. This is one of the simplest and most effective steps you can take to reduce toxins in your body.

Many of these foods are included in the recipes, which will help you to more easily include them in your diet.

Dr. Singleton's Special Dietary Considerations for Problem Headaches

Most people suffer from occasional headaches that are easily relieved by simple measures, such as rest or acetaminophen. If you suffer from chronic or frequent headaches, food sensitivities could be playing a significant role. An offending food can cause headaches by triggering changes to the blood vessels in the head, with or without the presence of other inflammation in the body. Migraines are an example of this kind of headache.

Identifying which foods are the culprits is difficult. Here are five steps you can take in the process of elimination.

1. **Avoid additives and artificial sweeteners.** Many foods contain artificial flavors, colors or sweeteners that can alter the blood flow to the brain and trigger a nasty headache. An especially common culprit is the artificial sweetener aspartame, which can even cause neurological problems. The foods recommended for the diet are all additive-free.

2. **Consider tyramine elimination.** Tyramine is a common, natural substance formed from the breakdown of protein as food ages. Generally speaking, the longer a high-protein food ages, the greater its tyramine content. Common signs of tyramine sensitivity include: acute and often severe headache, increase in blood pressure, anxiety, depression, tiredness, heart palpitations, nausea, vomiting or dizziness. Such foods include aged cheeses, yogurt, alcoholic beverages, bananas, prunes, raisins, ripe avocado, pineapple, vanilla, broad beans, eggplant, snow peas, lentils, most nuts, chocolate, soy sauce, Chinese vegetables, pickled herring, canned meats, sausages and preserved meats and brewer's yeast. Aged cheeses have the highest levels, and the toxic effect of tyramine is sometimes called "the cheese effect."

3. **Beware of caffeine.** Widely used in coffee, tea, chocolate, soft drinks and even some medications, regular consumption of caffeine can lead to dependency, and withdrawal from it can cause severe headaches. Consider avoiding caffeine completely, or limiting its use (such as only drinking it in green tea).

4. **Watch out for MSG.** Monosodium glutamate is a flavoring additive found in many Asian foods that's commonly linked to headaches and migraines. When dining out, request that your meal be prepared without MSG.

5. **Go alcohol-free.** You should avoid alcohol when recovering from inflammation or other health problems. In addition to containing tyramine, alcohol increases blood flow to the brain – which can cause headaches – and certain alcohols have other components that may induce headaches, such as the nitrates found in wine.

Using the Symptom Journal with the Diet

As you're learning, the diet is both an anti-inflammation diet and an elimination diet that helps you to determine if you have unidentified food sensitivities. Being in tune with your body while following the diet will result in a truly customized nutrition plan that works best for you and is likely the most accurate "food sensitivity test" available.

Recipes for Repair: *Symptom Journal*

PHASE 1 Date	headache	insomnia	light sensitivity	sound sensitivity	nausea	joint pain	brain fog	forgetfulness	swollen glands	ringing in ears	burning in feet	confusion	heartburn	daily fatigue	fatigue upon waking	dizziness	Meditation	Weight	Exercise?	Hours of sleep	Menstrual cycle
2/10	2	1	3	1	1	0	2	1	0	2	1	1	2	2	3	1	X	126	X	8.5	
2/11	1	2	3	1	1	0	2	1	0	2	0	1	1	2	3	2	X	126	X	7.0	
2/12	1	1	3	1	0	1	2	1	0	2	0	1	0	1	2	1	X	125		7.5	
2/13	2	1	3	1	0	0	1	1	0	2	0	1	0	2	2	1	X	125	X	8.5	
2/14	1	1	3	1	0	0	2	1	0	2	0	1	0	2	3	2	X	124	X	9	
2/15	2	1	3	1	0	0	2	1	0	2	0	1	0	2	3	1		125		8.5	x
2/16	1	1	3	1	0	0	2	1	0	2	0	1	0	2	3	1	X	124	X	8	x

Directions: Date the upper left hand corner with the day you start Phase 1. Date each row below with the days to come. Write in your persistent symptoms at the top of each column. Each morning, fill in how many hours you slept the night before on the new row for that day. If you have night symptoms write in a rating for each from the night you just finished. In the evening finish filling out the day's row by considering which symptoms you experienced through the day using the scale below. Weight loss is a welcome side effect of the diet. Record your weight, if desired, and check off if you exercised. If you have another weekly practice, such as meditation, add it in the column before "weight."

Degree of each symptom: **0**=none **1**=mild **2**=moderate **3**=severe

Use the space below to document any events, appointments, changes in treatment protocol, etc. and/or notable changes that may affect how you're feeling. For example, if you have a cold make a note of it so when you look back you'll realize the increase in fatigue was due to the cold.

Record notable events *(see above instructions)*

2/10 - Excited and a little nervous to start the diet

2/11 - Rather than my normal mild yoga routine I went out for an hour-long xc ski today.
I also had an extra stressful day because we discovered that we need a new hot water heater.

2/12 - I slept worse than usual because I had the water heater expense on my mind.

2/13 - I had an acupuncture appt. today. I've noticed an increase in appetite today.

2/14 - Today my doctor had me increase the NAC I've been taking by 100 mg.

Dr. Singleton suggests adding one single food or food group back into your diet no sooner than every other day. Be aware that a food sensitivity is different than a food allergy in that the reaction generally is delayed (page 16).

You may eat something you're sensitive to and not see the reaction manifest itself as a symptom until anywhere from an hour to a few days later. This is why it's critical to be in tune with your body during the entire elimination portion of the diet (approximately the first 10 weeks).

It's important to track your symptoms as you progress through the diet. We've developed a downloadable Symptom Journal that you can download at www.recipesforrepair.com/resources, which will help you with this. Over time, this grid-like journal allows you to visually track the progression of your specific symptoms, and makes it easier to determine if something you've been doing – such as eliminating a certain food – is helping.

Emily's Success Story: IBS and Hashimoto's Disease

A year before discovering the diet, Emily was diagnosed with Hashimoto's Disease; a thyroid condition that can be extremely debilitating and affect all areas of health. She exhibited over 20 symptoms of the illness, including extreme fatigue, abnormal skin and hair texture, chronic stomach aches, high blood pressure, swollen eyes, as well as severe menstrual cycles. Additionally, she was 30 pounds overweight and as she describes, "felt like a 'sick person' all the time."

Suspecting that food may be playing a role in some of her symptoms, she tried reducing her lactose intake, stopped eating fried foods and generally ate more healthy foods. But these modifications didn't help. The real changes came when she decided to try the Lyme Inflammation Diet.

About 3 weeks into it, she noticed that her stomach issues were greatly reduced and that her skin and hair looked more normal. After 6 weeks, she noticed that she was starting to lose weight and have more energy. At around 6 months, though, was when the full transformation took place.

She went into complete remission from both the IBS and thyroid condition and found that all of her symptoms were completely eliminated. She lost over 30 pounds and felt strong, energetic and better than she did when she was in her twenties.

Before implementing the diet, she ate very little, but could not even lose a pound. She did indulge in a lot of pre-packaged and frozen junk food.

By paying close attention to her body and how it reacted to the foods she was eating, she noticed that she had a low-tolerance for raw tomatoes and some pesto sauces, which caused her a lot of stomach irritation. She felt that tracking symptoms was important even with her new, clean diet, as it helped her to identify and cut out any foods causing her discomfort.

Not surprisingly, this transformation has kept her motivated to stay in Phase 4 of the diet indefinitely. She doesn't think that it is "worth the risk" to eat any other way, as she doesn't want to ever feel the way she did prior to going on the diet.

She keeps this cookbook on her counter and says that she uses it every, single day. She feels it is well-structured and well thought out making the diet easy to incorporate into her life.

Lyme Inflammation Diet Food Glossary

Some of the ingredients included in the diet and/or used in the recipes may be new to you. Below, we have defined some of the lesser-known foods and have noted the nutritional value of some that are exceptionally good for you.

Grains

Buckwheat is a fruit in the rhubarb family. It is not a grain, and does not contain wheat or gluten. It is very high in protein and a good source of manganese, magnesium and dietary fiber.

Groats are grains, such as oats or buckwheat, with their hulls only partially removed, leaving a coarse grain that's higher in nutritional value and natural fiber than more refined cereals.

Millet is an ancient, wheat- and gluten-free grain that retains its alkaline properties after being cooked. It's rich in B vitamins, iron and other important minerals, and is also considered to be a good source of protein.

Quinoa is often thought to be a grain; however, it is not a grain, but is rather the gluten-free seed of a leafy plant that's distantly related to spinach. Quinoa has excellent reserves of protein and, unlike most grains, is not missing the amino acid lysine, which provides you with a more complete protein.

Sorghum is a gluten-free grain that when milled into a flour can be used in gluten-free baking. It is a neutral tasting, light flour and is high in protein.

Teff is an ancient, gluten-free, African grain and is the smallest of all grains. There are two types of teff, ivory and dark. Ivory teff is higher in protein, while dark teff has higher levels of iron. Both varieties are high in calcium and zinc, with the nutrition concentrated in the germ and the bran. When cooked, teff makes a nutritious breakfast cereal with the consistency and texture of wheat farina. When milled into flour, teff can be used in baking.

Fats

Expeller Pressed Oil is oil extracted by pressing the seed without the use of chemical solvents.

Extra Virgin Coconut Oil has anti-inflammatory properties and is the ultimate super food. Of all the foods in nature, coconuts contain the highest level (50%) of lauric acid, which is a powerful tool to enhance the immune system. Clinical studies have shown that lauric acid has anti-microbial and anti-viral properties. Coconut oil can be found and purchased as either unrefined or refined. Unrefined is the ideal choice.

Ghee is clarified butter. In the clarifying process the butter is heated and milk solids are removed, leaving the butter oil without the lactose and casein that people with dairy sensitivity cannot tolerate. See page 258 for instructions on how to make your own ghee.

Palm Oil is a tropical oil. Long perceived as unhealthy, palm oil is actually a beneficial fat source when used in its natural form. Palm oil is indeed high in saturated fatty acids, but these are actually good for you. Unrefined palm oil remains a much healthier oil than any hydrogenated vegetable oil. Palm kernel oil, however, is heavily processed and entirely different than palm oil and in general is unhealthy and should be avoided.

Palm Shortening is derived from palm oil (see above), is not hydrogenated, contains no trans fats and isn't prone to rancidity. Two trusted brands that we use are Spectrum (called vegetable shortening on their label) and Tropical Traditions.

Safflower Oil is oil expeller-pressed from the seeds of the safflower plant, which is a member of the sunflower family. Safflower oil is often used for cooking, because it is healthier than most other oils.

Sweeteners

The allowable sweeteners in the diet are all-natural, but as with any treat, sweet recipes should be enjoyed in moderation. While xylitol has the same sweetening power as cane sugar (which is never allowed in the diet), the other allowable choices are sweeter. Therefore, if you would like to swap one for another, look online for a natural sweetener conversion chart. Below you will find a description of some of the allowable sweeteners:

Coconut Palm Sugar is an unrefined sugar made from the nectar of the coconut palm tree flower and tastes similar to brown sugar. It is lower on the glycemic index than cane sugar and has trace amounts of vitamin C, potassium, phosphorous, magnesium, calcium, zinc, iron and copper.

Dates are a great all-natural sweetener and are rich in dietary fiber. They include tannins, which are said to have anti-inflammatory properties. They are also rich in vitamins and minerals, most notably potassium, copper, manganese, magnesium and vitamin B6. We use Medjool dates in the recipes, but you can easily substitute other varieties in their place if you prefer a different type of date.

Lakanto is an all-natural, zero calorie sweetener with a glycemic index value of zero. It's made from a proprietary blend of the sweet extract of the

Chinese-grown fruit, luo han guo. This sweetener is pricey and not easily available so we have chosen not to use it in any of the recipes. If you prefer to use this sweetener though, you can use it as a one-for-one replacement for either xylitol or coconut palm sugar. See the Resources section (page 290) for more information.

Raw Honey is a natural antimicrobial and antioxidant. It enhances the immune and digestive systems because of the various amino acids, minerals and beneficial live enzymes found naturally in raw honey. "Raw" means it has never been pasteurized, filtered or heated, all of which destroy these powerful nutrients. In the recipes that call for raw honey, the honey is never heated above 117°F, so as not to damage the enzymes. If you plan to cook with honey at temperatures above 117°F, use regular honey, rather than raw.

Stevia is a bush (Stevia rebaudiana Bertoni), the leaves of which are used to produce extracts with up to 300 times the sweetness of sugar. It comes in both a liquid and powdered version and we use the liquid version exclusively in the book. You can bake with stevia because it is stable to 392°F, but because its sweetness is so concentrated, substituting the correct amount is crucial.

Xylitol is a sugar alcohol and differs from other sweeteners, such as sorbitol, fructose and glucose, in that its molecule has five, rather than six carbon atoms. This this is important because the body does not need to create insulin to break it down. Its sweetening power is the same as that of sucrose (table sugar), which is why it was chosen as the sweetener for some of the recipes in this book. It can act as a laxative in some and may produce flatulence and gastric upset if used in excess. Until you know how this sweetener affects you, limit its use to one recipe a day at most (in fact, this is a good precaution to take with all sweeteners ending in -tol).

Starches

Starches are also used in gluten-free baking to balance and lighten the mix. The popular options are **arrowroot starch** (described below), **corn starch**, **potato starch** (different from potato flour and not interchangeable), and **tapioca starch** (described below) which is also sometimes referred to as tapioca flour. If you have a sensitivity to a specific starch called for in a recipe, they are similar and can be substituted one-for-one, if needed.

Arrowroot is a neutral-flavored starch used in cooking as a thickening agent. It can be found in co-ops, health food stores or online.

Tapioca (Cassava) is a starch extracted from the root of the cassava or yucca plant. It is granular and is frequently used to thicken puddings.

Thickeners

Guar Gum is the ground-up extract of the guar bean, which comes from a plant grown primarily in India.

Xanthan Gum is a corn-based fermented product. Both of these gluten-free gums help hold gluten-free baked goods together, which would otherwise crumble. Guar gum is the less expensive of the two, and is the best option if you are sensitive to corn, but these gums can be used interchangeably. Recipes typically call for very small amounts of these products, which can be found in the bulk section of your local co-op or health food store, and thus can be purchased in small quantities.

Psyllium husk powder is a good source of fiber that can be added to many recipes to help boost your fiber intake. It can be used in gluten-free baking as a replacement for xanthin gum but it will make the baked good more compact and dense. Use no more than 1 tablespoon in your baking because it will alter the texture.

Sea Vegetables

Arame, Dulse, Hijiki, Kelp, Kombu, Nori and Wakame are the most common edible seaweeds and have a salty (and sometimes spicy) taste that adds flavor and nutrition to soups, stews and salads. They are nature's richest sources of iodine and contain high levels of vitamin K, folate, magnesium and other trace minerals. Lignans, which are plant compounds that may help ward off some serious health threats such as cancer, are found in these super foods of the sea. Vegans especially should turn to sea vegetables, as they are an excellent source of vitamin B12, a nutrient mostly found in meat. Refer to the package for cooking and rehydration instruction.

Traditional Soy Products

Miso and **Natto** are traditional fermented soy products. Miso is a thick, paste-like substance, whereas natto retains the soybean shape and has a stringier texture. Both provide you with high levels of protein and a low calorie count.

Tamari is the liquid that's collected from miso as it ages. Tamari is used like soy sauce but is wheat-free so is a gluten-free alternative.

Tempeh is made by a natural culturing and controlled fermentation process that binds soybeans into a cake form. Originating in Indonesia, tempeh is high in protein and very easy to digest.

Other

Coconut Aminos is a condiment made from coconut sap. It is a good substitution for tamari if you can't tolerate soy and can be used as a one-for-one substitution. It's an abundant source of 17 amino acids, minerals, vitamins, and has a nearly neutral pH.

Coconut Kefir is fermented coconut water from young coconuts. This water contains minerals, vitamins, antioxidants, amino acids and enzymes. It also has a high sugar content, and when the water is fermented, the sugars are converted into probiotics, which are an especially important addition to your diet when you are taking antibiotics. You can buy ready-made coconut kefir, or you can make your own using a culture starter kit. See the Resources section (page 290) for more information. When buying coconut kefir, be sure to purchase the unsweetened variety.

Herbes de Provence is a mixture of herbs invented in the 1970s. It generally includes a combination of thyme, oregano, marjoram, bay leaf, basil and rosemary. The Mediterranean flavor of these herbs goes well with meat, poultry, game, vegetables and tomato-based and grilled dishes. Some of the recipes in this book call for this blend. If you do not have this blend, you can make it yourself using a small amount of any or all of these seasonings.

Kefir is similar to yogurt, but contains more strains of beneficial bacteria. These healthy bacteria can actually colonize in the intestinal tract, while those from yogurt do not. Kefir is traditionally made from cow or goat's milk. When buying kefir, be sure you are buying the unsweetened variety.

Nutritional yeast is a deactivated yeast, rich in vitamin B12 , has 6 grams of protein per serving and has a cheese-like flavor. It comes in in Phase 3 of the diet, but it should be avoided if you have an active yeast problem like candida.

Raw Apple Cider Vinegar differs from apple cider vinegar in that it has never been filtered, heated or pasteurized. These processes destroy the "mother of vinegar," which is the organic matter that results from the fermentation process. Raw apple cider vinegar aids in detoxification and is rich in natural minerals, vitamins and enzymes.

Sea Salt is allowable on the diet and called for in the recipes. Choose from either Celtic sea salt or Himalayan crystal salt, as they are unrefined and contain a number of naturally occurring, essential minerals. Today's "table salt" is different from natural salt and should be avoided on the diet.

Nuts and Seeds

High in fiber and protein, nuts and seeds are not only delicious, but are extremely nutritious. Nuts and some seeds contain an enzyme-inhibiting substance which make them difficult to digest. Soaking removes this layer and stimulates the process of germination, which increases the nutrients. An alternative to soaking is to dry roast. This also increases the vitamin content, although not as much as germination.

Germination

Soaking: Combine sea salt with filtered water in a large bowl. The salt activates enzymes that neutralize the enzyme inhibitors. Add the nuts to the water (the water level should be two to three inches over the top of the nuts). Soak at room temperature for the time specified in the chart below. Drain well before drying.

Drying: Drying time can vary, depending on the nut or seed. Lay nuts out on a baking sheet and bake them at 150°F, or dry them in a dehydrator until they are dry and crispy. Refer to the chart below for general drying guidelines.

Nut or seed	Soak time (at room temperature)	Sea salt	Drying time [2]
Almonds	8 to 12 hours	1 tablespoon	12 to 24 hours
Cashews (whole)	4 hours (no longer than 6 hours)	1 tablespoon	6 to 12 hours
Peanuts, pecans, walnuts	7 hours to overnight	2 teaspoons	12 to 24 hours
Pumpkin seeds	7 hours to overnight	2 tablespoons	12 to 24 hours
All others	6 to 24 hours	Varies	12 to 24 hours

Dry Roasting

Spread nuts on a baking pan and cook in a preheated 350°F oven for a few minutes. Not all nuts cook in the same amount of time, so watch them closely as they can burn very quickly.

Storage

Nuts have a high fat content so they can become rancid. They should be stored in airtight containers away from heat, light or humidity. If you buy in bulk, keep a small amount on hand for cooking or snacking. Store the remainder in airtight containers in either the refrigerator or freezer. Nuts freeze very well and defrost in just minutes.

[1] Not all ovens can be set at temperatures as low as 150°F. Drying at higher temperatures will destroy the good enzymes created by the germination process.

[2] Drying times vary. Be sure nuts are fully dry to avoid the possibility of mold growing.

Beans, Peas and Lentils

Dried beans, peas and lentils are an excellent source of protein, dietary fiber and complex carbohydrates. Also called legumes or pulses, they are flavorful, nutritionally dense, inexpensive and versatile, and are a great alternative protein source for vegetarians. Cooking dried beans takes more time than opening a can, but dried beans are more flavorful, have a more pleasing texture and are less expensive than canned beans.

Always Do the Following Before Cooking Dried Beans

Sort: Arrange dried beans on a sheet pan or clean kitchen towel, and sort through them to pick out any shriveled or broken beans, stones or debris.

Rinse: Thoroughly rinse the sorted beans in cold, running water.

Soak: Soaking beans before cooking is vital for digestibility. Soaking aids in reducing the hard-to-digest sugars that cause gastrointestinal upset. Never cook beans in the same water used to soak them.

Two Methods for Soaking

Quick soak: Put the beans in a large pot and cover them with two to three inches of cool, clean water. Bring to a boil, and then boil briskly for two to three minutes. Remove from the heat, cover the pot and let sit for one hour. Rinse and drain well before cooking.

Regular soak: Place the beans in a large bowl and cover with filtered water (the water level should be at least three inches over the top of the beans, as the beans will absorb a lot of the water). Let sit at room temperature for eight hours or overnight, and then rinse and drain before cooking.

Suggested Cooking Methods

Stovetop: Put the beans in a large pot and cover them with filtered water or stock until the water or stock is at least two inches above the beans. Don't add salt at this point, because salt toughens the skins and this will cause it to take longer for the beans to soften. Slowly bring to a boil, skimming off any foam that collects on the surface. Reduce the heat, cover the pot and simmer, stirring occasionally and adding more liquid if necessary, until the beans are tender when mashed or pierced with a fork. Refer to the chart on page 41 for cooking times.

Slow cooking: Put the soaked beans in the slow cooker with the other recipe ingredients, and add a two-inch strip of kombu, rather than salt. The kombu will help make the beans more digestible.

Storage

Uncooked: Keep dried beans, peas and lentils in airtight containers and store them in a dry, cool, dark place. Beans stored this way will keep for up to a year, and peas and lentils will keep for up to six months.

Cooked: Refrigerate cooked beans in a covered container for up to 5 days. Beans freeze very well and will last for up to 6 months in an airtight freezer container.

Peas and Lentils

Sort and rinse dried peas and lentils as you would dried beans. Bring 1½ cups of water per cup of peas or lentils to a boil. Once the water boils, add the peas or lentils, return to a boil and then reduce the heat and simmer, partially covered, until tender. Check the chart below for cooking times.

When making soups and stews, you do not need to precook peas or lentils. Simply add them uncooked, but be sure to add enough liquid because they will absorb liquid as they cook.

Preparation of Beans, Peas and Lentils

Refer to the chart below for guidelines on cooking time, water amount and yield for one cup of dried beans, peas or lentils, as well as information on whether or not they need to be soaked.

Bean, pea or lentil	Presoak	Water (cups)	Stovetop cook time	Approximate yield (cups)
Black beans	yes	3 cups	60 to 90 minutes	2¼ cups
Black-eyed peas	no	3 cups	45 to 60 minutes	2 cups
Cannellini beans	yes	3-4 cups	60 to 90 minutes	2½ cups
Chickpeas	yes	4 cups	90 to 150 minutes	2 cups
Great Northern beans	yes	3-4 cups	60 to 90 minutes	2½ cups
Kidney beans	yes	3 cups	60 to 90 minutes	2 cups
Lentils, green or brown	no	1 ½ cups	30 to 40 minutes	2¼ cups
Lentils, red	no	3 cups	15 to 30 minutes	2 cups
Lentils, French or black	no	1 ½ cups	20 to 30 minutes	2 cups
Navy beans	yes	3-4 cups	90 to 120 minutes	2 cups
Split peas (green)	no	3-4 cups	50 to 60 minutes	2 cups
Split peas (yellow)	no	3-4 cups	50 to 60 minutes	2 cups
Pinto beans	yes	3 cups	90 to 120 minutes	2¾ cups
Soybeans	yes	4 cups	3 to 4 hours	2 cups

Whole Grains

Whole grains and whole grain flours have more flavor than refined white flour, because when grains are milled to make refined flours, up to 80% of the grain's nutrients are removed, along with most of its characteristic nutty flavor and chewy texture. See page 266 to learn how to make your own flours.

When you eat a whole grain, you ingest the complete form of the grain, which means that you get all of its vitamins and nutrients and enjoy its complex texture and rich taste. Whole grains include: the bran, which is an important source of most of the B-complex vitamins and of fiber, and which adds body, texture and flavor to the grain; the germ, which contains minerals, B vitamins, protein, vitamin E and oils; and finally, the endosperm, which consists mostly of starch, as well as some protein and other nutrients.

Like nuts and some seeds, grains contain an enzyme-inhibiting substance which make them difficult to digest. Soaking removes this layer and stimulates the process of germination, which increases the nutrients. This traditional practice suggests that whole grains should be soaked overnight, at a minimum. As an additional benefit, your cooking time will be shortened and the bitter taste that some notice with millet and quinoa is minimized. For more information on traditionally preparing grains, nuts and seeds go to www.westonaprice.org or pick up a copy of *Nourishing Traditions* by Sally Fallon.

Look for grains with undamaged kernels, because the outer bran layer protects the kernel's flavor and nutrients from destruction by light and air.

Store whole grains in airtight containers in a cool, dry place out of direct light. Always check the cooking instructions on the package before preparing whole grains. The following are general instructions:

Germination: Combine sea salt with filtered water in a large bowl. The salt activates enzymes that neutralize the enzyme inhibitors. Add the grains to the water (the water level should be two to three inches over the top of the grains). Soak at room temperature overnight. Rinse and drain before adding to a fresh pot of water for cooking. Note: If you do not have time to soak the grains overnight, thoroughly rinse whole grains in cold water until water runs clear immediately prior to cooking.

Cook: As a general rule, you can cook whole grains by simply boiling water (or broth, for added flavor), adding the grain and returning to a boil, and then lowering the heat and simmering, covered, until tender.

Test: As with pasta, always test for doneness a minute before the estimated cooking time. Most whole grains should be slightly chewy when cooked.

Fluff: When grains are done cooking, remove them from the heat and gently fluff them with a fork. Then, cover them and set them aside to sit for five to ten minutes before serving.

Gluten is the substance in some grains that gives dough (made from particular grains) its elasticity and helps bread to rise properly. Many people have gluten intolerances, but to varying degrees. Some can tolerate low levels, but to be safe, gluten is not a suggested allowable ingredient on the diet. You may try to introduce gluten-containing grains at a point when your inflammation has lessened and you are feeling better to see if you can tolerate it (see page 234).

Fats

Grades of Olive Oil

Extra virgin olive oil comes from the first cold pressing of the olives, done by methods that do not refine the oil. The word "cold" is important because if heat is used, the olive oil's chemistry is changed. It also means that no chemicals have been used in the extraction of the oil. Extra virgin olive oil is judged to have a superior taste because its acidity rate of less than 1%.

Like extra virgin olive oil, there is no refined oil in virgin olive oil. Virgin olive oil has an acidity rate of less than 2%, and is judged to have a good taste.

Oils labeled as pure olive oil, olive oil, 100% pure olive oil and light olive oil are all refined oils. Bear in mind, all olive oil contains 120 calories per tablespoon. The only olive oils used in the diet are extra virgin olive oil and virgin olive oil.

Smoke Point

Some oils are better for high temperature cooking than others, because it is important that an oil not reach its smoke point during cooking. The smoke point generally refers to the temperature at which a cooking fat or oil begins to break down into glycerol and free fatty acids. The smoke point also marks the beginning of both flavor and nutritional degradation.

The higher an oil's smoke point, the better it is for high temperature cooking. Oils with similar smoke points are interchangeable in the recipes. The only stipulation is that any fat or oil you wish to substitute for a given oil must be permitted in whichever Phase you are in. Check the list of allowable foods at the beginning of each Phase.

Refer to the product's label for exact recommendations on ideal cooking temperatures, as they differ from product to product.

Refined Foods: Progress or Setback?

As you've learned in Part 1 there are many benefits to changing the way you eat, including reducing your inflammation. It may be interesting to explore history to learn how the way food as we now know it has changed and how this may be to our detriment.

Over one hundred years ago, preparing a meal was a much more complex task than it is today. Meals depended on hunting, fishing and farming. Cooking involved preparation of foods that were bought locally and fresh, or that came from your own land. While this type of food preparation may be inconvenient or impossible in our fast-paced, busy lives, food in those days was fresh, eaten in season, and as close to the original food source as possible, and thus was filled with the nutrients our bodies need.

In the late 1800s, new technology for grinding flour was invented. No longer did whole grains need to be ground by the tedious process of stone grinding. Grains could now be ground using iron, steel or porcelain rollers, which produced a much finer, whiter flour, but which also stripped nutrients away from the original grain.

This new, finely ground flour no longer attracted insects, bacteria or rodents, which might seem like a benefit, except that what had attracted them in the first place were the nutrients that were now missing. Additionally, the new flour lasted months on the shelves and was much easier to transport, a positive change. Eventually, though, people became deficient in certain vitamins because the vitamins had been removed from the whole grains. With current technology, this is no longer a problem, as flours can be enriched with the missing vitamins and minerals.

This was the start of a new modern diet. It truly is a convenient way of eating. We can have a fully prepared meal (from the freezer section) in a matter of minutes. And our food can last months or years in our cupboards. But at what cost?

The modern diet is high in refined fats and sugars and lacking in vegetables and whole grains, and it contains artificial ingredients. Our bodies are not getting the nutrients they require, and we are consuming ingredients that are artificial, sometimes useless and sometimes harmful.

Eating and preparing the freshest foods that do not contain refined ingredients can do wonders for your health. In the pages to come, it is our hope that you realize that eating fresh, unrefined whole foods is worth the extra effort.

Organic Versus Conventional

As you are learning, the diet suggests that foods be eaten as close to their natural state as possible and foods that promote detoxification. Foods grown through conventional methods, however, may involve the use of synthetic fertilizers, pesticides, and herbicides, which in contrast, may contribute to body's toxic burden. To avoid this, organic foods should be used, when possible.

What Does "Organic" Really Mean?

Foods bearing the organic seal require that specific practices be observed in the production and processing of agricultural ingredients. These standards apply to the methods, practices and substances used in producing and handling crops, livestock and processed agricultural products, and they are strictly enforced. Organic growers and handlers must be certified by the USDA, and anyone who knowingly labels or sells an unqualified product as organic can be subject to a penalty of up to $10,000 per violation.

Below are seven good reasons to buy organic food, excerpted from the Northeast Organic Farming Association of NH's "Why Buy Organic?" brochure.

No persistent chemicals. Instead of using chemical fertilizers, herbicides, or fungicides that are often highly toxic, persist in the environment, and leach into soil and groundwater, organic standards require a program of soil building that protects against soil erosion and water pollution.

No synthetic pesticides. Organic standards prohibit the use of synthetic pesticides. No amount of scrubbing will remove pesticides that have been absorbed into a crop.

No genetic engineering. Organic standards prohibit the use of genetically modified organisms (GMOs) for seed or stock. Until compulsory GMO labeling is adopted in this country, buying certified 100% organic products is the best way to keep genetic engineering out of your food.

No antibiotics. Organic standards prohibit routine use of antibiotics in livestock operations. US government regulations permit conventionally-raised animals to be regularly fed subtherapeutic levels of antibiotics to promote growth and prevent disease due to their overcrowded conditions.

No growth hormones. Organic standards prohibit the use of growth hormones, which are used in conventional livestock operations to increase the growth rate of animals or to stimulate the production of milk.

No sludge. Organic standards prohibit the use of sewage sludge as fertilizer, relying instead on the use of composted manure, crop residues, green manures, cover crops, crop rotations, companion planting, and natural mineral supplements to provide needed nutrients to plants.

No irradiation. Organic standards prohibit the use of ionizing radiation to preserve food. Proponents argue that irradiation extends shelf life by killing microbes that spoil food and cause illness. Opponents argue that it also breaks down the enzymes and vitamins that make the food healthy in the first place. They suggest cleaning up industrial feedlots and food processing operations as a better way to protect the public from E. coli and other pathogens.

Where Can I Find Organic Food?
Organic products can be found in grocery stores, cooperatives, specialty stores, farmers' markets, farm stands, online and in many restaurants.

What Should I Look For to Be Sure the Foods I Buy Are Certified Organic?
When you shop, look for the "USDA Organic" seal (shown here). Products labeled "100% Organic" and that carry the "USDA Organic" seal contain only organically produced ingredients. Products made from at least 95% organic ingredients, with the remaining ingredients approved for use in organic products, may also carry the "USDA Organic" seal. In addition, products that contain at least 70% organic ingredients may list those ingredients as organic on the packaging.

What About Non-GMO Labels?
If a food has the USDA organic seal (as seen above) on it, you can trust that it's also non-GMO. When purchasing non-organic foods, some dishonest manufactures have been caught mislabeling their products so you can't always trust that a product is "non-GMO" even if it says so on  the packaging. *Smart Shop,* a magazine that used to be published by *Consumer Reports* had done some investigating on the topic and did find that packages sporting the "non-GMO Project" label (seen here) were in fact, non-GMO.

What About Unlabeled Locally Grown or Imported Foods?
At farmers' markets, it is not uncommon to see hand-written signs that say "grown without the use of pesticides" or "raised without antibiotics or growth hormones" alongside the produce and meats. While these products might not bear the official "USDA Organic" seal, that may be only because these local farmers have not applied for official organic status, which can be costly for a small farm. When buying your meat, eggs, dairy and produce at local farm

stands or farmers' markets, talk to the farmer. You'll often find that the local food you're buying is meeting, or close to meeting, the organic standards.

According to the Organic Trade Association, the organic food industry is the most heavily regulated and closely monitored production system in the United States. When buying food that is imported, such as nuts or coffee, be aware that food grown in other countries is not always subject to the same standards as domestically grown foods.

What If I Can't Afford to Buy Organic?

Unfortunately, organic food does cost more than non-organic, and eating a full diet of 100% organic food is often not financially possible. If you must choose which foods to spend the extra money on, keep the following points in mind.

For meats, fish, poultry, dairy, eggs and other animal-derived products, it is well worth spending the extra money to buy organic. Organic livestock production guidelines ensure that the livestock are fed 100% organically, and are raised without the use of antibiotics and synthetic growth hormones.

Eating only organic fruits and vegetables is quite difficult to do. Not only is it more expensive, but for some fruits and vegetables, an organic option isn't always available. Each year the Environmental Working Group tests and analyzes pesticide residue from 48 popular conventionally grown produce items and ranks them from worst to best. They use this data to compile their Clean 15 and the Dirty Dozen lists, which identify the fruits and vegetables most or least likely to contain pesticides or other harmful toxins. If eating all organic produce is not an option, refer to the chart to the right to see which foods are the cleanest, and which are most at risk for contamination. To get a downloadable version of the guide or view the full list, visit www.ewg.com/foodlist.

EWG's 2016 Clean 15
This list includes conventional produce least likely to hold pesticide residues, avocado being the cleanest choice
1. Avocados
2. Sweet Corn
3. Pineapples
4. Cabbage
5. Sweet peas frozen
6. Onions
7. Asparagus
8. Mangos
9. Papayas
10. Kiwi
11. Eggplant
12. Honeydew Melon
13. Grapefruit
14. Cantaloupe
15. Cauliflower

EWG's 2016 Dirty Dozen
Conventional produce with the highest pesticide loads, strawberries being the "dirtiest"
1. Strawberries
2. Apples
3. Nectarines
4. Peaches
5. Celery
6. Grapes
7. Cherries
8. Spinach
9. Tomatoes
10. Sweet bell peppers
11. Cherry tomatoes
12. Cucumbers

Source: ewg.org/foodnews

Recipes for Repair

How to Read "Nutrition Facts" Food Labels

The Nutrition Facts food label on every packaged food contains all the information you need to make an informed decision about which foods to buy. It is important that you become an avid label reader, as many packaged foods often contain sugars and other sweeteners, as well as artificial and refined ingredients, all of which should be avoided for the best possible outcome in your recovery. The secret to reading a food label is knowing what to look for. In June 2016 the FDA announced that new nutrition labels are coming and they look to be much more beneficial to the consumer.

How to Read a Nutrition Label

Important and reliable information can be found on the nutrition Nutrition Facts panel and ingredient listing. Below is a label from a can of organic tomato paste, with each section of the label defined.

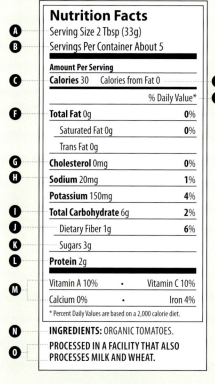

A. **Serving Size:** A serving size is the amount of food that should be eaten in one serving. It is listed by a general household measurement, such as pieces, cups or ounces (i.e., 10 nuts or ½ cup of rice). Serving size is an important part of a healthy diet. Eating larger portions than the recommended amount will contribute to weight gain.

B. **Servings Per Container:** Sometimes that small package that you assume is one serving is really two or more. If manufacturers think that you will be scared off by the high number of calories, they sometimes make two servings out of what appears to be a single serving nutrition bar or bag of nuts. So, always check the number of servings as well as the calorie count.

C. **Calories:** The number of calories in a serving, not in the whole container.

D. **Calories From Fat:** The number of calories per serving that come from fat.

E. **Daily Value (% DV):** A healthy person should consume a certain amount of fats, carbohydrates, fiber, protein and vitamins and minerals each day. The nutrition label provides a list of percentages (called the Percent Daily Value) which tells you what percentage of your daily requirement of a given nutrient one serving of the food provides. The Percent Daily Value is based on a daily diet of 2,000 calories. Calorie adjustments must be made

Recipes for Repair

for age, gender and exercise level. See www.mypyramid.gov for more information.

F. **Total Fat:** The number of grams of fat per serving. The information is broken down into Saturated Fat and Trans Fat. Companies are allowed to list the amount of trans fat as 0 grams if one serving contains less than .5 grams of trans fat. Always check the ingredient list for trans fat, which may be listed as hydrogenated vegetable oil or partially hydrogenated vegetable oil.

G. **Cholesterol:** The number of grams of cholesterol per serving. You should pay close attention to this number if you have heart disease.

H. **Sodium:** Processed foods tend to be very high in sodium. Look closely to make sure your diet is not too high in it.

I. **Total Carbohydrate:** The number of grams of carbohydrates per serving.

J. **Dietary Fiber:** Fiber helps your body digest the food you eat, and it can help lower your risk of diabetes and heart disease. A food is considered high in fiber if it contains 5 grams of fiber or more per serving. Fiber is found in fruits, vegetables and whole grains.

K. **Sugars:** The total amount of sugar per serving. Sugars add calories, and are often listed on the label in other terms, such as "high fructose corn syrup," "dextrose," "invert sugar" or "turbinado." Pay extra attention to the ingredients list to be sure you are not consuming sugars that are not part of the LID.

L. **Protein:** The number of grams of protein per serving.

M. **Vitamins and Minerals:** The nutrition label lists vitamin A, vitamin C, calcium and iron. You should try to get more of these nutrients in your daily diet, as well as other vitamins and minerals that are not listed on the label.

N. **Ingredient List:** Manufacturers are required to list all of the ingredients contained in the product by weight and in order of amount, from most to least. A jar of tomato sauce with tomatoes as the first ingredient lets you know that tomatoes are the main ingredient. A spice or herb listed last is present in the least amount. This information is critical for anyone who has allergies, and for prudent shoppers who want more tomatoes than water, or whole foods rather than refined.

O. **Allergens:** Manufacturers will include a warning on the label if the food was made in a factory where foods containing allergens (such as nuts) have been processed on the same manufacturing lines.

Don't Be Confused By the Words Printed On the Labels

Labels found on the front of packaged foods can be misleading or downright inaccurate. Words such as "fresh," "no additives" and "all-natural" may look good, but these terms are not regulated, and so should be taken with a grain of salt. Your best bet is to review the Nutrition Facts food label (page 48) and look at the actual ingredients in the product. If you can't pronounce or don't recognize an ingredient, chances are you should steer clear of that particular product.

A good rule of thumb when buying packaged foods is to choose ones with a limited amount of ingredients.

How to Save

It is unfortunate that eating well and providing our bodies with the best possible nutrition comes at a much higher price tag than does eating convenient or processed foods. With savvy and a little extra effort, however, a whole foods diet doesn't need to be a financial burden. Below are 14 tips on how to save money when buying whole and/or organic foods for the diet.

1. **Make your own.** In the Pantry and Sauces and Condiments sections of this book (pages 256-289), you'll find some recipes that give you the option of making your own basic ingredients, which can save you a significant amount of money. For example, learn how to make your own ghee and ketchup. Additionally, lesser known grains, ground into flour, can be bought pre-packaged at any natural foods store, but the cost is often quite high. For the best possible bargain, you can buy the grain itself and grind your own flour for a fraction of the store price. (See page 266 for homemade flours.)

2. **Buy a coffee grinder.** Having a coffee grinder dedicated to items other than coffee beans will save you an extraordinary amount of money. Organic nut butters can cost more than $20 per jar! You can grind your own nut butters at home. After grinding your first few jars, the investment of an inexpensive coffee grinder will be more than paid for. In the Pantry section (page 256), you'll find recipes that explain how to use a coffee grinder to make nut butters, flours and more.

3. **Pick your own.** A fun activity to share with friends and family is to go berry, apple or peach picking. There's nothing more delicious than freshly picked berries, and their lower-than-store price is an added bonus. Freeze blueberries or peaches to use throughout the year.

4. **Grow your own.** If you have a green thumb, consider growing your own vegetable or herb garden. Plant your favorite herbs in pots so you can have them for cooking all year round. Grow an extra crop of your favorite vegetables, and can or freeze them to use throughout the winter.

5. **Join a CSA.** CSA, or community supported agriculture, gives consumers the opportunity to purchase a membership to cover production costs of local farmers. In exchange, consumers receive a weekly share of the farm's seasonal produce throughout the harvest period. Being a member of a CSA introduces new and different in-season vegetables to your diet, providing you with a wider range of nutrients.

6. **Shop at a farmers' market.** Farmers' markets are very popular and have similar advantages to a CSA: you can buy local, freshly picked produce, farm-fresh eggs, cheeses, meats, herbs and more. Prices are often less than you'd find at your local grocery store, and the food is fresher, generally picked that day.

7. **Become a member.** A food co-op is a collectively owned grocery store that allows shoppers to become members. Some co-ops have special offers for members that are not available to the general public.

8. **Browse closeout stores.** Closeout stores are a great place to find affordable, delicious, organic foods. We have found organic extra virgin olive oil at a local chain closeout store for $6.99 per bottle. Compare that price to the same-sized bottle at the grocery store, priced at a whopping $18.99. Make sure to check the expiration dates.

9. **Buy ingredients or foods online.** You'll be surprised at the variety of high quality, organic foods you can find online for a significant bargain. See the Resources section (page 290) for some websites to try out.

10. **Sign up for online savings.** Some stores have online programs that you can join by providing an email address. They offer perks like extra savings on certain days and printable coupons that are not published anywhere else.

11. **Take advantage of sales, circulars and coupons.** Stores run specials all the time, and when one of your favorite foods is on sale, buying in bulk is the way to go. If you have internet access, you can go online to sign up for coupons, or to look up the weekly specials. One time we discovered organic almonds were discounted by $4.00 per pound at a local natural foods store. You never know what kind of deal you might snag by being an informed shopper.

12. **Know your prices.** Product prices can vary by dollars from one store to another. Develop a list of your favorite products and compile a price comparison for each store where you shop. You'll be surprised by how much you can save just by knowing what foods to buy at which store.

13. **Buy in bulk.** The savings from buying bulk over packaged can be substantial. Co-ops, natural food stores and some chain grocery stores offer foods in bulk. From nuts to grains to herbs and spices, you can buy the amount that suits your needs.

14. **Ask for it.** A company wants nothing more than a new customer. If you would like to try a new product, but price is a factor, you can contact the company and tell them so. Often they will send you coupons or samples.

Pickled Beets, page 88

Shredded Carrot Salad, page 97

Part III
Getting Started

Green Beans with Shiitake Mushrooms and Almonds, page 98

Stir-Fried Bok Choy, Leeks and Pine Nuts, page 99

"Week Zero"— Preparing for the Diet

By now you have learned about the Lyme Inflammation Diet and how implementing it can help you discover food sensitivities and help reduce inflammation and symptoms caused by dietary inflammation. But preparation is the secret to success, both when cooking and when implementing the diet, so we recommend that you begin with what we like to call "week zero" in the days leading up to Phase 1. During this time, we suggest you do the following, which will help prepare for the start of the diet:

- **Learn the diet.** Before starting the diet, take time to familiarize yourself with it. Read all of the information in Parts 1 and 2 so that you gain a full understanding of the diet before you even begin.
- **Try the recipes.** Thumb through all the recipes and pick out and make some that appeal to you. It is important that you try the recipes from all Phases because once you do you will realize that they all taste really great. This realization will help alleviate some of the common fears people have, like the concern that the food will taste like "diet" food or that you will feel deprived.
- **Make extra.** We always say "cook once, eat many times." As you prepare some of the recipes (as suggested above), consider doubling some of the recipes. This does not take much more time or effort, but will give you extra servings that you can freeze. There's nothing better than coming home after a long day and reheating a meal that has already been prepared.
- **Stock your pantry.** As you familiarize yourself with the diet's allowable foods, also take note on what foods are never allowed. Spend some time reading labels on the foods in your refrigerator and pantry. If any contain sugar, artificial ingredients, trans-fats and other ingredients that are not permitted on the diet do not restock them next time you shop. The goal is to start replacing processed, convenience foods with healthier alternatives. You can't be tempted by foods that are not in your kitchen, so it's best to remove foods that do not comply with the diet.
- **Make a meal plan.** For ease, we have created a meal plan for Phase 1 (pages 70-71). This can be used as a starting point or followed to the letter. Decide which recipes you want to make, and plan your menu during this preparation stage. Once you have nailed down your meal plan, review each recipe and determine which recipes from the Pantry and Sauces and Condiments sections (pages 256-289) are called for in the recipes you will be making. Write them down with the page number. There are a good number of recipes within the recipes, so we suggest that you make them over a few days. This will help you not to feel overwhelmed once you begin Phase 1.

- **Shopping.** Download and print out a copy of our Shopping List from our website. Read each recipe that you plan to make, and determine which grocery items you'll need to buy, including the quantity. Write these down on the Shopping List. If you plan to buy any ingredients online, be sure to check our Resources section (page 290), as well as our resources section of our website, www.recipesforrepair.com/resources, for recommendations.

Once you begin cooking the recipes, we suggest you:

- **Group recipes.** Choose a few similar recipes, that have similar preparation methods, cooking methods or ingredients to make on the same day. For instance, make the almond butter and almond flour on the same day.
- **Rely on small appliances.** Some kitchen gadgets and small appliances can become your best friend in the kitchen. The tools we rely on most are a digital food scale, a food processor, a blender and a stand mixer. If you are not sure whether you want to make the investment in a certain small appliance or kitchen gadget, borrow one. We'll bet that if you put a post up on Facebook or email friends and family asking to borrow a food processor or blender, for example, you will find several people would be happy to loan you one.
- **Recruit help.** Maybe your family members don't know how to cook, but chances are they can measure, clean or chop (adults, not children). If you have small kids, get them in the kitchen with you and have them do simple tasks like breaking the stems off the green beans. Teenagers or adults can help you measure the ingredients, wash fruits and vegetables, slice and dice them, and clean up the mess when you're done.
- **Precook the rice.** Brown rice is a staple in the diet, especially in Phase 1. Cook a 2-pound bag of brown rice, short grain brown rice, and brown and wild rice before you start the diet. It keeps in the refrigerator for up to a week and in the freezer indefinitely.
- **Mix dry ingredients in advance.** Some recipes, like the Sloppy Joes (page 205) have a mixture of herbs and spices that can be measured in advance. You can measure out enough for one or more recipes' worth. When combined, the seasoning mixture measures out to just under 2 tablespoons. Store the mixture in a jar with instructions so you know when it was made and how much you need to add. Next time you want to make this recipe, all you will have to do is sauté an onion and meat, add 2 tablespoons of the already-prepared seasonings, and measure out the tomato paste and water. That cuts the prep time in half! You can also do this with any of the baked goods to make your own pre-packaged baked goods mix!
- **Pre-cook onions and garlic.** Many of the recipes call for sautéed onions and garlic. A helpful practice to get into is to refer to your meal plan for

the week to assess how many onions and garlic cloves will be needed for all of the recipes. Chop and cook that quantity on a day you have some spare time and store the cooked mixture in a container in the refrigerator for later use. We generally weigh the cooked onion and garlic mixture and divide it by the number of onions we used to get a weight per onion. This helps us to know how much to use in the recipes we will be preparing.

All of the suggestions are good habits to get into, and as time goes on it will be of great benefit in all the Phases of the diet.

Snack Ideas and Easy Meal Suggestions

It's important to keep in mind that not all of your meals and snacks need to have been made from a recipe. If you are feeling tired or simply don't have enough time to prepare a meal, you can always try some the following ideas (just be sure you're eating foods that are permissible with your current diet Phase):

- For breakfast, scramble up some eggs and serve them with leftover veggies.
- Cut up apple slices and have them with almond butter or have celery sticks dipped in your favorite nut butter.
- Make a trail mix with allowable nuts and dried unsweetened fruits.
- Grill your favorite allowable protein and serve with steamed or grilled veggies.
- Cook a turkey or beef burger and top it with avocado slices on a bed of baby spinach tossed with a salad dressing of your choice.
- Grill or bake some chicken and use it on top of salads. Easier yet, buy a plain rotisserie turkey or chicken and serve with steamed veggies for dinner. Use leftovers to make chicken stock and/or chicken salad.
- Try brown rice cakes (i.e., Lundberg Brown Rice Cakes) with a nut butter as a tasty snack. Add some Berry Compote (page 75) or Cran-Raspberry Sauce (page 275) and Cashew Honey Butter (page 263) for a nut butter and "jelly" cake.
- Make a cold salad with leftover cooked grains, chopped vegetables, nuts and/ or seeds, herbs, extra virgin olive oil and an allowable vinegar of your choice.
- Have a baked sweet potato as a snack or side dish with dinner.
- Once you reach Phase 3, make air-popped popcorn and add melted ghee (if tolerated) and sea salt for super, easy snack.
- Dehydrate your favorite fruits for an easy, on-the-go snack.
- Make a quick and simple veggie stir-fry with frozen vegetables. As an example: Sauté onions and garlic, add ground beef, peas, artichoke hearts, and broccoli. When cooked, sprinkle on sesame seeds and mix in a splash of tamari.

Packaged Foods That Comply with the Diet

While making meals from scratch ensures that you know exactly what you are eating, we understand that not everyone has the energy, time or desire to do so. Luckily, there are wonderful packaged foods on the market that comply with the diet. We list our favorite products, including which Phase they comply with, at www.recipesforrepair.com/our-favorite-products. Check back often, as we make updates when we find tasty new products. Below are just a few examples!

Adding Cultured Foods to Your Diet

Another easy way to cut down on your time in the kitchen is to add cultured vegetables to your meals. Rather than cooking a side dish, you simply have to open a jar and serve. How easy is that?

Taking a high-quality probiotic (see related box on page 58) that your doctor recommends is important, but adding cultured foods to your diet is another, much tastier way to introduce good bacteria to your gut.

Helping to restore healthy intestinal flora is not the only health benefit from eating cultured foods. They also increase the bioavailability of nutrients; improve digestion and absorption; have cleansing properties; and are rich in enzymes.

Yogurt (made from either cow or goat milk) is a very commonly used cultured food, but unfortunately is not generally an option for the dairy intolerant. You can also buy, or even make yourself, yogurt from non-dairy types of milk such as coconut and soy milks. However, be sure to read the product labels closely, as quite often the store bought varieties have large amounts of added sugar. Other non-dairy cultured foods include cultured vegetables, cultured tea (kombucha) and cultured beet juice (kvass), to name a few.

Try purchasing cultured foods and adding them to your diet. Or better yet, if you'd like to make your own cultured vegetables, there are many helpful resources online, including videos that take you through the process step-by-step. There are also wonderful cookbooks with a wide variety of recipes for cultured foods. (See page 291 for some suggestions.)

Below are a few recipes with suggested cultured foods that work well with those particular meals:

- Calico Slaw (page 95) is delicious when made with cultured red cabbage. The tartness of the cabbage is a tasty contrast to the sweetness of the other ingredients.
- The Cook's Note to the recipe for Deviled Eggs (page 85) suggests transforming the recipe into egg salad. When making this egg salad, chop up real kosher pickles (cultured cucumbers) and add them to the eggs.
- Shredded Carrot Salad (page 97) can be revised by using ½ cup grated raw carrots and ½ cup cultured carrots.
- Kimchi has a kick and is a nice addition to the Stir-Fried Chicken with Red Peppers and Cashews (page 203).
- Add sauerkraut (also known as cultured cabbage) to the Slow Cooked Pulled Chicken (page 207). Please note that canned sauerkraut, while fermented, has no significant healthy bacteria left in the product. Unfortunately the heat of the canning process destroys the beneficial bacteria. Like all other healthy probiotic-rich cultured or fermented foods, you will find raw sauerkraut in the refrigerated section of the store.
- You can purchase (or make your own) fermented nut cheeses that are delicious! This makes a great edition to the stuffing in the Stuffed Turkey Burgers (page 154).

You can also just serve any type of cultured vegetable as a side dish with lunch or dinner or use them in place of salad dressing on any of your favorite salads.

Dr. Singleton's Tips on Probiotics with the Use of Antibiotics

Patients using antibiotics – as is typical for Lyme disease – must be concerned about balancing the negative effects of those drugs with the healthful benefits of probiotics.

Antibiotics can destroy the intestinal tract bacteria responsible for food digestion. Probiotics introduce new healthy bacteria to your system. It's normally sufficient to consume foods that are good natural sources of probiotics (fermented foods such as kefir, yogurt, kombucha, tempeh and sauerkraut are especially good sources). When taking antibiotics, however, it's generally best to supplement your diet with a high-quality probiotic formula on a daily basis.

Be sure to carefully time and sequence your daily antibiotic and probiotic doses. If you take them together, they'll in effect cancel each other out. Generally, a separation of two or more hours ensures that both work effectively.

Also, note that it is important to continue taking probiotics for several weeks (and sometimes months) after antibiotics have been discontinued to restore the balance of intestinal bacteria.

Using Recipes as a Template

We've had readers comment on how they decide against a recipe because they don't have or don't like one of the secondary ingredients. If there is a particular vegetable or spice that you don't have or don't like you can use a substitution as long as it's an allowable food in the Phase you're currently in.

If you're new to cooking and aren't sure what the right substitution would be, you can either do an Internet search to find a suitable substitute or contact us on Facebook or via email. We are always happy to help. Recipes can be used as a template, so feel free to experiment and make modifications to any of the recipes. If you come up with something that you really enjoy, make a notation of it in your book for future use.

Introductory Cooking Terms for Beginners

If you don't have much experience cooking from scratch, use the following explanation of cooking supplies and cooking terms as your reference.

Baking supplies

Cake pans: 8- or 9-inch round pans, used for cakes; or 8x8x2- or 9x9x2-inch square pans, used for brownies, bar cookies and general cooking and baking.

Cooling racks: Wire racks of assorted sizes, used to cool cakes, cookies and other baked goods.

Custard cups: Heat resistant cups (usually about 5 ounces in size) that can be placed in the oven, used to make individual servings of custard and pudding.

Flour sifters, with handles: Used to sift (remove lumps and lighten texture) flour (wire sieves can also be used for this purpose).

Loaf pans: 9x5x3- or 8½x4½x2½-inch pans, used for quick breads.

Muffin pans: 6- or 12-cup muffin pans, used for muffins.

Tart pans: 8-, 9- or 10-inch pans with removable bottoms, used for tarts and quiches.

Pie plates: 8-, 9- or 10-inch pans (also 9-inch deep dish pie plates), used for pies and quiches.

Measuring cups

Nesting measuring cups: A set of cups, which are known as "dry measure" cups because they are used to measure dry ingredients. A set usually consists of one each of ¼-cup, ⅓-cup, ½-cup and 1-cup measures. Some sets also include ¾-cup and ⅔-cup measures. You should own at least one set of measuring cups.

Graduated measuring cups: Glass or plastic cups with spouts and handles, in a variety of sizes from 1-cup to 10-cup, used to measure liquids. They are marked by ounces and by fractions of a cup: ¼-cup, ⅓ cup, ⅔-cup, ¾-cup and 1-cup.

Measuring spoons: A set of spoons, usually nesting and connected at the handles, used to measure small amounts from ¼-teaspoon up to 1-tablespoon.

Mixers

Hand mixers: Used for light-duty mixing, although some of these mixers are very powerful and come with dough hooks.

Stand mixers: Heavy-duty mixers with detachable bowls, dough hooks and more powerful motors; can be used for long-term mixing and kneading.

Stick (immersion) blenders: Hand-held blenders that are used for blending soups, making smoothies and more.

Other Kitchen Equipment

Blenders and food processors: If you don't have both types of equipment, these two appliances can be used interchangeably. However, blenders are better for making homemade mayonnaise and for liquefying fruits and vegetables for drinks. Food processors are better for slicing, chopping and shredding large quantities of food in a few seconds.

Cheesecloth: Cheesecloth is light-weight cotton mesh cloth commonly used to strain foods. It can be purchased in the baking section of the grocery store, or by the yard at the fabric store.

Citrus zesters: used to remove the skins, commonly called the "zest," from citrus fruits).

Colanders: Used to drain water from pasta and cooked vegetables.

Cutting boards: Boards made from wood or plastic, used for cutting, chopping and many other kitchen tasks. For food safety reasons, you should have several cutting boards reserved for different purposes: one for meats, one for poultry and one for vegetables and fruits. Be sure to keep them clean and sanitized by washing them in the dishwasher, or with a mild solution of bleach.

Double boiler: Pot with a separate insert that fits into its top. To cook with a double boiler, fill the bottom section with 2 inches of water and bring the water almost to a boil. Place the food in the top of part of the double boiler, set it over the bottom section and cook as the recipe directs. If you don't have a double boiler, you can make one by using a bowl and a pot that fit together, so that the bowl rests in the pot without touching the pot's contents. Never allow the boiling or hot water in the bottom section of a double boiler to touch the bottom of the double boiler's top section.

Sieves/strainers: Usually made of fine, stainless steel mesh; can be used to drain liquid, or as sifters.

Cooking Methods

Below you will find definitions for various cooking methods and techniques used in recipes in this and other cookbooks.

Bake: Cook in an oven, usually in one that has been preheated.

Baste: Moisten roasting food, usually using the pan juices.

Beat: Combine a mixture until smooth by bringing the depths to the surface and vice-versa, usually using a mixer, wire whisk or spoon.

Blanch: Drop in boiling water for about a minute, usually done to remove the skin from fruits, vegetables or nuts.

Blend: Thoroughly combine two or more ingredients, usually using a spoon, wire whisk or electric mixer.

Boil: Heat a liquid until bubbles constantly rise to the surface (water boils at 212ºF). A full, rolling boil is reached when stirring the liquid will not quell the bubbling. Most recipes instruct you to lower the heat once a liquid comes to a boil, at which lower temperature, the liquid will simmer.

Braise: Brown on all sides in a hot pan using a small amount of oil. After the food is browned, add liquid and cover the pan. Simmer until tender on medium to low heat. Braising is generally done to tenderize tougher cuts of meat.

Broil: Cook on the oven rack directly below the heating source, using a pan with a drip tray. In outdoor broiling, cook indirectly above the heated coals.

Caramelize: Use intense dry heat, as in roasting or sautéing, to break down the natural sugars contained in all meats and vegetables, resulting in brown color and rich flavor.

Chop: Cut into roughly equal-sized pieces – either coarse larger-sized pieces, or finely chopped, smaller-sized pieces.

Coat: Evenly cover with a substance, such as nut or bread crumbs.

Cool: Allow to stand at room temperature until no longer warm.

Cream: Combine softened shortening, butter or with sweetener until the mixture is light and fluffy, usually using an electric mixer.

Cube: Cut into equal-sized pieces, such as ½-inch pieces.

Cut in: Use two knives or a pastry cutter to slice fat, such as butter, into flour until the fat and flour form pea-sized pieces.

Dice: Cut into very small (¼-inch) cubes.

Dissolve: Mix a dry substance into a liquid until it forms a solution.

Dredge: Coat lightly with a substance, such as flour or breadcrumbs.

Fold: Incorporate into a mixture by using an under-over motion, often using a rubber spatula. Most often, recipes will instruct you to fold beaten egg whites into a mixture. Unlike stirring, which breaks up the egg whites and causes them to deflate, folding egg whites incorporates air into the mixture.

Grate: Shred into small uniform pieces, using a grater, zester or the grating disc of a food processor.

Grease: Rub the surface of a pan with butter or shortening, or spray with non-stick cooking spray. Greasing helps keep food from sticking to the pan, and makes removing food from the pan easier.

Marinate: Let stand in a marinade mixture for a prescribed period of time, usually in the refrigerator in order to flavor and/or tenderize meat.

Mince: Cut very fine.

Pan-broil: Cook uncovered in an ungreased or lightly greased frying pan, pouring off any accumulated fat.

Pan-fry: Cook in a frying pan using a small amount of hot fat.

Par-boil: Cook or boil partially. Parboiling is usually a preliminary part of the cooking process, with parboiled foods later being fried, baked or roasted.

Pare: Remove the skin or outer coating of a fruit or vegetable.

Peel: Remove the skin or outer coating of a fruit, such as a banana or orange, usually by hand.

Preheat: Heat an oven or griddle to a desired temperature before using it for baking or cooking.

Pulse: Process or blend in a food processor or blender by holding down the "on" button for a second or two, and then releasing.

Purée: Reduce to paste or a sauce-like consistency, using a blender, food processor or food mill.

Sauté: Cook in a small amount of hot fat.

Score: Cut shallow slits in the surface.

Sear: Brown the surface quickly over high heat in a frying pan, or on a grill pan.

Season: Sprinkle with salt, pepper, herbs and/or spices.

Sift: Pass through a flour sifter or sieve, in order to make a substance (usually flour) lighter and to remove any lumps.

Simmer: Cook just below the boiling point, at about 185°F.

Sliver: Cut into long, thin pieces.

Stir: Blend with a spoon in a circular motion, widening the circle until all the ingredients are incorporated.

Thicken: Blend a thickening agent, such as arrowroot, cornstarch or flour, with a small amount of liquid until it forms a smooth paste. Whisk the resulting paste into the liquid to be thickened and continue to stir (usually while heating to a boil) until the liquid becomes thick.

Toss: Mix lightly with two forks, or a fork and spoon, usually done to coat salad greens with dressing.

Whip: Beat with an electric mixer or wire whisk, in order to incorporate air and increase volume.

Zest: Zest is the thin outer skin of a citrus fruit and contains the essential oils of the fruit. It adds the flavor of the fruit, without the acid.

Before You Cook, Remember...

- Read the recipe thoroughly.
- Take time to learn the basic cooking techniques used in the recipe.
- Be sure you have all the ingredients assembled and enough time to prepare the recipe before you begin to cook. If you are missing ingredients, feel free to substitute something similar for the missing item.
- Always wash produce, grains and beans, even if they are organic. Vegetables that have an outer skin, such as melons and squash, should also be washed, because when you cut them, germs on the skin can spread into the edible portion.
- Always wash your hands before cooking, and after touching raw poultry.
- Wash cooking surfaces and place cutting boards in the dishwasher after preparing foods, especially poultry and meats. This will help ensure food safety.
- Always marinate food in the refrigerator, unless it marinates for less than 30 minutes, or the recipe specifically instructs otherwise.

Explanation of the Recipes

The recipes are organized according to the four Phases of the diet. At the beginning of each Phase there is a table of contents for that specific Phase and a list of the foods introduced in that Phase. You will then find recipes specific to that Phase of the diet and each recipe page has the following features:

A **Category** indicates Breakfast, Soups/Salads/Sides/Snacks, Entrees or Desserts/Drinks

B **Symbols** indicate support of the following dietary modifications:

Dairy-free   Egg-free   Vegetarian   PALEO

We interpret the above dietary modifications as follows:

Dairy-free recipes do not include milk or any foods derived from milk. Any recipes that contain ghee (also known as clarified butter) as the only form of dairy can be adapted to be dairy-free by using the alternate oil suggested in the ingredients list, which we make note of in the recipe. Please note that in many instances, those who are lactose intolerant can eat ghee without ill effects.

Egg-free recipes do not contain eggs. In some instances, a recipe may have an egg-free symbol, despite having an egg in the ingredients list. In these cases, you will find a substitution and revised list of instructions so that it can be made egg-free.

Vegetarian recipes don't include meat or poultry, but may include fish, eggs, honey and/or dairy products.

Paleo meals have been identified for those who discover that they feel best with the elimination of beans, starches, grains and dairy.

C **Phase** numbers are color coded as follows:
■ Phase 1 ■ Phase 2 ■ Phase 3 ■ Phase 4

D **Title** and comments for the recipe

E **Recipe time and serving size**

F **Ingredients**

G **Directions**

H **Variations** of the recipe suitable for other Phases. As you progress through the diet, be sure to look back to recipes in previous Phases so that you can enjoy the recipe with the addition of a new, allowable food.

I **Notes** giving nutritional details or cooking tips.

Note: At the beginning of each diet Phase you will find a table of contents with recipes to that Phase (pages 66, 118, 164, 234, 256 and 269). Here we have identified if a recipe is dairy-free, egg-free, vegetarian and/or Paleo so that you can quickly see which recipes are suitable for your specific needs.

Soups/Salads/Sides/Snacks PALEO PHASE 1

Creamy Asparagus Soup

Coconut milk adds a creamy feel to this nutritious, easy-to-make dairy-free Creamy Asparagus Soup.

Prep time: 10 minutes
Cook time: 40 minutes

Makes: 4 servings

- 2 tablespoons extra virgin olive oil
- 1 medium onion, chopped
- 2 cloves garlic, chopped
- 1 large carrot, peeled and chopped
- 1 stalk celery, chopped
- 8 ounces asparagus, chopped
- 2 teaspoons freshly chopped dill
- ½ teaspoon freshly chopped tarragon
- 1 tablespoon freshly chopped parsley
- 1 teaspoon sea salt
- 3 cups Vegetable Broth (page 259)
- 1 cup Coconut Milk (page 261)

1. Heat the oil in a 2-quart saucepot over medium heat for 1-2 minutes, or until hot.
2. Sauté the onions for 3 minutes, or until they are limp and just starting to brown.
3. Add the garlic, carrots, celery, and asparagus and sauté for 5 minutes.
4. Add the remaining ingredients, stir well to combine and bring the soup to a boil over medium-high heat. Lower to medium heat and simmer for 30 minutes.
5. Pour the soup into a blender container. Cover the container. Remove the center cup from the cover.
6. Place a clean, folded kitchen towel over the blender cover and press down with your hand.
7. Purée the soup until smooth.
8. Serve immediately and refrigerate leftovers.

PHASE 3 variation: Once you reach Phase 3, you may substitute Chicken Bone Broth (page 264). Bone broth is rich in minerals, is very healing, aids in digestion and tastes wonderful.

Cook's Note: If you can't tolerate coconuts, replace the 1 cup of coconut milk with an extra cup of broth. It will not be creamy but still tastes great. Enjoy this and other soups with the Savory Vegetable and Herb Biscotti (page 89). For an even creamier version of this soup, use canned organic full-fat coconut milk with guar gum (an ingredient introduced into the diet in Phase 3).

Recipes for Repair

Phase 1 Contents

Carrot Almond Pancakes	73
Make-Ahead Brown Rice Porridge with Mixed Berry Compote	75
Coconut Berry Smoothie	77
Cherry Vanilla Almond Blast	77
Poached Eggs Florentine with Béarnaise Sauce	79
Herb Scrambled Eggs with Shiitake Mushrooms	81
Brown Rice Pancake	82
Apple and Nut Skillet	83
Green Smoothie	84
Deviled Eggs	85
Egg Salad	85
Creamy Asparagus Soup	87
Pickled Beets	88
Savory Vegetable and Herb Biscotti	89
Cauliflower Carrot Soup	91
Steamed Vegetables and Brown & Wild Rice w/ Fresh Herb Vinaigrette	93
Grilled Salmon over Assorted Greens w/ Fresh Herb Vinaigrette	94
Calico Slaw	95
Crispy Kale	95
Mashed Cauliflower	96
Cinnamon Applesauce	96
Shredded Carrot Salad	97
Green Beans with Shiitake Mushrooms and Almonds	98
Stir-Fried Bok Choy, Leeks and Pine Nuts	99
Stir-Fried Brown Rice and Vegetables	101
Moroccan Spice-Rubbed Salmon	103
Brown and Wild Rice Cauliflower and Mushroom Curry	104
Almond and Herb Crusted Tilapia	105
Sautéed Salmon Cakes	107
Slow Cooked Brown Rice Risotto and Mushrooms	109
Sautéed Filet of Sole with Artichoke Pesto	110
Berry Frozen Dessert	111
Nutty Coconut Delight	113
Chewy Coconut Almond Cookies	115
Coconut Almond Custard	116
Açai and Blueberry Spritzer	117
Mint Tea	117
Ginger Mint Tea	117

Phase 1: The Induction Phase *(one week)*

Phase 1 is to be followed for one week. Its goal is to help your body quickly shut down the mechanisms of chronic inflammation and begin detoxifying. This is accomplished by eating a primarily vegetarian diet consisting of fiber-rich foods with anti-inflammatory properties which will help your body to quickly and effectively begin to control inflammation.

In addition to restricting yourself to the foods permitted in Phase 1 (see the list on the next page), you should strive to follow these guidelines:

- Choose wild-caught fish rather than farm-raised, which are often full of antibiotics and coloring dyes.
- Broil, bake, or sauté fish and eggs. Do not fry fish (or eggs), as fried foods significantly contribute to inflammation in the body.
- Eat at least 5-8 servings of vegetables and 2-3 servings of fruit each day.
- Eat almonds, walnuts, pine nuts and freshly ground flaxseed, which are loaded with anti-inflammatory oils and nutrient.
- Drink pure, filtered water, or unsweetened fruit juices (sparingly) from the beverage list. Juice the fruits yourself, or buy high-quality fruit juices with no added sugar or artificial ingredients. If you get bored with water, toss in a piece of fresh mint or ginger to mix things up a bit!
- During this (and every) Phase, you should avoid eating foods you know you are allergic or sensitive to, even if they are on the list of allowable foods
- Follow the General Food Guidelines and Food Choices for Detoxification on pages 28-30 during all Phases of the diet.

> **Modifying Fruit Consumption While Using Antibiotics**
>
> When taking antibiotics, you should generally limit your intake of most fruits because their naturally high sugar content can lead to yeast overgrowth in the intestinal system.
>
> An unfortunate side effect of antibiotics is the death of healthy bacteria along with the unhealthy. Healthy bacteria help prevent the uncontrolled growth of potentially harmful organisms such as yeast, so their absence sets the stage for intestinal yeast infection. Because yeast feeds on sugar – even that from healthy fruits – the combination of antibiotics and fruit can lead to serious problems.
>
> Therefore, when following the diet while taking antibiotics, observe these additional guidelines:
>
> **Eat Phase 1** fruits only two to three times per week.
> **Eat Phase 2** fruits only one to two times per week.
> **In Phase 3**, eat low-sugar fruits, such as lemon, lime and grapefruit, daily if desired.
>
> Any time you're taking antibiotics, also take probiotics to replace the friendly bacteria. *(See the sidebar on page 58 for more on probiotics.)*

Foods Allowed During Phase 1

Beverages [1]
  Açai juice
  Blackberry juice
  Blueberry juice
  Cherry juice [2]
  Cranberry juice
  Pomegranate juice [2]
  Pure filtered water
  Raspberry juice
  Rooibos tea

Fruits
  Açai
  Avocado
  Blackberries
  Blueberries
  Cherries [2]
  Coconut (or
    coconut milk) [3]
  Cranberries
  Green apple NEW
  Pomegranate [2]
  Raspberry

Nuts and Seeds
  Almonds (or
    almond milk) [3]
  Chia seeds NEW
  Flaxseed
  Pine nuts
  Walnuts

Vegetables
  Artichoke
  Arugula
  Asparagus
  Beets
  Bok choy
  Broccoli
  Cauliflower
  Brussels sprouts
  Cabbage
  Carrots
  Celery
  Chard
  Collard greens
  Cucumber
  Garlic
  Kale
  Leeks
  Mushrooms (shiitake
    are the best choice)
  Mustard greens
  Onions
  Lettuce
  Scallions
  Spinach
  Sprouts
  String beans
  Watercress

Grains
  Brown rice
  Wild rice

Protein
  Eggs (organic, free-
    range recommended)
  Haddock
  Halibut
  Flounder
  Mackerel
  Salmon
  Sardines
  Sole
  Tilapia

Herbs and Spices
  Basil
  Bay leaf NEW
  Cardamom
  Chives
  Cilantro
  Cinnamon
  Cloves
  Cumin NEW
  Curry
  Ginger
  Lemon grass NEW
  Mint NEW
  Mustard [4] NEW
  Mustard powder NEW
  Mustard seed NEW
  Oregano
  Parsley
  Rosemary
  Sage NEW
  Sea salt
  Thyme NEW

Fats
  Extra virgin coconut
    oil NEW
  Extra virgin olive oil [5]
  Ghee
  Virgin olive oil NEW

Sweeteners
  Lakanto NEW
  Raw honey [2,6]
  Stevia

Other
  Almond extract NEW
  Baking soda NEW
  Coconut aminos NEW
  Coconut extract NEW
  Cream of tartar NEW
  Mint extract NEW
  Raw apple cider vinegar
  Vanilla extract

NEW : Foods added or shifted to earlier Phases of the diet, since the original version of the diet.

[1] Unsweetened fruit juice only.

[2] Use sparingly, as they are very high in sugar.

[3] Read label closely as sweeteners and/or stabilizers are often added. It's best to make your own. See page 261 for recipe.

[4] Mustard is not permitted until Phase 3 because most mustards are made with varieties of vinegar other than apple cider. Some varieties of mustard are made with apple cider vinegar, however, making them allowable for Phase 1. (See the Resources section on page 290). Additionally, dry mustard can be substituted for prepared mustard at a ratio of one teaspoon dry for every one tablespoon prepared.

[5] Mixed with a small amount of sesame oil is also acceptable.

[6] Limit to two teaspoons per day. Learn the difference between honey and raw honey on page 36.

Food Sensitivies and Testing

By Dr. Kenneth B. Singleton, MD, MPH

For the majority of Lyme patients I've worked with, the Lyme Inflammation Diet has worked extremely well. However, there are occasions when a person may need more specific testing for food sensitivities. For instance, a person may be hypersensitive to eggs (which are allowed early in the diet) and as a result may have ongoing body inflammation symptoms despite following the program faithfully.

A few years ago I was introduced to the Alcat Test by the late Dr. Robert Atkins (author of *The Atkins Diet*). Based on his recommendation, I've been using this test in my practice for a number of years. I have found this test to be the most helpful of all the food sensitivity tests that I have utilized.

It's a simple blood test done in your doctor's office. The sample is over-nighted to the lab, where up to 450 substances can be evaluated for a hypersensitivity reaction. (By the way, the hypersensitivity reaction detected by the Alcat Test is very different from the life-threating "allergic" reaction that an Allergist works with.)

The test results from the Alcat Test can help determine which foods and other substances may trigger unwanted inflammation. The personalized nutrition plan based on your immune response can greatly assist with specific food choices that are better for your particular health and well-being. When complying with the Alcat Test results, many clinical symptoms associated with food sensitivity may be substantially improved or possibly prevented altogether. You can learn more about the test at www.cellsciencesystems.com.

Why Eggs are Included in Phase 1

As mentioned above by Dr. Singleton some people can't tolerate eggs. I, Laura, am one of those people, which can pose a challenge with implementing the first Phase of the diet. I discovered this a few years ago, which is interesting as I had been eating eggs on nearly a daily basis for years and never realized that I had a sensitivity. Many of the recipes in the first edition of this book used eggs, but after I found out I couldn't eat them anymore my mom went back into her test kitchen to recraft many of these recipes to be egg-free. You will notice that on a number of the baked goods recipes that call for eggs, that there is an alternative ingredient and set of instructions to make the recipe egg-free.

So why are eggs in Phase 1? Dr. Singleton has told us the reason he included them is because they are a complete protein and that around 75% of his patients have no problem with them. If you do have any concern about having a sensitivity to eggs, you should avoid eating them in Phase 1 and slowly introduce them in a later Phase of the diet. You can also consider having the Alcat food sensitivity test mentioned above.

Phase 1 Meal Plan

Below is a week-long suggested meal plan created to help you more easily implement Phase 1. Most of the suggested recipes make 4 servings and can all be doubled if you would like leftovers for lunch. Plan to prepare the soup and cooked side dish recipes before you even begin the diet. They may be frozen and thawed and enjoyed on days when you are short on time in this or later Phase of the diet. You may make extra soup and serve them it with a salad for a light supper. To save time cook 6 cups of long-grain brown rice, 4 cups of short-grain brown rice and 4 cups of wild rice at once if you plan to follow this meal plan to the letter. Add cultured vegetables to any meal as this involves no work at all (more on this on pages 57-58). For further preparation tips, especially if you are not accustomed to cooking from scratch, review pages 54-59.

This meal plan has egg-free alternatives listed for those who can't tolerate eggs. If you don't see an alternative that means the meal is already egg-free. If you suspect an egg sensitivity, follow the egg-free plan.

	Breakfast:	Lunch:	Dinner:
Day 1	Poached Eggs Florentine with Béarnaise Sauce (page 79) Egg-free option: Apple and Nut Skillet (page 83)	Steamed Vegetables and Brown & Wild Rice with Fresh Herb Vinaigrette (page 93)	Almond and Herb Crusted Tilapia (page 105) with a side of Crispy Kale (page 95) and Calico Slaw (page 95)
Day 2	Make-Ahead Brown Rice Porridge with Mixed Berry Compote (page 75)	Egg Salad (page 85) with assorted greens with Fresh Herb Vinaigrette (page 93) Egg-free option: Creamy Asparagus Soup (page 87) with Savory Vegetable and Herb Biscotti (page 89)	Sautéed Filet of Sole with Artichoke Pesto (page 110) served with Stir-Fried Bok Choy, Leeks and Pine Nuts (page 99)
Day 3	Carrot Almond Pancakes (page 73) Egg-free option: Make-Ahead Brown Rice Porridge with Mixed Berry Compote (page 75)	Grilled Salmon over Assorted Greens with Fresh Herb Vinaigrette (page 94) served with a side of Calico Slaw (page 95)	Brown and Wild Rice Cauliflower and Mushroom Curry (page 104)
Day 4	Coconut Berry Smoothie (page 77) or Green Smoothie (page 84)	Deviled Eggs (page 85) served over Assorted Greens with Fresh Herb Vinaigrette (page 94) and a side of Pickled Beets (page 88) Egg-free option: Brown rice with Artichoke Pesto (page 110) topped with pine nuts and spinach	Moroccan Spice-Rubbed Salmon (page 103) with Green Beans with Shiitake Mushrooms and Almonds (page 98) and Shredded Carrot Salad (page 97) or Crispy Kale (page 95, for egg-free option)

Recipes for Repair

	Breakfast:	Lunch:	Dinner:
Day 5	Herb Scrambled Eggs with Shiitake Mushrooms (page 81) on a Brown Rice Pancake (page 82) **Egg-free option:** Cherry Vanilla Almond Blast (page 77)	Day 3 leftovers: Brown and Wild Rice Cauliflower and Mushroom Curry (page 104)	Sautéed Salmon Cakes (page 107) served with Mashed Cauliflower (page 96) and green beans **Egg-free option:** Sautéed Filet of Sole with Artichoke Pesto (page 110)
Day 6	Apple and Nut Skillet (page 83)	Day 1 leftovers: Steamed Vegetables and Brown & Wild Rice with Fresh Herb Vinaigrette (page 93)	Day 3 leftovers: Stir-Fried Brown Rice and Vegetables (page 101) <u>or</u> Cauliflower Carrot Soup (page 91) with Savory Vegetable and Herb Biscotti (page 89)
Day 7	Day 2 leftovers: Make-Ahead Brown Rice Porridge with Mixed Berry Compote (page 75)	Day 5 leftovers: Sautéed Salmon Cakes (page 107) **Egg-free option:** Leftover soup option with Savory Vegetable and Herb Biscotti (page 89)	Slow Cooked Brown Rice Risotto and Mushrooms (page 109) served with a side salad

Snack, dessert and drink options:

Remember, this is not a calorie-restricted diet. If you'd like to have snacks throughout the day, go for it! Also plan to enjoy the delicious dessert options that we have available to you, if you'd like. But remember not to overdo it with the sweets. Below we have listed snack and dessert options and have indicated if these options contain eggs with an asterisk (*). We have also given you some suggestions for drink options in this limited Phase of the diet.

Snack Options
- Deviled Eggs* (page 85)
- Shredded Carrot Salad * (page 97)
- Raw carrots, celery and broccoli served with Pesto Mayonnaise or Curried Mayonnaise* (page 270)
- Coconut Berry Smoothie (page 77)
- Cherry Vanilla Almond Blast (page 77)
- Apple and Nut Skillet (page 83)
- Green Smoothie (page 84)
- Savory Vegetable and Herb Biscotti (page 89)
- Calico Slaw (page 95)
- Crispy Kale (page 95)
- Cinnamon Applesauce (page 96)
- Green apple or celery sticks with Almond Butter (page 262)

- A mixture of any allowable Phase 1 nuts and seeds
- Brown rice cake served with Mixed Berry Compote (page 75) and/or Almond Butter (Page 262)

Dessert Options
- Coconut Almond Custard * (page 116)
- Berry Frozen Dessert (page 111)
- Nutty Coconut Delight (page 113)
- Chewy Coconut Almond Cookies (page 115)

Drink Options
- Açai and Blueberry Spritzer (page 117)
- Rooibos tea
- Mint Tea or Ginger Mint Tea (page 117)
- Filtered water

Bonus! You can also download a blank meal planning grid on our website, www.recipesforrepair.com/resources, if you prefer to create your own meal plan. This document can be used in any of Phase of the diet.

Breakfast   PHASE 1

Carrot Almond Pancakes

These pancakes may look a little different than what you're used to, but they taste sweet and nutty and are very satisfying. Top them with a teaspoon of raw honey and some blueberries for a complete breakfast treat.

Prep time: 10 minutes
Cook time: 12 minutes

Makes: 4 pancakes

- 1 cup peeled and grated carrots (2-3 large carrots)
- ¼ cup almonds
- 1 slice fresh ginger (⅛-inch thick)
- 1 teaspoon flaxseed meal
- 2 tablespoons unsweetened shredded coconut
- ½ teaspoon ground cinnamon
- 1 egg
- ¼ teaspoon sea salt
- ½ teaspoon vanilla
- 1-2 tablespoons Ghee* (page 258) or extra virgin coconut oil
- 1 teaspoon raw honey
- Blueberries (optional)

For dairy-free use the olive oil in place of the ghee.

1. Place the grated carrots in a medium-sized bowl.
2. Place the almonds, ginger and flaxseed in the bowl of a food processor. Pulse 5-6 times until the almonds are finely ground.
3. Add the almond mixture and all of the remaining ingredients, except for the ghee, honey and blueberries, to the grated carrots.
4. Heat the ghee in a small frying pan over medium heat for 1-2 minutes, or until hot.
5. Spoon 4 ¼-cup portions of the mixture into the frying pan, and cook for about 1-2 minutes per side, or until lightly browned.
6. Top with honey and blueberries if desired, and serve hot.

Cook's Note: Prepare and refrigerate the pancake mixture the night before, so that you can make your breakfast in a few minutes.

Breakfast

PHASE 1

Make-Ahead Brown Rice Porridge with Mixed Berry Compote

Save some time by preparing the compote the night before. All that's left to do in the morning is cook, serve and enjoy.

Soaking time: 8-12 hours
Prep time: 5 minutes
Cook time: 20 minutes

Makes: 4 servings

Porridge
1½ cups cooked short grain brown rice
3 cups Coconut Milk (page 261) or Almond Milk (page 260)
1 teaspoon vanilla extract
2 teaspoons extra virgin coconut oil
½ teaspoon ground cinnamon
¼ teaspoon ground ginger
¼ teaspoon sea salt
4-8 drops liquid stevia

Compote
½ cup each raspberries, blackberries and blueberries
2 tablespoons filtered water
¼ cup pomegranate juice
¼ teaspoon ground cinnamon
6 drops liquid stevia
½ teaspoon almond extract
2 tablespoons chopped walnuts

1. Place all the ingredients for the porridge into a 2-quart sauce pot, stir well and cover.
2. Place the covered pot into the refrigerator overnight for use in the morning.
3. Remove the pot from the refrigerator and bring the mixture to a boil over medium-high heat. Lower the heat to medium-low, uncover and simmer for 20 minutes or until most of the liquid is absorbed and the rice is tender.
4. While the porridge is cooking combine all the compote ingredients except for the walnuts in a small sauce pot. Cook over medium heat for 5 minutes.
5. Serve the porridge topped with berries and chopped walnuts.

Cook's Note: The key to this recipe is soaking the cooked rice over night as instructed. This softens up the rice to the point where it becomes the consistency of traditional porridge. Make extra compote, purée it and use it as a syrup on the Carrot Pancakes (page 73).

Breakfast PALEO PHASE 1

Coconut Berry Smoothie

This recipe makes enough for two smoothies, so share with someone, or take the extra to work for a mid-afternoon snack.

Prep time: 5 minutes

Makes: 2 drinks (3 cups)

1 cup Coconut Milk (page 261)

½ cup unsweetened pomegranate juice

½ cup blueberries

½ cup raspberries or blackberries

2 teaspoons raw honey or 3-5 drops stevia* (optional)

½ cup ice

1. Place all the ingredients in a blender container in the order listed. Cover, and blend on High, or on a frozen drink setting, until the ice is crushed and the fruits are blended.

Not suitable for Paleo.

Cherry Vanilla Almond Blast

Cherries have a short season, but that doesn't mean that you can't enjoy this smoothie year-round. Frozen cherries are a fine substitute for fresh.

Prep time: 5 minutes

Makes: 1 drink

1 cup frozen or fresh pitted cherries

1 teaspoon flaxseed meal

1 cup Almond Milk (page 260)

½ teaspoon vanilla

⅛ teaspoon almond extract

1 teaspoon raw honey or 3-5 drops stevia* (optional)

½ cup ice cubes

1. Place all the ingredients in a blender container. Cover, and blend until smooth.
2. Pour into a tall glass and serve immediately.

Not suitable for Paleo.

Cook's Note: If you don't like cherries, substitute raspberries, blueberries or any other fruit that is permitted in Phase 1.

Breakfast

Poached Eggs Florentine with Béarnaise Sauce

This recipe is perfect if you are hosting brunch, or if you just want to relax and enjoy a day at home.

Prep time: 30 minutes (including sauce preparation)

Cook time: 15-20 minutes

Makes: 4 servings

- 1 recipe Béarnaise Sauce (page 273)
- 1 tablespoon Ghee* (page 258) or extra virgin olive oil
- 1 small shallot, minced
- 1 small clove garlic, crushed
- 1 bag (1 pound) baby spinach
- 3 cups filtered water
- 4 eggs
- 1 teaspoon raw apple cider vinegar
- Chopped parsley (optional)

* For dairy-free use the oil in place of the ghee.

1. Prepare the Béarnaise Sauce and set aside.
2. Heat the ghee or oil in a small frying pan over medium heat for 1-2 minutes, or until hot.
3. Add the shallot and garlic and sauté over medium heat for 2 minutes, or until limp.
4. Add the spinach and sauté for 2 minutes, or until just limp. Set aside.
5. Pour the water into a frying pan, and bring it to a boil.
6. Crack each egg into a separate custard cup.
7. Once the water boils, add the vinegar and stir vigorously until a whirlpool forms.
8. Add the eggs one at a time, and poach for about 2 minutes.** Spoon any floating egg white back over the poaching egg. Continue until all the eggs are poached.
9. If necessary, reheat the spinach for a minute. Divide the spinach and place on four plates. Top each portion of spinach with a poached egg, and spoon Béarnaise Sauce over each. Garnish with chopped parsley if desired.

** *Cooking time for the eggs is a matter of personal preference. The cooking time given here will result in runny yolks. Cook longer if you prefer firmer yolks.*

Cook's Note: If you are making the Béarnaise Sauce in advance, you can reheat it over a double boiler, or on low in your microwave. When using a double boiler, be very careful never to let the water boil, or to let the hot water touch the bottom of the top section, as this will cause the sauce to curdle.

Breakfast   PALEO   PHASE 1

Herb Scrambled Eggs with Shiitake Mushrooms

This recipe for Herb Scrambled Eggs with Shiitake Mushrooms can top the Brown Rice Pancakes (page 82) or be eaten alone. When served on the Brown Rice Pancake it makes a wonderful meal that you can serve guests for brunch.

Prep time: 10 minutes
Cook time: 5 minutes

Makes: 2 servings

- 1 teaspoon extra virgin olive oil
- 1 cup chopped shiitake mushrooms
- 2 scallions, white part only, chopped
- 1 small clove of garlic, chopped
- 2 teaspoons of freshly chopped herbs, such as parsley, oregano, tarragon or lemon thyme
- ½ teaspoon sea salt
- 2 eggs, beaten

1. Heat the oil in a medium-sized frying pan over medium heat for 1-2 minutes, or until hot.
2. Add the mushrooms, scallions, and garlic and cook for 2 minutes, or until they begin to brown.
3. Combine the herbs and eggs in a bowl and mix well with a fork.
4. Pour the eggs into the frying pan and cook for two minutes mixing with a fork to scramble.
5. Serve on Brown Rice Pancake.

Cook's Note: This recipe can also be eaten alone (not on the Brown Rice Pancake) and makes a delicious and satisfying lunch or dinner.

Nutrition Note: Eggs are a healthy protein source with many dietary benefits. Egg yolks are high in phosphatidylcholine, lutein, and zeaxanthin. Choose eggs that are labeled "USDA certified organic." The nutrients in eggs are essential to maintaining the healthy function of your heart, immune system, skin and even your brain.

Breakfast   PHASE 1

Brown Rice Pancake

The recipe does call for one egg, but if you can't tolerate eggs we have a substitution in the notes section of the recipe making this an egg-free breakfast.

Prep time: 10 minutes
Cook time: 8 minutes

Makes: 2 servings

1 tablespoon extra virgin olive oil
1 cup cooked brown rice, chopped
1 teaspoon freshly chopped parsley
1 teaspoon freshly chopped chives or ½ teaspoon chopped green onions
½ teaspoon sea salt
¼ teaspoon garlic powder
1 egg*

*Substitute 1/4 cup of applesauce for the egg.

1. Heat the oil in a 10-inch fry pan over medium heat for 1-2 minutes, or until hot.
2. Combine all the ingredients in a small bowl.
3. Spoon the mixture into the hot frying pan pressing down with a wooden spoon or spatula until the whole pan is covered with the rice mixture.
4. Cook for about 3 minutes per side, or until golden brown.
5. Serve as a light breakfast, a side dish or top with Herb Scrambled Eggs with Shiitake Mushrooms (page 81) for a hearty breakfast.

Cook's Note: If you are making the egg-free version of these pancakes, the pancakes will not hold together as well, so make them into 2-4 smaller pancakes so they are easier to flip. This recipe also makes a great lunch-time meal.

Breakfast

PHASE 1

Apple and Nut Skillet

The chia seeds in this recipe give you a protein energy boost and the healthy fats from the nuts will help keep you going, right up until lunch.

Prep time: 10 minutes
Cook time: 5 minutes

Makes: 2 servings

- 1 tablespoon extra virgin coconut oil
- 1 large green apple, peeled, cored and sliced
- ½ teaspoon cinnamon
- ¼ teaspoon ground ginger
- a pinch of sea salt
- ½ cup filtered water
- 1½ tablespoon chia seeds
- 2 drops liquid stevia* (optional)
- 3 tablespoons walnuts, chopped

1. Heat the oil in a medium-sized frying pan over medium heat for 1 minute, or until hot.
2. Add the apples to the frying pan and sauté for 2-3 minutes, or just until tender.
3. Combine the cinnamon, ginger and salt and sprinkle over the apples. Stir well to coat.
4. Remove the apples to a bowl and reserve.
5. Add the water to the frying pan with the chia seeds and simmer for 30 seconds, stirring constantly.
6. Return the apples to the frying pan, stir in the walnuts and stevia, if desired, and sauté for 1 minute.
7. Serve immediately.

PHASE 2 variation: Once you reach Phase 2, you may substitute pears, apricots or mangos for the apples.

Not suitable for Paleo.

Cook's Note: For a little variety try making this recipe with mixed allowable Phase 1 berries in place of the apples.

Breakfast  PHASE 1

Green Smoothie

This easy-to-make blender smoothie combines vegetables and fruits in a surprisingly refreshing drink. We have it classified as a breakfast, but it can also be enjoyed as a drink or snack during the day.

Prep time: 5 minutes

Makes: 3 cups

- 1½ -2 cups filtered water
- 1 tablespoon flaxseed meal
- 1 tablespoon Almond Butter (page 262)
- 1 cup baby spinach
- 1 large green apple, peeled, cored, cut in 1-inch pieces
- 1 2-inch piece of cucumber, peeled, cut in half
- 1 medium carrot, peeled, cut in 1-inch pieces
- 1 small avocado, peeled, pitted, cut in 1-inch pieces
- ½ cup ice cubes

1. Pour 1½ cups of the water into a blender container. Add the remaining ingredients.
2. Cover and blend on high for 2 minutes or until the mixture is smooth. Add the remaining water if the drink is too thick and reblend for 15 seconds.
3. Pour into glasses and serve immediately. Refrigerate any leftover juice for future use. Reblend before serving.

Cook's Note: Add kale or some parsley to this drink for a more complex flavor. Add a few drops of liquid stevia to add a little sweetness, if desired.

Soups/Salads/Sides/Snacks PALEO   PHASE 1

Deviled Eggs

This old-time favorite has made a recent comeback. So if you haven't had it in a while, why not give it a try?

Prep time: 15 minutes

Makes: 12 pieces

- 6 eggs, hard boiled and peeled
- 3 tablespoons Herb Mayonnaise (page 270)
- 1 tablespoon mustard
- ¼ teaspoon sea salt

1. Cut the peeled, cooked eggs in half lengthwise. Remove the yolks to a small bowl and add the remaining ingredients. Break the yolks up with a fork and continue to mash until the mixture is smooth.
2. Spoon the filling back into the egg whites, or, if desired, pipe it back into the whites using a pastry bag fitted with a star tip.

Bonus Recipe: Egg Salad: If you prefer, you can make this recipe into egg salad by chopping the whole cooked eggs, and adding chopped celery and combining them with the mayonnaise, mustard and salt. Serve over mixed greens.

Savory Vegetable and Herb Biscotti, page 89

Soups/Salads/Sides/Snacks   PHASE 1

Creamy Asparagus Soup

Coconut milk adds a creamy feel to this nutritious, easy-to-make dairy-free Creamy Asparagus Soup.

Prep time: 10 minutes
Cook time: 40 minutes

Makes: 4 servings

2 tablespoons extra virgin olive oil
1 medium onion, chopped
2 cloves garlic, chopped
1 large carrot, peeled and chopped
1 stalk celery, chopped
8 ounces asparagus, chopped
2 teaspoons freshly chopped dill
½ teaspoon freshly chopped tarragon
1 tablespoon freshly chopped parsley
1 teaspoon sea salt
3 cups Vegetable Broth (page 259)
1 cup Coconut Milk (page 261)

1. Heat the oil in a 2-quart saucepot over medium heat for 1-2 minutes, or until hot.
2. Sauté the onions for 3 minutes, or until they are limp and just starting to brown.
3. Add the garlic, carrots, celery, and asparagus and sauté for 5 minutes.
4. Add the remaining ingredients, stir well to combine and bring the soup to a boil over medium-high heat. Lower to medium heat and simmer for 30 minutes.
5. Pour the soup into a blender container. Cover the container. Remove the center cup from the cover.
6. Place a clean, folded kitchen towel over the blender cover and press down with your hand.
7. Purée the soup until smooth.
8. Serve immediately and refrigerate leftovers.

PHASE 3 variation: Once you reach Phase 3, you may substitute Chicken Bone Broth (page 264). Bone broth is rich in minerals, is very healing, aids in digestion and tastes wonderful.

Cook's Note: If you can't tolerate coconuts, replace the 1 cup of coconut milk with an extra cup of broth. It will not be creamy but still tastes great. Enjoy this and other soups with the Savory Vegetable and Herb Biscotti (page 89). For an even creamier version of this soup, use canned organic full-fat coconut milk with guar gum (an ingredient introduced into the diet in Phase 3).

Soups/Salads/Sides/Snacks   PHASE 1

Pickled Beets

Pickled beets are great as an addition to a salad, or as a stand-alone side dish served hot or cold.

Prep time: 10 minutes
Cook time: 1 hour

Makes: 4-6 servings

1 bunch (4-5) beets (about 2 pounds)
¼ cup cider vinegar
½ cup filtered water
1 small onion, sliced
1 clove garlic, peeled and thinly sliced
½ teaspoon sea salt
2 tablespoons raw honey

1. Place the beets in a 3-quart saucepan and cover them with water. Cover the pan, and bring to a boil over high heat. Lower the heat to medium-high and cook for 45-50 minutes, or until a knife inserted in the middle of a beet comes out easily.
2. Drain, cool and peel the beets, and then slice them into ¼-inch thick slices.
3. Return the sliced beets to the saucepan and add the vinegar, water, onion, garlic and salt.
4. Cook over high heat until the mixture comes to a boil. Lower the heat and cook for about 10 minutes, or until tender.
5. Remove the beets from the heat and allow them to cool. Stir in the honey.
6. Serve hot or cold.

Nutrition Note: Beet greens are rich in potassium and an excellent source of carotenoids, flavonoid antioxidants, vitamin A and magnesium and are thought to have strong detoxification properties. Rather than throw them out, mix them into your salads. They taste great topped with a spoonful of pickled beets.

Soups/Salads/Sides/Snacks

PHASE 1

Savory Vegetable and Herb Biscotti

These savory biscuits are an excellent accompaniment to have with a soup or salad. Break them up into pieces and use them atop a salad like croutons.

Prep time: 10 minutes
Cook time: 50 minutes
Stand time: 30 minutes

Makes: 10 Biscottis

- 1½ cups Almond Flour (page 260)
- 2 tablespoons flaxseed meal
- ¼ cup baby spinach, packed and chopped
- 1 tablespoon onions, chopped
- ¼ cup carrots, chopped
- ¼ teaspoon celery salt
- ½ teaspoon sea salt
- ½ teaspoon Herbes de Provence
- 1 teaspoon garlic powder
- 1 teaspoon dried basil
- 2 tablespoons extra virgin olive oil

1. Preheat the over to 375°F.
2. Place all the ingredients in the bowl of a food processor. Pulse on and off about 10 times or until the mixture begins to form a ball.
3. Line a small baking sheet with parchment paper. Remove the mixture and place it on the parchment paper. Form the mixture into a 7 x 3½ x ¾-inch loaf.
4. Bake in the preheated oven for 30-35 minutes or until the edges start to brown.
5. Cool on a rack for 30 minutes.
6. Cut the cooled loaf into 10 half-inch diagonal slices on a cutting board using a serrated edge knife.
7. Put the slices flat side down onto the parchment lined sheet. Place the sheet back in the oven and bake 12-15 minutes, turning mid-way, until the biscotti is lightly browned. Do not over bake or else they will taste burned.

Cook's Note: This recipe is double baked so there is a cooling time of 30 minutes in between the first and second baking. Plan an extra 30 minutes for the standing time.

Soups/Salads/Sides/Snacks   PALEO PHASE 1

Cauliflower Carrot Soup

This smooth soup combines two basic vegetables into a delicious medley of flavors. Add cooked quinoa, brown rice or chicken for a heartier version.

Prep time: 35 minutes
Cook time: 45 minutes

Makes: 4 servings

- 2 tablespoons extra virgin olive oil
- 1 medium onion, chopped
- 2 cloves garlic, chopped
- ½ small head cauliflower (about 1 pound) cut into florets
- 2 carrots, peeled and chopped
- 1 quart Vegetable Broth (page 259)
- 2 tablespoon parsley, chopped
- 1 tablespoon chives, chopped
- 1 teaspoon rosemary, chopped
- 1 teaspoon fresh dill, chopped
- 1 teaspoon celery salt
- ½ teaspoon sea salt
- 1 ½ cup Coconut Milk (page 261)

1. Heat the oil in a 2-quart saucepot over medium heat for 1-2 minutes, or until hot.
2. Sauté the onions over medium heat for 3 minutes, or until they are limp and just starting to brown.
3. Add the garlic, cauliflower and carrots and sauté for 5 minutes.
4. Add the remaining ingredients, stir well to combine, and bring the soup to a boil over medium-high heat. Lower to medium heat and simmer for 35 minutes.
5. Pour the soup into a blender container. Cover the container. Remove the center cup from the cover.
6. Place a clean, folded kitchen towel over the blender cover and press down with your hand.
7. Purée the soup until smooth.
8. Serve immediately and refrigerate leftovers.

Cook's Note: An immersion blender is the ideal cooking tool for puréeing hot soup right in the saucepot. If you don't have an immersion blender, you can pour the hot soup into a food processor or blender.

Make a double batch and freeze in serving-sized portions to take to work.

Soups/**Salads**/Sides/Snacks

PHASE 1

Steamed Vegetables and Brown and Wild Rice with Fresh Herb Vinaigrette

Leftover rice and vegetables make a great salad when topped with Fresh Herb Vinaigrette.

Prep time: 15 minutes

Makes: 4 servings

2 cups cooked brown and wild rice

3 ounces steamed green beans

1 cup steamed bok choy

1 cup steamed julienned carrots

Fresh Herb Vinaigrette
¼ cup apple cider vinegar

1 teaspoon each freshly chopped basil and parsley

½ teaspoon freshly chopped tarragon or thyme

½ teaspoon dry mustard

¼ teaspoon each garlic and onion powder

1 teaspoon raw honey

¼ teaspoon sea salt

⅓ cup extra virgin olive oil

1. Place the cooked rice on a serving plate and top with the green beans, bok choy and carrots.
2. Combine all of the ingredients for the vinaigrette.
3. Spoon a small amount of the vinaigrette over the vegetables, and serve the remaining vinaigrette on the side.

Cook's Note: Any cooked vegetables can be used in this recipe. Use whatever you have on hand, or your family's favorites. It's a perfect way to use up your leftovers.

Soups/Salads/Sides/Snacks

Grilled Salmon over Assorted Greens with Fresh Herb Vinaigrette

Serve this healthy, delicious salmon salad for lunch or dinner any time of the year. You can broil the fish in the colder months, and grill it outdoors in the summer.

Prep time: 10 minutes
Cook time: 8 minutes

Makes: 2 servings

1 recipe Fresh Herb Vinaigrette (page 93)

Salmon
2 (6-ounce) salmon filets
1 teaspoon extra virgin olive oil
⅛ teaspoon sea salt

Greens
1 cup mixed greens, such as romaine and arugula
¼ cup shredded carrots
¼ cup chopped celery
¼ cup cooked string beans
2 tablespoons fruit-juice sweetened, dried cranberries
2 asparagus spears, cooked and cut into 1-inch pieces
1 tablespoon toasted, chopped nuts, such as walnuts, almonds or pine nuts

1. Preheat the oven to Broil.
2. Prepare and set aside the Fresh Herb Vinaigrette.
3. Brush the salmon filets with the oil and season them with the salt.
4. Broil the filets for 8 minutes, or until the fish flakes easily with a fork.
5. While the fish is cooking, combine all of the ingredients for the mixed greens. Pour ½ the vinaigrette over the greens and toss well to coat.
6. Plate the greens and top each plate with a grilled filet. Drizzle the remaining vinaigrette over the fish, and serve immediately.

Cook's Note: Save yourself some time on future meals by preparing double the recipe of Fresh Herb Vinaigrette and broiling a couple of extra salmon filets to use for Sautéed Salmon Cakes (page 107).

Soups/Salads/Sides/Snacks   PALEO   PHASE 1

Calico Slaw

This colorful slaw partners well with the fish recipes in this Phase. Prepare it in advance, and allow it to set in the refrigerator for at least a few hours, preferably overnight, before serving.

Prep time: 20 minutes

Makes: about 6 cups

- 8 ounces white cabbage, shredded
- 8 ounces red cabbage, shredded
- 1 carrot, peeled and shredded
- 1 recipe Fresh Herb Vinaigrette (page 93)
- 1 teaspoon dry mustard
- 1 teaspoon sea salt
- 1 teaspoon raw honey
- ½ teaspoon celery salt

1. Place the cabbage in a large bowl. Combine all the remaining ingredients and stir them into the cabbage. Mix until all the cabbage is coated.
2. Refrigerate for several hours or overnight before serving.

Cook's Note: Substitute 1 recipe of Garlic Shallot Mayonnaise (page 271) for the Fresh Herb Vinaigrette for a creamy version of this slaw. You may add fruit-juice sweetened, dried cranberries to this recipe, if desired.

Crispy Kale

This simple recipe is a great accompaniment to most entrees!

Prep time: 5 minutes

Cook time: 10-12 minutes

Makes: 4 servings

- 1 bunch kale, about 10 ounces
- 1-2 tablespoons extra virgin olive oil
- ½ teaspoon each garlic and onion powder
- ⅛ teaspoon sea salt

1. Preheat the over to 375°F.
2. Tear the kale leaves from the rib and then rip into bite size pieces.
3. Place the kale on a baking sheet. Drizzle the oil over the kale and toss well to coat each piece.
4. Combine the remaining ingredients and sprinkle over the kale. Toss again.
5. Bake for 10-12 minutes. Keep an eye on it during the last few minutes. The kale should be bright green not brown.

Soups/Salads/Sides/Snacks   PALEO   PHASE 1

Mashed Cauliflower

Yearning for some mashed potatoes? Here is a Phase 1 substitution that is healthier and sure to please.

Prep time: 5 minutes
Cook time: 8 minutes

Makes: 4 servings

½ small head cauliflower (about 1 pound) cut into florets

¼ cup Coconut Milk (page 261), Almond Milk (page 260) or Vegetable Broth (page 259)

2 tablespoons Ghee (page 258)

½ teaspoon each garlic and onion powder

⅛ teaspoon sea salt

1. Steam the cauliflower for 5-6 minutes or until it's soft enough to break apart with a fork.
2. Place the remaining ingredients in a food processor and then add the drained cauliflower.
3. Process for 1-2 minutes or until it is a smooth consistency, similar to a very smooth batch or mashed potatoes.

PHASE 3 **Variation:** Once you reach Phase 3, try adding Cheddar or any other favorite cheese for cheesy mashed cauliflower. You can also add 1 tablespoon of nutritional yeast for a cheesy-flavored, dairy-free option.

  PALEO

Cinnamon Applesauce

Green apples are the only apples permitted in Phase 1. They are available year-round and make wonderful applesauce.

Prep time: 10 minutes
Makes: 2½ cups

2 pounds green apples (about 4 large apples), peeled and cut into 1-inch pieces

⅔ cup filtered water

½ teaspoon cinnamon

⅛ teaspoon sea salt

2-3 teaspoons raw honey

1. Combine all the ingredients, except for the honey, in a 2-quart saucepot. Bring the mixture to a boil over medium-high heat. Cover the pot, and lower the temperature to medium. Cook for about 20 minutes, or until the apples soften and begin to fall apart.
2. Remove the sauce from the heat and allow it to cool for about 15 minutes before stirring in the honey.
3. Applesauce can be served warm or cold. Refrigerate or freeze any leftovers.

Cook's Note: This recipe can be doubled or cut in half.

Soups/Salads/Sides/Snacks   PHASE 1

Shredded Carrot Salad

Make this salad to take to work for lunch, or serve as a dinner side dish with Almond and Herb Crusted Tilapia (page 105).

Prep time: 20 minutes
Stand time: 1 hour

Makes: 4 servings

- 2 cups shredded carrots (about 8 ounces)
- ¼ cup Homemade Mayonnaise (page 270)
- ½–1½ teaspoons raw honey
- 1 teaspoon freshly chopped chives
- ½ teaspoon lemon thyme
- ¼ teaspoon sea salt
- 2 teaspoons raw apple cider vinegar
- 2 tablespoons fruit-juice sweetened, dried cranberries
- 2 tablespoons chopped walnuts

1. Combine all the ingredients in a bowl and stir well.
2. Refrigerate for at least an hour before serving.

Cook's Note: Lemon thyme is a type of thyme that has a lemon scent and taste. If it is not available, you can substitute regular fresh thyme.

Soups/Salads/Sides/Snacks   PHASE 1

Green Beans with Shiitake Mushrooms and Almonds

Green beans and almonds are a classic combination. This side dish pairs perfectly with fish. Try it with a fish dish, like the Moroccan Spice-Rubbed Salmon (page 103).

Prep time: 15 minutes
Cook time: 10 minutes

Makes: 4 servings

- ½ pound green beans
- 2 tablespoons extra virgin olive oil
- 1 shallot, chopped
- 2 cloves garlic
- 4 ounces shiitake mushrooms (caps only), sliced
- ½ teaspoon sea salt
- ½ teaspoon thyme leaves
- ½ teaspoon freshly chopped basil
- 1 teaspoon raw apple cider vinegar
- 2 tablespoons almonds, sliced

1. Steam the green beans for 5-6 minutes.
2. Heat a medium-sized frying pan over medium heat for about 1 minute, or until hot.
3. Add the oil and sauté the shallot and garlic for 1 minute, or until just limp.
4. Add the steamed green beans and the mushrooms and sauté for 2 minutes.
5. Stir in the salt, thyme, basil and vinegar and sauté for 1 minute.
6. Sprinkle on the almonds and serve immediately.

Cook's Note: Next time you make green beans, cook some extra and use the leftovers in this quick side dish. You can even use these beans as a salad topping.

Soups/Salads/Sides/Snacks   PHASE 1

Stir-Fried Bok Choy, Leeks and Pine Nuts

If bok choy is not available, or if you prefer, you can substitute Chinese cabbage.

Prep time: 10 minutes
Cook time: about 8 minutes

Makes: 4 servings

3 extra virgin olive oil, divided
2 leeks, white part only, cut into ¼-inch thick rounds and very well rinsed
1 clove garlic, crushed
1 head (1 pound) bok choy, cut horizontally into ½-inch slices
½ teaspoon sea salt
3 tablespoons pine nuts

1. Heat 1 tablespoon of the oil in a large frying pan over medium heat for 1-2 minutes, or until hot.
2. Add the leeks and sauté for 2 minutes, or until limp.
3. Add the garlic and sauté for 30 seconds.
4. Add the remaining oil and the bok choy, and stir fry for about 3 minutes, or until it is wilted.
5. Stir in the salt and pine nuts and stir fry for an additional minute.

PHASE 3 Variation: Once you reach Phase 3, you may add 1 tablespoon of tamari with the pine nuts, and stir fry for 1 minute.

Entrees PHASE 1

Stir-Fried Brown Rice and Vegetables

Brown rice has a nutty taste, and stir-frying gives it a little crunch and enhances the flavor. Adding chopped nuts and blueberries ties all the flavors together for a satisfying, meatless meal.

Prep time: 20 minutes
Cook time: 8 minutes

Makes: 2 main dish servings

- 3 tablespoons extra virgin olive oil, divided
- 4 scallions, chopped
- 2 cloves garlic, chopped
- 1 cup broccoli, broken into small florets or coarsely chopped
- 1 cup diced carrots
- 1 cup sliced celery
- ½ teaspoon sea salt
- 1 cup cooked brown rice
- ½ teaspoon extra virgin olive oil
- 1 egg*, lightly beaten
- 2 tablespoons chopped, toasted almonds, pine nuts or walnuts
- 2 tablespoons blueberries

* Omit egg for egg-free

1. Heat 2 tablespoons of the oil in a large frying pan over medium heat for 1-2 minutes, or until hot.
2. Add the scallions, garlic, broccoli, carrots, celery and salt stir fry for 3 minutes, or until nicely browned.
3. Add the remaining 1 tablespoon of oil and the rice, and stir fry for another minute. Remove the rice and vegetables from the frying pan.
4. Add the ½ teaspoon of oil to the frying pan and heat for 30 seconds.
5. Pour the egg into the frying pan, making sure to cover the bottom of the pan. Cook for 1 minute, turn, and cook for 1 minute, or until set. Remove the egg and slice into thin strips.
6. Top the rice with the egg strips, and add the chopped nuts and blueberries. Serve immediately.

PHASE 3 Variation: Once you reach Phase 3, you may add 1 tablespoon of tamari at the same time as you add the rice. Continue as directed.

Cook's Note: Add chicken, beef or any other favorite protein to this meal once you reach the appropriate Phase of the diet for a more substantial meal.

Entrees  PALEO   PHASE 1

Moroccan Spice-Rubbed Salmon

This blend of spices gives the salmon an Indian/Moroccan taste. The sautéed onions are optional, but highly recommended.

Prep time: 20 minutes
Cook time: 8 minutes

Makes: 2 servings

Rub
1 teaspoon garlic powder
½ teaspoon onion powder
½ teaspoon ground turmeric
¼ teaspoon sea salt
¼ teaspoon dried oregano
½ teaspoon garam masala or curry powder
⅛ teaspoon ground ginger

Fish
2 (6-ounce) salmon filets

Topping (not pictured)
1 small onion, sliced in rounds
1 tablespoon extra virgin olive oil

1. Preheat the oven to 450°F.
2. Combine all the ingredients for the rub.
3. Spread the rub on the flesh side of the salmon filets.
4. Cook the fish without turning for 8 minutes, or until the fish flakes easily with a fork.
5. While the fish is cooking, sauté the onion in the oil. Place the sautéed onions on top of the fish for the last 2 minutes of cooking.

Cook's Note: If you have never used these spices, you might be hesitant about this recipe, but giving it a try might just open a whole new world of delicious possibilities to you and your family.

Entrees   PHASE 1

Brown and Wild Rice Cauliflower and Mushroom Curry

This recipe uses all leftovers so you can be eating dinner in just a matter of minutes. It is a meal that your whole family will enjoy, even your vegan family members!

Prep time: 15 minutes
Cook time: 5 minutes

Makes: 2 servings

- 2 tablespoons extra virgin coconut oil or extra virgin olive oil
- 1 small onion, chopped
- 1 clove garlic, chopped
- 4 ounces mushrooms, sliced
- 1½ cups cooked brown and wild rice
- 6 ounces cooked, steamed cauliflower
- 1 teaspoon curry powder
- ½ teaspoon tumeric
- ¼ teaspoon cumin
- 1 teaspoon sea salt
- ½ teaspoon celery salt
- ½ teaspoon garlic powder
- 1 tablespoon each, chopped parsley and chopped basil
- 1 cup Coconut Milk (pg. 261)
- ½ cup Vegetable Broth (page 259)
- 1½ cups baby spinach leaves
- 2 tablespoons walnuts, chopped
- 2 tablespoons unsweetened shredded coconut

1. Heat the coconut oil in a large fry pan over medium heat for 1 minute, or until hot.
2. Add the onions and sauté for two minutes or until limp. Add the garlic and sauté for 30 seconds. Add the mushrooms and sauté for three minutes or until limp.
3. Add the rice and the remaining ingredients except the spinach, chopped walnuts and shredded coconut. Stir well and cook for 2 minutes.
4. Stir in the spinach and cook for 1 minute, just to warm the spinach. Do not allow it to wilt.
5. Serve topped with chopped walnuts and shredded coconut.

Cook's Note: Once you reach Phase 2 of the diet, you can stir in chunks of grilled or baked white meat chicken.

Entrees VG PALEO   PHASE 1

Almond and Herb Crusted Tilapia

The coating in this recipe, which replaces breadcrumbs, is one of many that you will find in the various Phases of this book. Best of all, these replacements add variety to your menus.

Prep time: 10 minutes
Stand time: 30 minutes
Cook time: 10-14 minutes

Makes: 4 servings

⅔ cup Almond Flour (page 260)

2 teaspoons each freshly chopped parsley, thyme, oregano and chives

½ teaspoon each onion and garlic powder

½ teaspoon sea salt

4 (4- to 6-ounce) tilapia filets

3 tablespoons extra virgin coconut oil or Ghee* (page 258)

Herb Mayonnaise (page 270)

For dairy-free use the oil in place of the ghee.

1. Combine the almond flour, herbs, onion and garlic powder, and salt on a dinner plate. Mix well.
2. Coat both sides of each filet with the mixture. Press the crumbs into the fish using your hands.
3. Place the fish on a small rack and let it sit in the refrigerator, uncovered, for at least 30 minutes, to allow the crumbs to dry and set in place.
4. Heat the oil or ghee in a frying pan over medium heat for 1-2 minutes, or until hot.
5. Place the fish in the pan and cook for 5-7 minutes per side (depending on the thickness of the fish), until the crust is nicely browned.
6. Serve immediately with Herb Mayonnaise.

Cook's Note: Breadcrumbs are generally made from breads that are not permitted in this diet. This book provides a recipe for gluten-free breadcrumbs (Italian Breadcrumbs, page 267), but they are not permitted until Phase 4 of the diet. Almond flour blended with fresh herbs makes a delicious coating that is approved for Phase 1. You may never want to use breadcrumbs again!

Entrees | PHASE 1

Sautéed Salmon Cakes

In this recipe, chopped, cooked brown rice takes the place of breadcrumbs, which are generally used as a binding agent. The rice adds a nutty flavor, as well as some crunch after it browns.

Prep time: 25 minutes
Stand time: 30 minutes
Cook time: 12 minutes

Makes: 6 cakes

3-4 tablespoons extra virgin olive oil or Ghee* (page 258), divided
1 small onion, finely chopped
1 clove garlic, finely chopped
1 stalk celery, finely chopped
2 shiitake mushrooms, finely chopped
½ teaspoon sea salt
⅓ cup Herb Mayonnaise (page 270)
1 tablespoon flaxseed meal
1 teaspoon dry mustard powder
1½ cups cooked brown rice
½ pound cooked salmon, broken into large chunks
⅔ Almond Flour (page 260), divided

For dairy-free use the oil in place of the ghee.

1. Heat 2 tablespoons of the oil or ghee in a medium-sized frying pan over medium-high heat for 2 minutes or until hot.
2. Add the onions, garlic, celery, mushrooms and salt and sauté for 3 minutes, or until lightly browned.
3. Remove the mixture to a bowl and allow it to cool for about 10 minutes.
4. Add the remaining ingredients except for ⅓ cup of almond flour, and mix well.
5. Fill a ½-cup measuring cup with the mixture and form into 6 cakes. Coat each cake with the remaining almond flour and refrigerate for an additional 30 minutes to allow to set.
6. Heat the remaining tablespoon of oil in a large frying pan and sauté 3 cakes at a time for about 3-4 minutes per side, or until nicely browned, adding additional olive oil if needed.

Cook's Note: The cakes can be frozen, either fully cooked or before being cooked. Defrost and sauté raw cakes as directed. Fully cooked cakes can be reheated in a 350°F oven for 10 minutes, or until hot.

Slow Cooked Brown Rice Risotto and Mushrooms

Don't have time to stir that risotto? The best part is that this risotto is made in a slow cooker so no stirring is necessary.

Prep time: 15 minutes
Cook time: 1 hour and 40 minutes

Makes: 4 servings

- 3 tablespoons extra virgin olive oil, divided
- 2 shallots, peeled and chopped
- 2 cloves garlic, peeled and chopped
- 1 cup short grain brown rice
- 8 ounces baby bella or cremini mushrooms, sliced
- 2¼-2½ cups Vegetable Broth (page 259)
- 1 teaspoon sea salt
- 2 tablespoons each, freshly chopped parsley and basil
- ½ teaspoon each, freshly chopped thyme and mint
- 1 teaspoon, freshly chopped dill

1. Heat 2 tablespoons of the oil in a large fry pan over medium heat for 1-2 minutes, or until hot.
2. Add the shallots and sauté for one minute. Stir in the garlic and cook 30 seconds.
3. Add the remaining oil and uncooked rice and cook stirring for about 2 minutes.
4. Add the mushrooms and sauté for 3 minute, or until just limp. Stir in salt.
5. Add the sautéed ingredients to the slow cooker. Add 2¼ cups of the vegetable broth and stir well.
6. Cover and cook on low for 1½ hours. Stir in the herbs and the remaining broth, if needed, in the last ½ hour.
7. Serve immediately.

Cook's Note: Double or even triple this recipe and serve the leftovers for lunch or store away in the freezer to enjoy on another day. As you get into later Phases of the diet feel free to add in a protein of your choice. Grilled chicken, for instance, goes nicely with this recipe.

Entrees   　　　　　　　　　　　PHASE 1

Sautéed Filet of Sole with Artichoke Pesto

Try this unique pesto on your fish. For a snack, use any extra sauce as a dip for celery and carrots.

Prep time: 10 minutes
Cook time: 10 minutes

Makes: 1½ cups pesto and 4 servings fish with pesto

Pesto
- 1 tablespoon extra virgin olive oil or extra virgin coconut oil
- 1 small shallot, chopped
- 1 clove garlic, chopped
- 8 almonds
- 1 can (14 ounces) artichoke hearts, drained
- ½ teaspoon sea salt
- ¼ cup basil leaves
- 2 tablespoons parsley leaves, stems removed
- ¼ cup baby spinach
- ¼ cup Homemade Mayonnaise* (page 270)

Fish
- 1 tablespoon extra virgin olive oil
- ½ teaspoon garlic powder
- ½ teaspoon onion powder
- ¼ teaspoon sea salt
- 4 filets of sole

Omit for egg-free

1. Heat the oil in a small frying pan over medium heat for 1-2 minutes, or until hot.
2. Add the shallots and garlic and sauté for 1 minute, or until limp.
3. Place the sautéed shallots and garlic, almonds, artichoke hearts, salt, basil, parsley, spinach and mayonnaise in the bowl of a food processor. Cover, and pulse several times until you reach the desired consistency—the pesto can be served chunky or smooth, to your taste.
4. Heat the oil in a medium-sized frying pan over medium heat for 1-2 minutes, or until hot.
5. Combine the garlic powder, onion powder and salt.
6. Season the fish on both sides with the garlic salt mixture. Place 2 filets in the frying pan and cook 2 minutes. Carefully turn the fish and cook for 2 minutes. Remove the cooked filets to a platter.
7. Repeat Step 6 with the remaining filets.
8. Serve each filet topped with 2-3 tablespoons of the pesto.
9. Store any remaining pesto in the refrigerator, for future use as a dip with carrots and celery.

PHASE 3 Variation: Once you reach Phase 3, you may add ¼ cup grated Parmesan cheese to this pesto before serving. Try it over buckwheat pasta, topped with additional grated cheese and freshly chopped tomatoes.

Desserts/Drinks  PALEO   PHASE 1

Berry Frozen Dessert

Try this Phase 1 version of "ice cream." No ice cream maker is needed.

Prep time: 10 minutes
Stand time: 2 hours

Makes: 4 servings

6 ounces frozen strawberries, raspberries, blackberries or blueberries or a combination
1 cup coconut milk, canned*
a pinch of sea salt
1 teaspoon vanilla
2-4 drops stevia** (optional)**

1. Put the frozen berries into the food processor. Pulse several times until coarsely chopped.
2. Add the remaining ingredients. Pulse until smooth.
3. Place in a container and freeze for two hours before serving.

* Most commercially available canned coconut milk contains guar gum, which isn't introduced into the diet until Phase 3. We did find one brand, however, called Natural Value Organic that doesn't contain guar gum! So while in Phase 1 use this brand. Otherwise hold this recipe until you reach Phase 3.

** Not suitable for Paleo. May add 1 teaspoon raw honey in its place.

Cook's Note: We call for canned coconut milk, rather than homemade because the canned milk separates from the liquid, making a very thick cream. Unfortunately, without that cream, your frozen ice cream-like dessert doesn't resemble ice cream. It's best to eat this soft-served ice cream imposter the day you make it. If not, be sure to take it out of the freezer at least a half an hour before serving.

Desserts/Drinks

PHASE 1

Nutty Coconut Delight

This recipe is a real treat. During Phase 1 of this diet, you are urged to keep your intake of sweets to a minimum, so restrict yourself to one. Be forewarned, however, that once you taste these treats, stopping at one might be easier said than done!

Prep time: 10 minutes
Cook time: 15 minutes
Set up time: several hours

Makes: 15 (2-inch) balls

¼ cup Ghee (page 258) or extra virgin coconut oil
¼-½ cup raw honey
½ cup almonds
1 teaspoon cinnamon
¾ cup unsweetened shredded coconut
½ cup walnuts, chopped

1. Preheat the oven to 350°F.
2. Place the ghee, honey, almonds and cinnamon in the bowl of a food processor. Pulse 6 or 7 times, or until the nuts are ground.
3. Grease the bottom of an 8-inch square baking pan. Spread the nut and honey mixture over the bottom of the greased pan.
4. Sprinkle the coconut over the honey nut mixture, and then sprinkle the chopped walnuts over the coconut.
5. Place the pan in the oven and bake for 15-20 minutes, or until the edges bubble and begin to brown.
6. Allow the pan to cool and then refrigerate it for several hours or overnight.
7. Scoop the mixture into balls using a small ice cream scoop or serving spoon.
8. Serve immediately and refrigerate any leftovers.

Cook's Note: Store in a sealed container in the refrigerator, or freeze them and defrost later for a take-along snack. Of course, everyone in your family will love these treats so much you might not have many leftovers to freeze.

Desserts/Drinks  PALEO   PHASE 1

Chewy Coconut Almond Cookies

This delicious dessert is a welcomed treat during this Phase, when the allowable foods are limited. Enjoy with a cup of hot tea.

Prep time: 10 minutes

Cook time: 10 minutes

Makes: 12 cookies

- 1 cup Almond Flour (page 260)
- ⅓ cup unsweetened shredded coconut
- 2 tablespoons raw honey
- 1 tablespoon extra virgin coconut oil
- 1 teaspoon vanilla extract
- ¼ teaspoon almond extract
- a pinch of sea salt

1. Preheat the over to 350°F.
2. Place all the ingredients in the bowl of a food processor. Pulse on and off about 10 times or until the mixture begins to form a ball.
3. Line a small baking sheet with parchment paper. Remove the mixture and place it on the parchment paper. Divide the dough into 12 portions. Form each into a ball.
4. Place the cookies on the parchment paper and press down to flatten.
5. Bake for 8-10 minutes or until the edges start to brown. Do not over bake.

Nutrition Note: Of all the foods in nature, coconut contains the highest level (50%) of lauric acid, which is a powerful tool to enhance the immune system. Clinical studies have shown that lauric acid has anti-microbial and anti-viral properties.

Desserts/Drinks

PHASE 1

Coconut Almond Custard

If you have never made custard and think that it is beyond your skill level, you will be pleasantly surprised by just how easy this recipe is to make.

Prep time: 15 minutes
Cook time: 35-40 minutes

Makes: 4 servings

2 eggs
1 cup Coconut Milk (page 261)
1 tablespoon raw honey
1 teaspoon vanilla
⅛ teaspoon almond extract
⅛ teaspoon sea salt
¾ cup unsweetened shredded coconut
Toasted coconut (see Cook's Note) **and chopped almonds for topping**

1. Preheat the oven to 400°F.
2. Combine all of the ingredients, except for the coconut, in a mixing bowl. Using a wire whisk or electric hand mixer whisk or beat for 1 minute or until the egg whites are thoroughly combined with the other ingredients.
3. Stir in the coconut.
4. Pour ½ cup of the mixture into each of four 6-ounce custard cups or heat-proof bowls. Place the filled cups in a baking dish. Fill the baking dish with enough hot water to reach about ⅓ of the way up the sides of the cups, being careful not to get any water into the cups.
5. Bake in the preheated oven for 35-40 minutes, or until the custard is set and a knife inserted about an inch from a cup's center comes out clean.
6. Carefully remove the custards from the water and allow them to cool for at least 30 minutes before serving, or refrigerate and serve chilled.
7. Sprinkle with toasted coconut and chopped almonds before serving.

Cook's Note: To toast the coconut for the topping, spread ½ cup of unsweetened shredded coconut in a thin layer on a baking tray. Place the tray in the preheated oven before you begin preparing the custards, and bake for 5 minutes, or until the coconut is lightly browned. Keep a close eye on it, as coconut toasts very quickly. Allow the coconut to cool, and store any unused portion in an airtight container for later use.

Desserts/Drinks

Açai and Blueberry Spritzer

Have this cool spritzer any time of day for a great pick-me-up.

Prep time: 5 minutes

Makes: 1 drink

- 3 ounces unsweetened acai juice
- 3 ounces unsweetened pomegranate-blueberry or blueberry juice
- 1 teaspoon raw honey or 3-5 drops liquid stevia* (optional)
- 2 ounces sparkling water

* Not suitable for Paleo. Use raw honey in its place.

1. Combine the juices and the honey and pour into a tall, ice-filled glass.
2. Top with the sparkling water and stir.

Mint Tea

Mint tea is as refreshing on a cold night as it is a on a hot summer day. If you like mint, give this super simple recipe a try.

Prep time: 15 minutes

Makes: 1 cup

- ¼ cup mint leaves
- 1 cup boiling filtered water

1. Place the mint leaves in the boiling water and allow them to steep for up to 10 minutes.
2. Strain the mint leaves from the water, and drink immediately.

VARIATION: Add a 1-inch slice of peeled ginger to the mint leaves and steep for 10 minutes to make Ginger Mint Tea.

Nutrition Note: Peppermint is said to have an antispasmodic effect on the muscles, so herbalists use it to treat respiratory problems and to soothe stomach cramps, irritable bowel symptoms and nausea. Ginger is also said to have soothing properties for upset stomachs, and its anti-inflammatory properties might help with migraine headaches, muscle aches and joint pain. Combining these two herbs can help to alleviate a variety of ailments.

Phase 2 Contents

- Granola 121
- Blueberry Oatmeal Pancakes 123
- Apricot Oat Muffins 125
- Overnight Oatmeal with Dried Fruit and Almonds 127
- Oat Crepes 128
- Indian Chickpea and Spinach Fritters 129
- Spinach and Lentil Salad with Warm Honey Vinegar Dressing 131
- Autumn Mixed Green and Roasted Butternut Squash Salad 132
- Apple and Pear Salad with Honey Mustard Dressing 133
- Seed Sandwich Thins 134
- Seed Crackers 134
- Salted Roasted Chickpeas 135
- Curried Cashews 135
- Lentil Soup 137
- Artichoke Hummus 138
- Chickpea and Sweet Potato Patties 139
- Chicken Salad 140
- Sesame Chicken Tenders 141
- Olive Tapenade Baked Haddock 142
- Roast Rack of Lamb with Mustard Herb Crust 143
- Sweet and Tangy Baked Chicken 145
- Lamb with Apricots and Prunes Tagine 147
- Cran-Raspberry Glazed Salmon 149
- Coconut Chicken Tenders 150
- Grilled Chicken Souvlaki 151
- Mixed Herb Pesto with Brown Rice Pasta 153
- Stuffed Turkey Burger 154
- Pecan Cherry Cookies 155
- Pavlova 157
- Honey Nut Bars 159
- Fruit and Nut Bars 161
- Pumpkin Custard 162
- Pumpkin Pie 162
- Iced Minted Raspberry Green Tea 163

Phase 2: The Early Reentry Phase *(three weeks)*

Phase 2 of the Lyme Inflammation Diet is to be followed for three weeks after the conclusion of Phase 1. The goal of this Phase is to slowly reintroduce healthy foods that have a low risk of triggering inflammation. This is done by slowly adding each food group's new foods to your diet. You'll add a new food from a food group every other or every few days. For example, on day one add the new fruits; on day three, add the new nuts, and so forth.

It is vitally important that you do not rush the reintroduction of foods. If you experience any symptoms of inflammation after the foods are reintroduced, this is a sign that you should continue to avoid them for the time being (the foods that carry the highest risk of triggering inflammation are nuts and certain fruits, such as mangos). While the suggested time frame of this Phase is three weeks, for some it may take some more time to reintroduce all the foods.

Remember a food sensitivity can appear anywhere from hours to days after you eat an offending food. Be sure to continue to use your Symptom Journal (downloadable at www.recipesforrepair.com/resources) which will help you assess if a food that you've recently added back in may be causing you a problem.

Don't forget to follow the General Food Guidelines and Food Choices for Detoxification on pages 28-30 during all Phases of the diet.

Phase 2 Preparation Tips (to start on day 4 of Phase 1)

Here are some suggestions and helpful steps that you can take starting on around day four of Phase 1 to help you prepare for your move into Phase 2.

- **Meal Plan.** As we suggest for Phase 1, you should start to come up with your meal plan for next week a few days before starting. Download and print the meal planning grid and shopping list available for download at www.recipesforrepair.com/resources so that you can plan a week's worth of recipes. Decide which foods you will add back and when before you come up with your meal plan.

- **Phase 2 Shopping List.** Once you planned your weekly meals it's time to shop. Many non perishables can be bought online for less. We have done the research and found some of the best prices available and share that information with you at www.recipesforrepair.com/our-favorite-products.

- **Phase Variations.** Some of the Phase 1 recipes that are vegetarian or call for fish can be made with poultry. So even though you are done with Phase 1 don't discount Phase 1 recipes; a simple change of a few ingredients can change the recipe into something new. Always look at the bottom of a recipe for a "Phase variation" where we give instruction on how to modify the recipe as you progress to later Phases of the diet.

Foods Allowed During Phase 2

Beverages
Black tea
Green tea
Vegetable juice[1]
Carbonated water, such as Perrier

Fruits[2]
Apricot
Cantaloupe
Date
Fig
Mango
Olives `NEW`
Pear
Pineapple
Plum `NEW`
Prune
Watermelon

Nuts and Seeds
Brazil nuts
Caraway seeds `NEW`
Cashews
Pecans
Poppy seeds `NEW`
Pumpkin seeds
Sesame seeds
Sunflower seeds

Vegetables
Arame [3] `NEW`
Celery root `NEW`
Dulse [3] `NEW`
Fennel `NEW`
Hijiki [3] `NEW`
Kelp [3] `NEW`
Kohlrabi `NEW`
Kombu [3] `NEW`
Nori [3] `NEW`
Pumpkin
Squash
Sweet potato
Tapioca (cassava)
Wakame [3] `NEW`
Wasabi `NEW`

Grains
Brown rice flour `NEW`
Oat flour `NEW`
Oatmeal

Beans and Legumes
Black beans
Chickpeas
Kidney beans
Lentils
Navy beans
Peas
Pinto beans

Protein
Lamb
Venison `NEW`
White meat chicken `NEW`
White meat turkey `NEW`

Herb and Spices
Black pepper

Fats
Margarines without trans fats [3]

Sweeteners [2]
Coconut palm sugar `NEW` or coconut nectar
Honey[5,6] `NEW`
Maple syrup
Sorbitol
Xylitol

Other
Coconut kefir[6,7]
Psyllium husk powder `NEW`

`NEW` : Foods added or shifted to earlier Phases of the diet, since the original version of the diet.

[1] Make sure it does not contain tomato, which is not permitted until Phase 3.

[2] Use sparingly, as they are very high in sugar.

[3] These are all sea vegetables. If you are unfamiliar with them, see page 37 for more information.

[4] Examples include Earth Balance and Smart Balance.

[5] If you are unsure about the difference between honey and raw honey, see page 36.

[6] For more information on where to purchase, see the Resources section (page 290).

[7] See page 38 for definition and health benefits.

Breakfast

PHASE 2

Granola

This granola can be eaten as a breakfast cereal with almond or coconut milk or as a snack anytime.

Prep time: 15 minutes
Cook time: 30-40 minutes

Makes: about 7 cups

2½ cups certified gluten-free old-fashioned oats
1 cup unsweetened shredded coconut
1 tablespoon flaxseed meal
1 cup chopped pecans
½ cup sunflower seeds
1 cup sliced almonds
2 teaspoons cinnamon
⅓ cup maple syrup
⅓ cup Ghee* (page 258) or ⅓ cup melted extra virgin coconut oil
1 teaspoon vanilla extract
½ cup fruit-juice sweetened, dried cranberries
½ cup chopped dried apricots

* For dairy-free use the oil in place of the ghee.

1. Preheat the oven to 350°F.
2. Combine the oats, coconut, flaxseed, pecans, sunflower seeds, almonds and cinnamon on a large baking sheet.
3. Combine the syrup, ghee or coconut oil and vanilla in a measuring cup.
4. Pour the syrup mixture over the oats and nuts, and toss well to coat.
5. Bake for 30-40 minutes, or until lightly browned.
6. Remove the granola from the oven and add the dried fruit.
7. Allow to cool completely before storing in an airtight container.

Cook's Note: If you prefer a less sweet version of this recipe, simply substitute any allowable seeds and nuts in place of the dried fruits. When you reach the later Phases of the diet, you may add different fruits and nuts where permitted, such as raisins in Phase 4.

PALEO For a Paleo version of this granola, you may substitute 2½ cups of a mix of shredded coconut and your favorite nuts and seeds for the old-fashioned oats.

Recipes for Repair

Blueberry Oatmeal Pancakes

This recipe contains a trifecta of "good for you" foods. Blueberries are the number one fruit for antioxidants, and oats and almonds are heart-healthy and may help lower cholesterol. Most importantly, though, these pancakes are delectable!

Prep time: 15 minutes
Stand time: 5 minutes
Cook time: 6-18 minutes

Makes: about 6 (4-inch) pancakes

- ¾ cup certified gluten-free old-fashioned oats
- 1 cup Almond Milk (page 260)
- 1 teaspoon vanilla
- 1 teaspoon cream of tartar
- ½ teaspoon baking soda
- ¾ cup oat flour
- ¼ teaspoon sea salt
- 1 egg, separated
- 2 tablespoons Ghee* (page 258) or extra virgin olive oil
- 1 cup blueberries

* For dairy-free use the olive oil in place of the ghee.

1. Combine the oats, almond milk, cream of tartar, baking soda and vanilla in a medium-sized bowl, and allow to stand for at least 5 minutes to soften.
2. Meanwhile, combine the flour and salt in a small bowl.
3. Combine the egg yolk and the ghee or oil, and stir into the softened oatmeal.
4. Add the flour and salt to the oatmeal mixture and stir well to combine.
5. Preheat a frying pan or griddle (nonstick preferred).
6. Using an electric mixer, beat the egg white until it forms soft peaks. Fold the beaten egg white into the mixture.
7. Before making the first pancake, wipe the hot pan or griddle with a folded paper towel soaked in a small amount of ghee or extra virgin olive oil.
8. Measure ⅓ cup of batter per pancake, and pour onto the griddle.
9. Scatter blueberries on the top of each pancake, and cook for about 3 minutes. The pancake is ready to turn when bubbles form on the surface, and the edges begin to set. Turn the pancakes, and cook for 2-3 minutes.

Cook's Note: Correct timing and griddle temperature may vary. Because cooktops and stoves vary so widely, it is difficult to give precise instructions. Cook these pancakes as you cook any other pancake recipe. Just make certain that the cooking surface is hot enough before you pour the batter. Otherwise, the pancakes will stick. If the surface is too hot, however, the pancakes will brown too quickly while remaining raw in the center. Jot down the timing and temperature that work for you in the margin of this recipe, so that the next time you make these pancakes, you will have the information at hand.

Breakfast

PHASE 2

Apricot Oat Muffins

Try this muffin for breakfast or a mid-morning snack with a cup of tea. It's sweet, fruity and nutty and a nice change of pace for Phase 2.

Prep time: 15 minutes
Cook time: 25 minutes

Makes: 6 servings

⅔ cup certified gluten-free old-fashioned oats

1 egg*

1 cup Brown Rice Milk (page 261)**

1 teaspoon vanilla

¼ cup maple syrup

¼ melted extra virgin coconut oil or Ghee (page 258)

¾ cup brown rice flour

¼ teaspoon sea salt

½ teaspoon cinnamon

¼ teaspoon ground ginger

2 teaspoons Homemade Baking Powder*** (page 262)

⅓ cup dried apricot, finely chopped

Topping

2 tablespoons gluten-free old-fashioned oats

3 tablespoons pecans, chopped

¼ teaspoon cinnamon

1. Preheat the oven to 350°F.
2. Grease a 6-cup muffin pan and set aside.
3. Combine the oats, chia seeds or egg, rice milk, vanilla, maple syrup and oil. Stir well and allow to stand while the oven is preheating.
4. Combine the flour, salt, cinnamon, ginger and baking powder in small bowl.
5. Add the flour mixture into the oatmeal mixture and stir well. Stir in chopped apricots.
6. Fill each muffin cup with a scant ⅓ cup of batter.
7. Combine the topping ingredients and sprinkle the mixture over the muffins.
8. Bake in the preheated oven for 25 minutes, or until a toothpick inserted into the middle of the muffin comes out clean.
9. Allow the muffins to cool in the pan completely before removing. Refrigerate or freeze leftovers.

   * To make this recipe egg free, add one tablespoon of chia seeds to the dry ingredients and reduce the amount of the almond milk by ¼ cup.

   ** You may substitute with coconut milk or almond milk in place of the brown rice milk.

   *** Most commercial baking powders contain cornstarch, which is not permitted in the first two Phases of this diet. Making your own baking powder enables you to make the recipes for baked goods found in Phase 2.

Cook's Note: Once you reach Phase 3 and add ¼ of a teaspoon of guar gum or xanthan gum during step 2 of the recipe. If you're already in a later Phase you may add the gum during step 2 when making the recipe. Additionally, we advise that you let the muffins cool completely in the pan before transferring them to a container to store in the refrigerator. If you don't, the muffins may crumble.

Breakfast

PHASE 2

Overnight Oatmeal with Dried Fruit and Almonds

This nutritious breakfast will start your day off right.

Prep time: 15 minutes
Cook time: 8 hours

Makes: 6-8 servings

1 cup steel-cut oats or oat groats

2½ cups Almond Milk (page 260)

2½ cups Coconut Milk (page 261)

1 cup filtered water

¼ teaspoon sea salt

2 tablespoons maple syrup

1 teaspoon vanilla extract

1 teaspoon ground cinnamon

½ teaspoon ground ginger

¼ teaspoon nutmeg

½-1 cup chopped, mixed, unsweetened, dried fruits, such as apricots, cranberries, cherries, blueberries or figs

2 tablespoons sliced almonds or chopped walnuts or pecans

Additional Almond Milk (page 260)

Additional cinnamon

1. Place all the ingredients, except for the nuts, additional almond milk and additional cinnamon in the bowl of a slow cooker. Cover the cooker and set it to cook on Low for 8 hours.
2. Spoon the oatmeal into bowls, and top with the nuts, additional almond milk and/or additional cinnamon if desired.
3. Refrigerate any leftovers, which can be reheated.

Cook's Note: Turn on the slow cooker, as directed in Step 1, just before you go to bed at night. The next morning, everyone will wake up to a delicious bowl of oatmeal, no matter what time they leave for their day of work or school.

Breakfast

Oat Crepes

These versatile crepes are great filled with scrambled eggs for breakfast, sliced chicken and avocado for lunch or with a Stuffed Turkey Burger (page 154) for dinner. And, for dessert, top with Berry Pear Sauce (page 274) or Blueberry or Raspberry Syrup (page 277).

Prep time: 15 minutes
Cook time: 24 minutes

Makes: about 12 crepes

- 2 eggs, well beaten
- 1 cup oat flour
- 1 cup Almond Milk (page 260)
- 2 tablespoons Ghee* (page 258) or extra virgin olive oil
- ⅛ teaspoon sea salt
- 1 teaspoon vanilla**

* For dairy-free use the olive oil in place of the ghee.
** Omit when using crepes for a savory dish.

1. Combine all the ingredients in a large mixing bowl. Mix well with a blender or electric mixer until the batter is smooth.
2. Preheat an 8- or 9-inch frying pan or crepe pan until water sprinkled on the pan sizzles.
3. Before making the first crepe, wipe the hot pan with a folded paper towel soaked in oil.
4. Fill a ladle with 3 tablespoons of batter, or use a not-quite-filled ¼-cup measuring cup. Pour the batter into the pan, quickly tilting the pan to spread the batter over the bottom. Allow the crepe to cook for about 1½ minutes, or until it is set and lightly browned. Using a nonstick spatula, turn the crepe and cook 1½ minutes.
5. Remove the crepe to a plate and cover with a piece of waxed paper.
6. Continue cooking as directed, placing a piece of waxed paper between each cooked crepe, until all are cooked.
7. Use in any recipe calling for crepes.

Cook's Note: There's a knack to making crepes, and it takes some practice to learn to make them perfectly every time. Here are two suggestions for success: first and most importantly, make sure the pan is the correct temperature. Heat the pan over medium-high heat for 3-5 minutes. If a drop of water sizzles in the pan, it is at the right temperature. Also, crepes should be thin, so after pouring the batter, remove the pan from the heat and tilt it in all directions to spread the batter over the bottom of the pan. If you follow these two guidelines, you will be much less likely to have problems with your crepes.

Soups/Salads/Sides/Snacks   PHASE 2

Indian Chickpea and Spinach Fritters

The curry in these fritters gives them a decidedly Indian flavor. If you don't like Indian food, take a chance and try this recipe anyway – you might be pleasantly surprised. Many of our taste testers who "don't like Indian food" ended up asking for the recipe!

Prep time: 20 minutes
Cook time: 10 minutes

Makes: 8 fritters

- ½ cup brown rice flour
- ½ teaspoon baking soda
- ¼ teaspoon cream of tartar
- ¼ teaspoon freshly ground black pepper
- ½ teaspoon sea salt
- 1 egg
- ¼ cup filtered water
- 1 cup chickpeas, drained, rinsed and coarsely chopped
- 3 cups fresh baby spinach, finely chopped
- ½ small onion, chopped
- 1 clove garlic, crushed
- 2 teaspoons curry powder
- 2 teaspoons sesame seeds
- 1 teaspoon chopped oregano
- 1-3 tablespoons Ghee* (page 258) or extra virgin olive oil, divided

For dairy-free use the oil in place of the ghee.

1. Preheat the oven to 250ºF.
2. Combine the flour, baking soda, cream of tartar, pepper and salt in a large bowl.
3. Combine the egg and water and whisk until smooth. Add it to the flour and stir until smooth.
4. Add all the remaining ingredients, except for the ghee or oil, and stir well to combine.
5. Heat 1 tablespoon of the ghee or oil in a medium-sized frying pan over medium heat for 1-2 minutes, or until hot.
6. Using a standard ice cream scoop, drop the mixture into the hot pan. Press each fritter flat to form a 3-inch circle.
7. Cook 4 fritters at a time for 2½ minutes per side, or until nicely browned.
8. Remove the cooked fritters to a baking sheet and keep them warm in the preheated oven while you prepare the remaining fritters, adding the additional tablespoons of oil, if needed.

Cook's Note: If you have a large enough frying pan, you can cook all the fritters at once. In that case, you need not preheat the oven.

Soups/Salads/Sides/Snacks

PHASE 2

Spinach and Lentil Salad with Warm Honey Vinegar Dressing

This easy-to-make salad looks and tastes like a restaurant-quality dish. Your family and friends will be impressed.

Prep time: 15 minutes
Cook time: 45 minutes

Makes: 2 servings

- ½ cup lentils
- 2 tablespoons extra virgin olive oil
- 1 medium onion, cut into quarters and then sliced into strips
- 2 cloves garlic, crushed
- 3 tablespoons raw apple cider vinegar
- 1 tablespoon honey
- ¼ cup extra virgin olive oil
- 2 cups baby spinach leaves
- 2 hard cooked eggs, sliced
- 10 toasted pecans
- ½ ripe avocado, sliced

1. Cook the lentils according to the package directions.
2. While the lentils are cooking, heat the oil in a small frying pan over medium heat for 1-2 minutes, or until hot.
3. Sauté the onion for about 5 minutes, or until golden-brown.
4. Add the garlic and cook for 1 minute.
5. Combine the vinegar and honey, and pour it over the onions in the pan. Stir well to combine, and cook for 30 seconds.
6. Add the remaining ¼ cup of oil to the pan and cook for 30 seconds.
7. Divide the spinach between two bowls. Top each with half of the onion vinaigrette mixture and toss well.
8. Spoon the cooked lentils over the salads. Top with a splash of the dressing, and the eggs, nuts and avocado.

Cook's Note: Cook the lentils and eggs in advance. Then, all that is left to do is to make the dressing. Reheat the lentils and eggs (before slicing), and then assemble the salad.

Soups/Salads/Sides/Snacks   PHASE 2

Autumn Mixed Green and Roasted Butternut Squash Salad

Prep time: 15 minutes
Cook time: 40 minutes

Makes: 2 servings

Butternut Squash
8 ounces butternut squash, cut into ½-inch cubes
2 tablespoons extra virgin olive oil
1 tablespoon maple syrup
½ teaspoon onion powder
½ teaspoon garlic powder
½ teaspoon sea salt
¼ teaspoon freshly ground black pepper

Dressing
2 tablespoons acai, raspberry or pomegranate juice
1 tablespoon mustard
1 tablespoon raw apple cider vinegar
1 tablespoon raw honey
2 teaspoons maple syrup
¼ teaspoon sea salt
⅛ teaspoon garlic powder
⅛ teaspoon onion powder
⅛ teaspoon freshly ground black pepper
¼ cup extra virgin olive oil

Salad
2 cups mixed greens
2 tablespoons toasted pine nuts or walnuts
2 tablespoons fruit-juice sweetened, dried cranberries

1. Preheat the oven to 425ºF.
2. Place the squash on a baking sheet in a single layer.
3. Combine the oil, syrup, onion and garlic powder, and salt and pepper, and pour the mixture over the squash. Toss well to coat.
4. Roast the squash for 30-40 minutes, or until the pieces start to caramelize.
5. Meanwhile, combine the dressing ingredients in the order given, whisking in the olive oil until the dressing forms an emulsion.
6. Place the greens on two salad plates and top with the roasted squash, nuts and cranberries.
7. Spoon 2 tablespoons of dressing over each salad and serve immediately.

Use mustard made with apple cider vinegar or substitute dry mustard (see footnote 4 on page 68 for more information).

Soups/Salads/Sides/Snacks

PHASE 2

Apple and Pear Salad with Honey Mustard Dressing

Boston lettuce is strangely under used in salads. Its soft, almost buttery leaf works especially well with the fruits in this recipe.

Prep time: 15 minutes

Makes: 2 servings
(½ cup dressing)

Salad
- 2 large Boston lettuce leaves
- 1 green apple, peeled and sliced
- 1 medium pear, peeled and sliced
- 2 tablespoons fruit-juice sweetened, dried cranberries or cherries
- ½ cup pecans

Dressing
- 1 tablespoon mustard*
- 2 tablespoons raw apple cider vinegar
- 1 tablespoon raw honey
- ½ tablespoon maple syrup
- ¼ teaspoon sea salt
- ⅛ teaspoon freshly ground black pepper
- ⅛ teaspoon each garlic powder and onion powder
- ¼ cup extra virgin olive oil

1. Place the lettuce leaves on two salad plates.
2. Top with the fruits and nuts.
3. Combine the dressing ingredients in the order given, whisking in the olive oil until the dressing forms an emulsion.
4. Spoon 2 tablespoons of dressing over the salads just before serving. Refrigerate any leftover dressing.

Use mustard made with apple cider vinegar or substitute dry mustard (see footnote 4 on page 68 for more information).

Cook's Note: This salad can be turned into a main dish by topping it with broiled fish or chicken.

Soups/Salads/Sides/Snacks   PALEO   PHASE 2

Seed Sandwich Thins

Longing for a sandwich? Use these unusual seed thins to make an open-faced Egg Salad (page 85) or Chicken Salad (page 140) sandwich, or cut them up and use them as crackers with soup or Artichoke Hummus (page 138). Anyway you eat them they are sure to become an instant hit.

Prep time: 20 minutes
Cook time: 25-30 minutes

Makes: 8 thins

⅔ cups sunflower seeds
1 tablespoon flaxseed meal
½ cup pumpkin seeds
2 tablespoons black sesame seeds
2 tablespoons white sesame seeds
1 tablespoon chia seeds
2 tablespoons psyllium husk powder
½ teaspoon caraway seeds
½ teaspoon poppy seeds
¼ cup Almond Flour (page 260)
1 teaspoon sea salt
¼ teaspoon each onion and garlic powder
½ cup filtered water
2 tablespoons maple syrup
3 tablespoons extra virgin coconut oil, solid

1. Preheat the oven to 350°F.
2. Combine the seeds, psyllium husk powder, almond flour, salt, and onion and garlic powder in a bowl and stir well.
3. Combine the water and maple syrup and pour it over the seeds. Stir well.
4. Stir in the solid coconut oil and mix well until it is completely dispersed.
5. Line a large baking sheet with parchment paper. Using a ¼ cup measuring cup divide the mixture into 8 portions and place them on the baking sheet.
6. Using the palm of your hand press the mixture into 3½-inch rounds.
7. Bake in the preheated oven for 25-30 minutes, or until the edges are starting to brown.
8. Allow the thins to stand on the baking sheet for 10 minutes before removing them to a cooling rack. Cool completely before storing in an airtight container.

Bonus Recipe: Seed Crackers – These thins can also be made into crackers by simply cooking the thins for a few extra minutes.

Soups/Salads/Sides/Snacks   PHASE 2

Salted Roasted Chickpeas

Grab a handful of this tasty, healthy snack whenever you have a craving for something salty and nutty.

Prep time: 5 minutes
Cook time: 55-65 minutes

Makes: about 1¼ cups

- 1 can (14 ounces) organic chickpeas, drained and rinsed
- ½ tablespoon extra virgin olive oil
- ¼ teaspoon garlic powder
- ½ teaspoon sea salt
- ⅛ teaspoon freshly ground black pepper

1. Preheat the oven to 400ºF.
2. Pour the rinsed chickpeas onto a paper towel and blot dry.
3. Place the chickpeas on a baking sheet. Pour the oil over the chickpeas and toss well to coat them all.
4. Combine the garlic powder, salt and pepper and sprinkle over the chickpeas.
5. Roast in the preheated oven for 55-65 minutes, or until browned and crunchy. Turn the chickpeas with a large spoon or spatula once or twice during cooking to ensure even roasting.

Cook's Note: Keep an eye on the chickpeas during the last few minutes of roasting, to make sure they do not burn. They should be crunchy as soon as you remove them from the oven; if they are still soft, they need more time.

Curried Cashews   PALEO

Nuts are a great snack. In this recipe, the curry adds an Indian flavor.

Prep time: 5 minutes
Cook time: 10 minutes

Makes: 2 cups

- 2 cups raw cashew nuts
- 1 tablespoon curry powder
- ½-1 teaspoon sea salt
- ¼ teaspoon garlic powder
- Olive oil cooking spray or ½ tablespoon extra virgin olive oil

1. Preheat the oven to 350ºF.
2. Place the cashews on a small baking tray in a single layer.
3. Roast in the preheated oven for 8-10 minutes, or until lightly browned.
4. Combine the curry powder, sea salt and garlic powder in a small bowl.
5. Remove the nuts from the oven and spray with cooking spray or coat with the oil.
6. Sprinkle the curry mixture over the warm nuts. Toss well to coat.
7. Cool completely before serving.

Recipes for Repair

Soups/Salads/Sides/Snacks   PHASE 2

Lentil Soup

Make this soup and freeze half of it for a busy day when you have no time to cook. It is hardy enough for dinner but can also be taken to work to have for lunch after a quick reheat.

Prep time: 25 minutes
Cook time: 50 minutes

Makes: about 1½ quarts

- 2 tablespoons extra virgin olive oil
- 1 large onion, chopped
- 4 cloves garlic, chopped
- 2 carrots, peeled and chopped
- 3 stalks celery, chopped
- 1 cup (2 ounces) chopped kale
- 1 small zucchini, chopped
- 1 teaspoon sea salt
- ½ teaspoon freshly ground black pepper
- 1 tablespoon chopped chives
- 1 tablespoon chopped parsley
- ½ teaspoon chopped thyme
- ½ teaspoon chopped rosemary
- 8 cups Vegetable Broth (page 259)
- ½ pound lentils, rinsed

1. Heat the oil in a large saucepan over medium heat for 1-2 minutes, or until hot.
2. Add the onion and sauté for about 5 minutes, or until lightly browned. Add the garlic and sauté for 1 minute.
3. Add the carrots, celery, kale, zucchini, salt, pepper and herbs and continue to sauté for about 2 minutes until the vegetables are limp.
4. Add the broth, and stir in the lentils.
5. Bring the soup to a boil. Reduce the heat and simmer for 40 minutes, or until the lentils are tender.
6. Adjust the seasoning to taste, and serve.

PHASE 3 **Variation:** Once you reach Phase 3, add a 14-ounce can of diced tomatoes with herbs at the same time as you add the broth. The tomatoes will add even more flavor to this hearty soup.

Cook's Note: This soup will thicken as it stands because the lentils continue to soak up the liquid. If the soup becomes too thick, you can add some extra Vegetable Broth or water and simmer for a few additional minutes.

Nutrition Note: Lentils are a good source of B-vitamins and minerals, including, but not limited to, iron. They are among the healthiest sources of plant-based protein and are very high in dietary fiber, yet low in fat.

Soups/Salads/Sides/Snacks

PHASE 2

Artichoke Hummus

Hummus has become a very popular food. Chickpeas are usually the star of the show, but in this recipe they share the stage with artichoke hearts.

Prep time: 15 minutes

Makes: 2 cups

- 1 can (15.5 ounces) chickpeas, drained, with 2 tablespoons liquid set aside
- 1 can (14 ounces) artichoke hearts, drained
- 2 tablespoons Tahini (page 263)
- 3 tablespoons extra virgin olive oil
- 1 clove garlic
- 1 tablespoon raw apple cider vinegar
- 1 sprig parsley, leaves only
- 4 basil leaves
- 1 sprig oregano, leaves or ¼ teaspoon dried oregano
- ½ teaspoon sea salt
- ¼ teaspoon freshly ground black pepper
- ½ teaspoon each garlic and onion powder

1. Combine all the ingredients in the bowl of a food processor. Pulse several times to chop, and then turn on and process continually until the hummus is a smooth consistency.
2. If the hummus is too thick, add 1 tablespoon at a time of chickpea liquid until you reach the desired consistency.
3. Serve as a dip with carrot and celery sticks.

Nutrition Note: Artichokes and chickpeas are good sources of fiber and rich in folates and vitamins A and B6. They are a winning flavor and nutrition combination.

Soups/Salads/Sides/Snacks   PHASE 2

Chickpea and Sweet Potato Patties

Chickpeas and sweet potatoes combine beautifully in these satisfying patties. Serve them over greens for lunch, or as a side dish with dinner.

Prep time: 10 minutes
Stand time: 30 minutes
Cook time: 6 minutes

Makes: 5 patties

- 1 cup (8 ounces) cooked sweet potato, mashed
- 1 cup chickpeas, chopped
- 1 clove garlic, crushed
- 4 scallions, white part only, chopped
- ¼ teaspoon sea salt
- ⅛ teaspoon freshly ground black pepper
- 2 tablespoons Homemade Mayonnaise (page 270)
- ½ tablespoon mustard*
- 1 teaspoon each freshly chopped parsley, oregano and basil
- ⅔ cup Almond Flour (page 260)
- 2 tablespoons Ghee* (page 258) or extra virgin olive oil
- ¼ cup Curried Mayonnaise (page 270), optional

1. Combine all the ingredients, except for the almond meal and oil, and mix well.
2. Form the mixture into 5 patties (about ⅓ cup each).
3. Dredge the patties in the almond meal and refrigerate them for at least 30 minutes.
4. Heat the oil in a small frying pan over medium heat for 1-2 minutes, or until hot.
5. Cook the patties in the hot oil for 2-3 minutes per side, or until nicely browned.
6. Serve topped with Curried Mayonnaise, if desired.

*Use mustard made with apple cider vinegar or substitute dry mustard (see footnote 4 on page 68 for more information).

**For dairy-free use the olive oil in place of the ghee.

Cook's Note: These patties reheat well in a toaster oven or frying pan. They can also be frozen and reheated any time you need a quick meal. They can be made into small patties and used as appetizers.

Soups/Salads/Sides/Snacks   PALEO   PHASE 2

Chicken Salad

This is a quick lunch if you have all the ingredients prepared in advance. Be sure to make the sauces and condiments for each Phase that are found in the Sauces and Condiments section, so that you will have what you need to prepare the recipes at a moment's notice.

Prep time: 10 minutes

Makes: 4 servings (about 3 cups)

- 2 cups cooked white meat chicken, cut into ½-inch chunks
- ½ cup chopped celery
- ½ cup fruit-juice sweetened, dried cranberries
- ½ cup cashews
- ¼ cup chopped dried apricots
- ½ teaspoon sea salt
- ½ teaspoon garlic powder
- ¼ teaspoon freshly ground black pepper
- 1 teaspoon raw apple cider vinegar
- 1 cup Herb Mayonnaise (page 270)

1. Combine all the ingredients in a medium-sized bowl and stir well, coating everything with the mayonnaise.
2. Refrigerate the salad for at least 30 minutes, or overnight, before serving.
3. Serve over mixed greens.

Cook's Note: The flavors in this chicken salad blend and taste better when it's refrigerated for a while, so make this recipe ahead of time whenever possible.

Entrees PHASE 2

Sesame Chicken Tenders

Puffed brown rice is usually eaten as a breakfast cereal, but in this recipe, it is ground in a coffee grinder and mixed with seasoning and toasted sesame seeds. This mixture makes an outstanding breading for chicken tenders that you and your family will love.

Prep time: 10 minutes
Cook time: 15-20 minutes

Makes: 4 servings

- ½ cup ground puffed brown rice
- 1 teaspoon garlic powder
- 1 teaspoon onion powder
- ½ teaspoon sea salt
- ¼ teaspoon freshly ground black pepper
- ¼ teaspoon paprika
- ½ cup toasted sesame seeds
- 1 egg, lightly beaten
- 1 teaspoon filtered water
- 1 pound white meat chicken, cut into 1-inch strips
- 2 tablespoons extra virgin coconut oil or Ghee* (page 258)

For dairy-free use the oil in place of the ghee.

1. Combine the first 7 ingredients on a flat dinner plate.
2. Combine the egg and water in a shallow bowl.
3. Dip the chicken into the egg mixture and then into the sesame seed mixture. Place the coated chicken on a flat plate (see Cook's Note below).
4. Heat the oil in a large frying pan over medium heat for 1-2 minutes, or until hot.
5. Place the coated chicken in the hot oil, being careful not to overcrowd the pan, and cook for about 3 minutes per side, or until nicely browned.
6. Continue until all the chicken is cooked. Add more oil if needed, and lower the heat if the pan starts to get too hot.
7. Serve immediately with Berry Pear Sauce (page 274), or with any of the sauces found in the Sauces and Condiments section of this book (page 256).

Cook's Note: You can prepare these tenders in advance and, when you reach the indicated step, store the raw, coated tenders in the refrigerator until you are ready to cook them. They only take 6 minutes to cook, so this is a very quick main dish.

Entrees  PHASE 2

Olive Tapenade Baked Haddock

This recipe is super-easy to make and is really delightful. Serve it with a stir-fried vegetable medley and cultured carrots.

Prep time: 10 minutes
Cook time: 20 minutes

Makes: 4 servings

1 pound skinless haddock fillet, cut in four pieces
½ teaspoon each, salt and garlic powder
½ teaspoon mustard powder
2 teaspoons extra virgin olive oil
16 large pitted green olives
½ teaspoon each, freshly chopped oregano* and lemon thyme**

1. Preheat the oven to 425° F.
2. Place the fish on a baking dish and sprinkle with salt, garlic powder and mustard powder.
3. Drizzle olive oil over each fillet.
4. Place the olives and herbs in the bowl of a food processor.
5. Pulse 5 or 6 times until evenly chopped.
6. Spread the chopped olives evenly over the fish fillets.
7. Bake for 18-20 minutes or until fish flakes easily with a fork.

* or ⅛ teaspoon dried oregano
** or ¼ teaspoon dried thyme

Entrees | PALEO | PHASE 2

Roast Rack of Lamb with Mustard Herb Crust

This elegant dinner is ideal for a special occasion. The recipe can easily be doubled, so make this the next time you have company for dinner.

Prep time: 25 minutes

Cook time: 18-30 minutes, depending on desired doneness

Makes: 2 servings

- 1 teaspoon dry mustard
- 2 teaspoons raw apple cider vinegar
- 2 teaspoons chopped chives
- 2 teaspoons chopped rosemary
- 1 teaspoon chopped thyme
- 8 roasted almonds, finely chopped
- 2 cloves garlic, crushed
- ¼ teaspoon sea salt
- ⅛ teaspoon freshly ground black pepper
- 1 teaspoon honey
- 1 rack of lamb (6-9 chops), trimmed of most of the fat

1. Preheat the oven to 425°F.
2. Combine all the ingredients, except for the honey and the lamb, in a small bowl.
3. Using a pastry brush, coat the fat side of the lamb with the honey.
4. Spoon the mustard herb mixture onto the lamb and spread it over the top, pressing it in with your fingers to form a crust.
5. Place the lamb, herb-coated side up, into a heavy frying pan or small roasting pan. Cook in the preheated oven to desired doneness: 18-20 minutes for rare meat, 25 minutes for medium-rare and 30 minutes for medium-well.
6. Cut the rack into chops and serve immediately.

Cook's Note: You can prepare the meat in advance of cooking – season and coat it earlier in the day, so that you can spend time with your guests instead of in the kitchen.

Entrees PALEO PHASE 2

Sweet and Tangy Baked Chicken

This chicken, with its dark, tangy sauce and moist, tender meat, is finger-licking good!

Prep time: 15 minutes
Cook time: 50 minutes

Makes: 4 servings

2 tablespoons extra virgin olive oil
1 medium onion, chopped
4 large garlic cloves, peeled and chopped
2 large (12 ounces each) chicken breasts with skin and bones, cut in half
½ teaspoon sea salt
¼ teaspoon freshly ground black pepper
2 sprigs rosemary
2 sprigs thyme
2 tablespoons honey
3 tablespoons raw apple cider vinegar
3 tablespoons filtered water or Vegetable Broth (page 259)
1 tablespoon mustard*
½-1 cup filtered water

1. Preheat the oven to 400°F.
2. Heat the oil in a heavy-bottomed frying pan (cast iron preferred) over medium heat for 1-2 minutes, or until hot.
3. Add the onion and sauté for 2 minutes.
4. Add the garlic and sauté for 1 minute.
5. Remove the onion and garlic from the pan and reserve for later use.
6. Season the skin of the chicken with salt and pepper and add the chicken to the hot pan, skin side down. Cook for 3 minutes, or until browned. Then, turn the chicken and cook for 3 minutes.
7. Add the rosemary and thyme to the pan.
8. Combine the honey, vinegar, water or broth and mustard, and stir the mixture into the chicken.
9. Return the onions and garlic to the pan and stir well.
10. Place the pan in the preheated oven and cook for 30 minutes. After 30 minutes, check to see if the sauce has become too thick and syrupy; if it has, stir in the remaining ½-1 cup water.
11. Turn the chicken breasts and cook for 15 minutes, or until the chicken is nicely browned.
12. Remove the rosemary and thyme sprigs. If the sauce is still too thick, stir in a little more water.
13. Place the chicken on a serving platter, and top with the sauce.

Use mustard made with apple cider vinegar or substitute dry mustard (see footnote 4 on page 68 for more information).

Cook's Note: If your family prefers dark meat chicken to white, wait until Phase 3 to make this recipe.

Entrees  PHASE 2

Lamb with Apricots and Prunes Tagine

The word "tagine" refers to either a stew or a Moroccan cooking vessel. This is a flavorful stew with exotic spices, lamb and dried fruits that can be cooked in a tagine or in the oven.

Prep time: 25 minutes

Cook time: 1½-2 hours, or until meat is tender

Makes: 6 servings

- 3 tablespoons extra virgin olive oil, divided
- 1 large onion, sliced
- 4 cloves garlic, chopped
- 2½-3 pounds boneless leg of lamb, cut into 2-inch pieces
- ½ teaspoon sea salt
- ¼ teaspoon pepper
- 1 teaspoon dry mustard
- ½ teaspoon chopped ginger
- 1 teaspoon turmeric
- 1 teaspoon garam masala or curry powder
- 1 cinnamon stick or ¼ teaspoon ground cinnamon
- ¼ teaspoon cumin
- 3½ cups Vegetable Broth (page 259) or Chicken Bone Broth (page 264)
- 1 cup whole dried apricots
- 1 cup dried prunes, or other mixed dried fruits (without added sugar)
- ¼ cup sliced almonds (optional)

1. Preheat the oven to 350°F.
2. Heat 2 tablespoons of the oil in a large frying pan over medium heat for 1-2 minutes, or until hot.
3. Sauté the onion for 4 minutes, or until it begins to brown.
4. Add the garlic and sauté for 1 minute.
5. Remove the onion and garlic to a 3-quart oven-proof casserole dish with a cover, or to a Dutch oven.
6. Add the remaining oil to the frying pan and heat for 1 minute.
7. Add half of the lamb to the frying pan and brown on all sides for about 5 minutes. Remove the cooked lamb to the casserole dish.
8. Adding more oil as needed, brown the remainder of the lamb in the frying pan. Once cooked, add it to the casserole dish.
9. Combine the salt, pepper, mustard and spices and add them, along with the vegetable or chicken broth and the dried fruits, to the casserole dish. Stir well to combine.
10. Cover the casserole dish and cook in the preheated oven for 1½-2 hours, or until the meat is tender.
11. Top with the sliced almonds before serving if desired.

PHASE 3 variation: Once you reach Phase 3, you may substitute stewing beef and Beef Broth (page 264), which results in a darker colored, fuller flavored sauce.

Cook's Note: If you prefer, you can cook this recipe in a slow cooker set to Cook on Low for 4-6 hours, or in a tagine on the stovetop for about 1½ hours, or until the meat is tender.

Entrees   PHASE 2

Cran-Raspberry Glazed Salmon

Salmon, which is high in omega-3 fatty acids, is recommended for everyone to eat at least once a week. Here is another enjoyable recipe to help you meet that goal.

Prep time: 10 minutes
Cook time: 8 minutes

Makes: 2 servings

Salmon
¾ pound salmon filet, 1-inch thick
Sea salt and pepper

Glaze
1 clove garlic, crushed
¼ cup Cran-Raspberry Sauce (page 275)
1 teaspoon mustard*
1 teaspoon oat flour
¼ teaspoon sea salt

1. Preheat the oven to Broil.
2. Season the salmon with the salt and pepper and place it on a baking sheet, flesh side up.
3. Combine the glaze ingredients and brush over the flesh side of the salmon.
4. Broil or grill for 8 minutes, or until the fish flakes easily with a fork. Do not turn the salmon while cooking.
5. Serve immediately.

Use mustard made with apple cider vinegar or substitute dry mustard (see footnote 4 on page 68 for more information).

Cook's Note: This glazed salmon is even more delicious when served over greens with mango dressing, to make an entrée salad. Top a cup of baby mixed greens with the cooked, glazed salmon, and dress with two tablespoons of Mango Dressing (page 276).

Recipes for Repair

Entrees | PALEO PHASE 2

Coconut Chicken Tenders

Kids and adults love chicken tenders, so try this healthy, easy-to-make version. Serve with Berry Pear Sauce (page 274).

Prep time: 20 minutes
Cook time: 10 minutes

Makes: 4 servings

- 1 egg
- 2 tablespoons Coconut Milk (page 261)
- ½ cup unsweetened shredded coconut
- ½ cup Almond Flour (page 260)
- ½ teaspoon sea salt
- ½ teaspoon garlic powder
- 1 pound skinless, white meat chicken strips
- 2 tablespoons extra virgin coconut oil or Ghee,* divided (page 258)

1. Combine the egg and the milk in a shallow dish.
2. Combine the remaining ingredients, except for the chicken and the oil or ghee, on a flat plate.
3. Dip the chicken into the egg mixture.
4. Dredge the egged chicken in the coconut mixture.
5. Heat 1 tablespoon of the oil or ghee in a medium-sized frying pan over medium heat for 1-2 minutes, or until hot.
6. Add half the tenders to the hot oil, being careful not to overcrowd the pan, and cook for 3-5 minutes per side, or until golden brown.
7. Add the remaining oil if needed, and cook the rest of the tenders.

*For dairy-free use the oil in place of the ghee.

Cook's Note: Once you've reached Phase 3, try serving them with Corn Fritters (page 186) and Peach and Pineapple Dipping Sauce (page 285).

Entrees  PHASE 2

Grilled Chicken Souvlaki

These chicken skewers can be grilled outdoors or in the kitchen. For extra flavor, let them marinate for several hours in the refrigerator.

Prep time: 20 minutes
Marinate time: 30 minutes to 3 hours
Cook time: 12-16 minutes

Makes: 4 servings

Marinade
- 2 tablespoons raw apple cider vinegar
- 2 tablespoons extra virgin olive oil
- ¼ teaspoon each sea salt and freshly ground black pepper
- 1 clove garlic, crushed
- ¼ teaspoon dry mustard
- ½ teaspoon dried oregano
- ½ teaspoon dried thyme
- ½ teaspoon dried parsley
- ½ teaspoon dried mint

Chicken
- 1 pound boneless chicken breasts, cut into 1-inch cubes
- 8 skewers

Creamy Herb Vinaigrette Sauce (optional)
- ¼ cup Homemade Mayonnaise (page 270)
- 1 tablespoon Fresh Herb Vinaigrette (page 93)

1. If you are using bamboo skewers, soak them in water for at least 30 minutes.
2. Combine all the marinade ingredients in a plastic freezer bag. Add the chicken cubes and place the bag in the refrigerator to marinate for 30 minutes to 3 hours.
3. Thread the marinated chicken onto the skewers. Grill on an outdoor grill* or on a preheated indoor grill pan for 6-8 minutes per side, or until nicely browned. Turn the skewers once during cooking.
4. Combine the mayonnaise and the herb vinaigrette, if desired, and serve as a sauce with the grilled, skewered chicken.

PHASE 3 variation: Once you reach Phase 3, you may add ½ teaspoon paprika.

* Some controversy exists regarding outdoor grilling, because of carcinogens found in grill smoke and in meats cooked over a high heat. To avoid any possible problems, try indirect grilling, as explained in the Cook's Note below.

Cook's Note: Start the fire to one side of the grill, rather than in the center. Then, when the fire and the grill grates are hot, cook next to the fire rather than directly over it, with the grill cover down. This method, called indirect grilling, can be used for cooking large cuts of meat and whole turkeys, as well as for smaller items like these chicken skewers.

Entrees　　　PALEO　　　　　　　　　　　　　　PHASE 2

Mixed Herb Pesto with Brown Rice Pasta

This recipe is a twist on standard pesto, which is typically made with just basil leaves and pine nuts. The inclusion of parsley, mint, chives, spinach and almonds adds a new dimension to this easy sauce.

Prep time: 15 minutes
Cook time: 12 minutes

Makes: 2 servings
(½ cup pesto)

4 ounces brown rice pasta
1 cup packed basil leaves
2 tablespoons roughly chopped chives
¼ cup parsley leaves, stems removed
2 tablespoons mint
¼ cup packed baby spinach
2 tablespoons pine nuts
2 tablespoons sliced almonds
1 small clove garlic
¼ teaspoon sea salt
¼ cup extra virgin olive oil

1. Cook the pasta according to the package directions.
2. While the pasta is cooking, place all the remaining ingredients except for the oil into a food processor and pulse until the herbs are completely chopped.
3. Drizzle the oil down the feed tube and continue to process until all the oil is incorporated.
4. Reserve a tablespoon or two of the pasta water before draining the pasta.
5. Toss the drained pasta with the pesto. If necessary, add some of the reserved pasta water to thin the pesto. Serve immediately.

PHASE 3 Variation: Once you reach Phase 3, you can stir 2 tablespoons of grated Parmesan cheese into the pesto before tossing it with the pasta. Top the pasta with chopped plum tomatoes and additional grated cheese.

Cook's Note: Try this pesto as a topping for broiled chicken or fish, or add some to Homemade Mayonnaise (page 270) for a tasty salad dressing. This recipe is called for in other upcoming meals so plan to make extra and freeze in ice cube trays. After it is frozen remove the cubes from the trays and store in a container in the freezer.

PALEO For a Paleo version of this recipe, serve this pesto over spaghetti squash (page 221) or spiralized zucchini "noodles" instead of the brown rice pasta.

Entrees PALEO PHASE 2

Stuffed Turkey Burger

This recipe sparks up the otherwise bland turkey burger by stuffing it with cooked vegetables and topping it with a mayonnaise, vegetable topping.

Prep time: 10 minutes
Cook time: 20 minutes

Makes: 4 stuffed burgers

- 1¼ pound ground white meat turkey
- 1 teaspoon sea salt
- ½ teaspoon each garlic and onion powder
- ⅛ teaspoon freshly ground black pepper
- 2 tablespoons extra virgin olive oil, divided
- 1 medium onion, chopped
- 4 ounces cremini mushrooms, finely chopped
- 3 ounces baby spinach, chopped
- ½ teaspoon sea salt
- 2 tablespoons Homemade Mayonnaise (page 270) (optional)

1. Combine the turkey, salt, garlic powder, onion powder and pepper in a small bowl. Divide the meat into 8 equal portions and reserve.
2. Heat 1½ tablespoons of the oil in a medium-sized frying pan over medium heat for 1-2 minutes, or until hot.
3. Sauté the onions over medium heat for 3 minutes. Add the mushrooms and sauté for 3 more minutes. Then add the spinach and salt and sauté for 3 more minutes or until the vegetables are limp and starting to brown.
4. Remove the vegetable to a bowl and reserve. Allow the pan to cool and wipe the pan with a wet paper towel. Reserve for further use.
5. Flatten half of the meat into 4 patties. Place 1 tablespoon of the cooled vegetable mixture in the center of each pattie. Reserve the remaining filling.
6. Form the remaining meat into four more patties and place one on each of the filled patties. Seal the edges of each stuffed burger.
7. Heat the remaining ½ tablespoon of the oil in the frying pan and heat for 1 minute or until hot. Cook the burgers for 4 minutes per side.
8. While the burgers are cooking, if desired, stir the mayonnaise into the reserved, remaining cooked vegetables.
9. Top each burger with 1 tablespoon of the vegetable mixture before serving.

Cook's Note: Once you reach Phase 3 top the burger with melted cheese and place it in a Traditional Soft Corn Tortilla (page 206) and spread with Easy Spicy Ketchup (page 287). You can also use any other ground meat once you reach the appropriate Phase of the diet.

Desserts/Drinks  PHASE 2

Pecan Cherry Cookies

Looking for a delicious cookie that is good for you too? These vegan cookies are just that. There are only a few ingredients, but each one provides you with an abundance of nutrients.

Prep time: 5 minutes
Cook time: 8-10 minutes

Makes: 9 cookies

1 cup raw pecans
¼ cup unsweetened shredded coconut
2 tablespoons coconut nectar*
1 tablespoon extra virgin coconut oil
⅓ cup unsweetened dried cherries
1 teaspoon vanilla
a pinch of sea salt

1. Preheat the over to 350°F
2. Place all of the ingredients into a bowl of a food processor. Process about 20 seconds or until the mixture resembles a fine granola.
3. Divide the dough into 9 portions. Form each into a ball.
4. Place the cookies on baking sheet and lightly press down to flatten.
5. Bake for 8-10 minutes or until the edges just begin to brown. Do not over bake.

* If you prefer, you may substitute raw honey, in which case the recipe will no longer be vegan.

Desserts/Drinks

PHASE 2

Pavlova

This recipe was named after the famous Russian ballerina, Anna Pavlova. In this version, a base of meringue shell is topped with Zabaglione Sauce (page 272) and fresh berries.

Prep time: 15 minutes
Cook time: 2 hours
Set up time: 12 hours

Makes: 4 meringue shells

2 egg whites
¼ cup xylitol
½ teaspoon raw apple cider vinegar
1 teaspoon vanilla
¾ cup Zabaglione Sauce (page 272)
Assorted mixed berries

1. Preheat the oven to 225°F.
2. Using an electric mixer, beat the egg whites on medium speed for about 30 seconds, or until blended.
3. Place the xylitol in a food processor and process until it is reduced to a fine powder.
4. Raise the speed of the mixer to High and add the vinegar.
5. Add the xylitol to the egg whites 1 tablespoon at a time while still mixing on High for about 1½ minutes, until stiff glossy peaks form.
6. Add the vanilla and mix for about 20 seconds.
7. Line a baking sheet with parchment paper.
8. Measure out 4 portions of meringue using a ½-cup measuring cup, and drop each onto the parchment-lined baking sheet, leaving a few inches of space between each shell.
9. Using a spoon or spatula, make a well in the center of each shell, so that it looks like a nest.
10. Bake in the preheated oven for 2 hours. Remove the meringues from the oven, but take care not to touch them, as they will be sticky.
11. Allow the shells to stand uncovered and set up for 12 hours, or until fully hardened, before removing them from the tray.
12. Fill the shells with the Zabaglione Sauce, top with the berries and serve.

Cook's Note: Unused shells will keep for weeks in a cookie tin, if stored in a cool, dry place.

Desserts/Drinks

PHASE 2

Honey Nut Bars

These delicious bars are perfect for a snack or for dessert. You may substitute any allowable nuts for those given in the recipe. Remember that sweets should be kept to a minimum, so make these a special treat.

Prep time: 15 minutes
Standing time: Several hours
Cook time: 15 minutes

Makes: 9 bars

¼ cup melted Ghee (page 258)
⅓ cup honey
½ teaspoon cinnamon
½ cup Almond Flour (page 260)
2 tablespoons brown rice flour
½ cup cashews
½ cup pecan halves
½ cup almonds
½ cup walnuts

1. Preheat the oven to 350ºF.
2. Combine the ghee, honey and cinnamon in a small bowl.
3. Combine the remaining ingredients, and stir in the honey mixture.
4. Grease an 8-inch square baking pan, and line the pan with parchment paper, trimming the edges.
5. Spoon the mixture into the prepared pan. Press the mixture down until the bottom of the pan is evenly covered.
6. Bake in the preheated oven for 15 minutes, or until the edges just start to brown.
7. Remove the pan from the oven and allow to cool for about 30 minutes.
8. Place the pan in the refrigerator for several hours to harden.
9. Once the mixture has hardened, cut it into bars. To store, wrap each bar in plastic wrap and keep refrigerated for up to 3 weeks.

Cook's Note: The bars are very sticky and will be difficult to remove from the pan if parchment paper is not used, or if the bars have not sufficiently hardened. Do not use waxed paper, because the bars will stick to it.

Desserts/Drinks PALEO PHASE 2

Fruit and Nut Bars

These fruit-sweetened bars are filled with nutritious ingredients and while we classify them as a dessert, they can also be enjoyed as a snack or breakfast. Break up into small pieces and add dairy-free milk to enjoy as a bowl of grain-free cereal.

Soaking time: 12 hours
Prep time: 25 minutes
Dehydration time: 20-24 hours

Makes: 28 bars

3 cups pecans
2 cups walnuts
1 cup hazelnuts
⅓ cup sesame seeds
½ cup pumpkin seeds
½ cup sunflower seeds
1 tablespoon sea salt
10 ounces pitted Medjool dates
Filtered water for soaking
1 apple, cored
1 cup fresh (or dried), shredded coconut
1 cup fruit-juice sweetened, dried cranberries
¼ cup flaxseed meal
3 tablespoons cinnamon
1½ teaspoons vanilla
½ teaspoon sea salt

1. Fill a large bowl with the nuts and seeds and stir in the salt. Place the dates in a separate bowl. Cover both bowls with filtered water. The water should be at least two inches above the nuts and seeds and dates. Soak overnight, or for 12 hours.

2. Drain nuts and seeds and add to the bowl of a food processor. Pulse until mixture is the consistency of granola. Remove and place in a large bowl.

3. Drain the dates and place them in the bowl of the food processor. Process for 1-2 minutes or until they become a thick, syrup-like consistency. Stir into the chopped nuts and seed mixture.

4. Shred the apple and fresh coconut* using the shredding attachment for your food processor.

5. Stir the shredded apple and coconut into the nut, seed and date mixture.

6. Add the dried cranberries, flaxseed, cinnamon and vanilla. Mix well.

7. Put ½ of the mixture on parchment paper and roll out into a ½ inch square. Cut into 28 (4x2½) bars and place parchment paper with bars onto a dehydrator tray. Repeat with the remainder of the mixture.

8. Dehydrate at 125°F for 20-24 hours or until crunchy. Allow to stand for 1 hour before storing and then store in a glass container.

*If using dried coconut in place of the fresh coconut, add in step 4 instead.

Cook's Note: Dehydrating time varies based on a number of factors, including humidity, altitude and your dehydrator. This recipe can be cut in half. You can substitute different nuts and seeds, if you prefer a different variety. Once you reach Phase 4, you may use raisins in place of the dried cranberries.

Desserts/Drinks   PALEO   PHASE 2

Pumpkin Custard

This recipe brings Thanksgiving to mind because it tastes like pumpkin pie without the crust.

Prep time: 15 minutes

Cook time: 1 hour and 20 minutes

Cool time: 30 minutes

Makes: 6 servings

- 2 eggs
- 1 cup Almond Milk (page 260)
- 3 tablespoons raw honey
- 2 tablespoons maple syrup
- 1 cup canned or cooked pumpkin
- 1 teaspoon vanilla
- ¼ teaspoon sea salt
- 1 teaspoon cinnamon
- ½ teaspoon freshly grated ginger or ¼ teaspoon dried ginger
- ¼ teaspoon allspice
- ⅛ teaspoon nutmeg
- ⅓ cup Cran-Raspberry Sauce (page 275)

1. Preheat the oven to 350°F.
2. Combine all the ingredients in a large bowl. Mix well using a wire whisk or hand mixer.
3. Pour ½ cup of the mixture into each of 6 custard cups.
4. Place the cups in a 13x9-inch baking dish. Fill the baking dish with enough hot water to reach about ⅓ of the way up the sides of the cups, being careful not to get any water into the cups.
5. Bake in the preheated oven for 1 hour and 10-20 minutes, or until the custards are set, their tops are shiny, and a knife inserted about 2 inches from a cup's center comes out clean.
6. Carefully remove the custards from the water bath and allow them to cool for 30 minutes, or refrigerate and serve chilled.
7. Spoon 1 tablespoon of Cran-Raspberry Sauce on top of the custard before serving, if desired.

Bonus Recipe: Pumpkin Pie – Once you reach Phase 3, use the pie crust found in the Spinach and Sun-Dried Tomato Quiche recipe (page 209) to make the pie. Bake the crust in a 9½x1½ tart pan or pie plate as directed for 10 minutes and allow it to cool completely. Fill the crust with a fully cooled recipe of Pumpkin Custard (above). Refrigerate the pie for several hours before serving. Serve topped with a spoonful of Cran-Raspberry Sauce (page 275).

Nutrition Note: As a rule of thumb, the deeper the color of a fruit or vegetable, the higher the nutritional content. Pumpkin, being a bright orange, is a rich source of vitamins and minerals, particularly beta-carotene, vitamin C and potassium.

Desserts/**Drinks**

PHASE 2

Iced Minted Raspberry Green Tea

Cool and refreshing on a summer day or anytime, this tea is a perfect substitute for soft drinks and other calorie-laden drinks. Your whole family will love this recipe!

Prep time: 5 minutes
Cook time: 10 minutes
Cool time: 2 hours

Makes: about 6 cups

- **4 cups filtered water**
- **¼-½ cup xylitol or raw honey***
- **1 cup fresh or frozen raspberries**
- **4 green tea bags**
- **2 cups ice cubes**
- **2 sprigs fresh mint**
- **6 sprigs fresh mint (garnish)**

* Xylitol is not suitable for Paleo.

1. Combine the water, xylitol or honey and raspberries in a 2-quart saucepot and stir well to distribute the xylitol. Bring the mixture to a boil, and boil for about 5 minutes to make a simple syrup. Reduce the heat to medium and simmer for 5 minutes.
2. Position a sieve in a bowl. Pour the mixture through the sieve and mash the raspberries with a spoon to squeeze out the juice while leaving the seeds in the sieve.
3. Immerse the tea bags in the liquid and allow the tea to steep for 4 minutes.
4. Allow the tea to cool, and then pour it into a pitcher, add the mint and refrigerate until ready to serve.
5. Add the ice to the pitcher just before serving. Serve in tall, ice-filled glasses, and garnish with the mint sprigs.

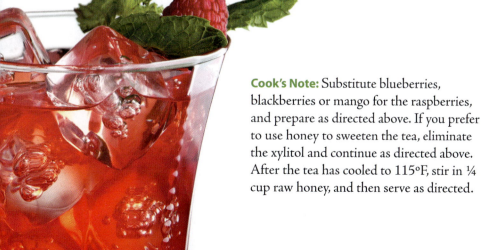

Cook's Note: Substitute blueberries, blackberries or mango for the raspberries, and prepare as directed above. If you prefer to use honey to sweeten the tea, eliminate the xylitol and continue as directed above. After the tea has cooled to 115°F, stir in ¼ cup raw honey, and then serve as directed.

Phase 3 Contents

Whole Grain Waffles with Assorted Berries		169
Pineapple Cherry Delight		170
Peanut Butter Banana Smoothie		170
Date Nut Bread		171
Toasted Coconut Almond Muffins		173
Applesauce Walnut Tea Bread		175
Breakfast Burritos		176
Soft Flour Tortillas		177
Tortilla Chips		177
Broccoli, Red Cabbage and Quinoa		179
Chicken with Wild Rice and Vegetable Soup		181
Red Pepper Hummus		182
White Bean and Sun-Dried Tomato Spread		183
Butternut Squash and Apple Soup		185
Corn Fritters		186
Roasted Vegetables		187
Summer Vegetable Medley Salad		189
Slow Cooked Baked Beans		191
Zucchini Corn Bake		193
Kale Chips		195
Fruit Salsa		196
Tomato Salsa		197
Guacamole		199
Cream of Tomato Bisque		200
Veggie Burgers		201
Stir-Fried Chicken with Red Peppers and Cashews		203
Sloppy Joes		205
Burritos		205
Traditional Soft Corn Tortillas		206
Slow Cooked Pulled Chicken		207
Spinach and Sun-Dried Tomato Quiche		209
Chicken Tamaki		210
Shepherd's Pie		211
Seared Peppered London Broil		213
Mediterranean Chicken		215
Multicolored Stuffed Peppers		217
Greek Ground Lamb Crumble		218
Chicken Fajitas		219
Meatballs and Spaghetti Squash		221
Honey Battered Chicken		222
Slow Cooked Vegetarian Tempeh Chili		223
Red and Green Pepper Frittata		225
Homemade Pasta		226

			Mixed Berries with Crème Patisserie (Vanilla Pastry Cream) 227
			Mixed Berry Tart 227
			Lime Ice 228
		PALEO	Strawberry Ice Cream 229
		PALEO	Watermelon Lime Cooler 231
			Raspberry Lemonade Slushie 231
			Maple Walnut Shortbread Cookies 232
			Oatmeal Craisin Cookies 233

Phase 3: The Late Reentry Phase *(four weeks)*

Phase 3 is to be followed for four weeks after the conclusion of Phase 2. Do not begin Phase 3 until you are certain the foods you reintroduced in Phase 2 have not triggered new bouts of inflammatory symptoms. If symptoms do recur, wait until they subside before moving on to the next Phase.

During Phase 3, your goal is to reintroduce additional foods that are normally healthy, but can trigger inflammation in some people. All these foods have a greater risk of doing so than the foods listed in Phase 2, so proceed cautiously, once again reintroducing Phase 3 foods no sooner than one every other day. Should health problems occur as a result of eating these additional foods, return to Phase 2 until you feel better. (The food and beverages that pose the highest risk of triggering inflammation during Phase 3 are indicated with an asterisk.)

At this point, you may include soybeans in your diet, but avoid soy milk, textured soy protein meat substitutes and soy powders. Instead, choose fermented soy foods, such as miso, natto and tempeh. Tofu is permissible as well, but fermented soy foods are better choices.

As a food group, grains carry a higher than normal risk of causing inflammation. Therefore, proceed with caution as you reintroduce grains to your diet. Whole grain gluten-free pastas made from Phase 3 allowable grains are also acceptable, provided no adverse reactions occur.

Proceed with caution when reintroducing nightshade foods [chilies, eggplant, peppers (both red and green), white potatoes and tomatoes, as well as the spices cayenne, chili powder and paprika], which can cause inflammation. You might need to avoid these foods altogether if you know you are sensitive to them, or if you suffer from arthritis symptoms that are aggravated by them.

Dairy is another food group with a higher than normal risk of causing inflammation. Proceed with caution as you reintroduce dairy products, and avoid them altogether if you are allergic or sensitive to them.

Be sure to follow the General Food Guidelines and Food Choices for Detoxification on pages 28-30 during all Phases of the diet.

Foods Allowed During Phase 3

Beverages
 Apple juice [4]
 Citrus juice*
 Coffee (organic)*
 Orange juice [4]

Fruits
 Apple (all varieties)
 Banana [4]
 Grapefruit*
 Lemon*
 Lime*
 Nectarine
 Orange*
 Peach
 Strawberry*

Nuts/Seeds
 Peanuts*[1]
 Pistachios*[1] NEW

Vegetables
 Dill pickles NEW
 Jicama NEW

Nightshade Foods
 Cayenne*
 Chili powder*
 Chilies*
 Eggplant*
 Green pepper*
 Hot pepper*
 Mild pepper*
 Paprika*

 Potato (white)*
 Red pepper*
 Tomato*

Grains
 Buckwheat
 Corn*
 Millet
 Oat groats
 Quinoa
 Sorghum NEW
 Teff NEW

Traditional Soy Bean Products
 Miso
 Natto NEW
 Tamari
 Tempeh
 Tofu

Protein Sources
(organic, if possible)
 Beef
 Bison (free-range)
 Chicken (dark meat)
 Turkey (dark meat)

Dairy
 Butter (organic)
 Cheeses*[2]
 Milk*[2]
 Cream*[2]
 Yogurt *[2,3]

Fats
 Almond oil NEW
 Avocado oil NEW
 Grapeseed oil NEW
 Palm oil NEW
 Safflower oil NEW
 Sunflower seed oil NEW

Other
 Air-popped popcorn NEW
 Arrowroot NEW
 Baking powder NEW
 Guar gum NEW
 Nutritional yeast [5] NEW
 Mustard
 Other vinegars NEW
 Xanthan gum NEW

 NEW : Foods added or shifted to earlier Phases of the diet, since the original version of the diet.

 * These foods and beverages pose the highest risk of triggering inflammation.
 [1] Have a high risk of mold, so buy raw and organic, and store in the refrigerator.
 [2] Raw cow or goat milk sources are highly preferable.
 [3] Plain, unsweetened and organic (if possible).
 [4] Use sparingly, as they are very high in sugar.
 [5] Nutritional yeast is best avoided if a person has an active yeast problem like candida.

Gluten-Free Baking Tips

There is no one gluten-free flour that can be used as a one-for-one substitution for all-purpose white or whole wheat flour. Instead, you need to use a mixture of gluten-free flours and starches in order to bake successfully.

You also need to use xanthan gum or guar gum, which are the key to successful gluten-free baking because they provide the binder that is needed to hold the baked good together. They also help give elasticity to the final baked goods. A little goes a long way, and if you use too much, your baked goods will have a gummy consistency.

To help make gluten-free baking easier for you we have developed a Gluten-Free Baking Mix (page 265) that is used in many of our recipes. We included xanthan gum in our mix, but no leavening agents were added. Instead, you will add them according to the directions given in the specific recipe you are making.

While many of the baked goods in this book call for our baking mix, others do not. We found that breads that use yeast are better when they are made using different flours and starches or the same flours and starches but in different proportions.

If you are new to gluten-free baking and plan to make some of the gluten-free baked goods in this Phase, read on for some important baking tips and information about gluten-free ingredients.

- Gluten-free baked goods don't age as well as those made with gluten-containing grains. This is just the nature of the ingredients and is why we have chosen to make smaller batches for the muffins. None of our recipes contain preservatives, so be sure to store your baked goods in the refrigerator or freezer to extend the shelf life.
- It is a good idea to reheat baked goods for a minute or two in the oven or in the microwave for a few seconds, prior to eating them. This will help bring back some of its original texture and flavor.
- If you really enjoy a recipe, double the dry ingredients and put them in a container until you are ready to make a fresh batch. Store in a covered container in the refrigerator and label with the name of the recipe, including the page number. When you are ready to make the recipe, all you will need to do is mix the wet ingredients and bake. It's like having your own packaged muffin, bread or cookie mix.

Breakfast PHASE 3

Whole Grain Waffles with Assorted Berries

These whole grain waffles are higher in nutritional value than waffles made from white flour, and they are every bit as delicious. Try topping them with berries and maple syrup, or, for an extra berry boost, with homemade Blueberry or Raspberry Syrup (page 277).

Prep time: 15 minutes
Cook time: 20 minutes

Makes: 3
7-inch round waffles

- 1½ cups Gluten-Free Baking Mix (page 265)
- 2 teaspoons baking powder
- ¼ teaspoon sea salt
- ½ teaspoon cinnamon
- 1 tablespoon xylitol or coconut palm sugar
- 1 egg, lightly beaten
- ⅓ cup Ghee (page 258)
- 1½ to 1¾ cups Almond Milk (page 260)
- 1 teaspoon vanilla
- Assorted berries, such as blueberries, blackberries and raspberries

1. Preheat the waffle maker.
2. Combine the dry ingredients in a medium-sized mixing bowl.
3. Combine the wet ingredients and whisk them into the dry ingredients. Initially, add 1½ cups almond milk; then, if the mixture is still too thick, add another ¼ cup.
4. Follow the instructions that came with your waffle maker to bake the waffles.
5. Top the finished waffles with an assortment of your favorite berries and maple or homemade berry syrup.

Cook's Note: Mornings are busy, so why not make the batter the night before and refrigerate it? That way, everyone can make their own waffles whenever they're ready for them. You can also make the waffles ahead of time, refrigerate or freeze them, and then reheat them in a toaster or toaster oven.

Nutrition Note: Blueberries rank number one in fruits that contain antioxidants, and they are also very high in vitamin C.

Recipes for Repair

Breakfast   PALEO   PHASE 3

Pineapple Cherry Delight

Prep time: 5 minutes

Makes: 2 cups

¾ cup frozen or fresh frozen cherries
¼ cup frozen pineapple
1 cup non-dairy milk of your choice*
1 teaspoon vanilla
1 teaspon honey or coconut palm sugar
¼ cup ice cubes

1. Place all the ingredients in a blender container in the order listed. Cover, and blend on High, or on a frozen drink setting, until smooth.
2. Pour into a tall glass and serve immediately.

* Choose your favorite homemade milk: Almond Milk (page 260), Coconut Milk (page 261) or our Brown Rick Milk (page 261).

Cook's Note: Use these recipes as a template, and substitute fruits or berries that are in season or that you especially like.

Peanut Butter Banana Smoothie

Who doesn't love the combination of peanut butter and banana? In this filling morning smoothie you will enjoy those wonderful flavors.

Prep time: 5 minutes

Makes: 2 cups

1½ cups non-dairy milk of your choice*
1 banana, cut in pieces
1 tablespoon flaxseed meal
2 pitted Medjool dates, soaked (optional)
2 tablespoons peanut butter**
¼ avocado
¼ cup ice cubes

** Use almond butter for Paleo.

1. Cut up a banana and place it into a container and freeze overnight.
2. If using, soak the dates in water overnight so they are very soft for blending in the morning.
3. Drain the dates and remove the banana from the freezer.
4. Place all the ingredients in a blender container in the order listed. Cover, and blend on High, or on a frozen drink setting, until smooth. If too thick, add more of the milk or some water to thin out.

Pour into a tall glass and serve immediately.

* Choose your favorite homemade milk: Almond Milk (page 260), Coconut Milk (page 261) or our Brown Rick Milk (page 261).

Cook's Note: Once you reach Phase 4, add 1 tablespoon of unsweetened cacao powder for a chocolatey treat.

Breakfast

PHASE 3

Date Nut Bread

Serve this bread to your family and friends. We assure you that no one will ever guess that it's gluten-, dairy- and egg-free.

Prep time: 15 minutes
Cook time: 45 minutes

Makes: 1 loaf

- 1 tablespoon chia seeds
- 1¼ cups Almond Milk or Coconut Milk (page 260)
- ⅓ cup safflower oil
- 1½ teaspoon vanilla
- 1½ cups Gluten-Free Baking Mix (page 265)
- 3 tablespoons coconut palm sugar
- ½ teaspoon ground cinnamon
- 2 teaspoons baking powder
- ⅛ teaspoon sea salt
- 1 cup coarsely chopped pecans or walnuts
- 1 cup pitted Medjool dates, chopped (about 9)

1. Preheat the oven to 350°F.
2. Combine the chia seeds with the liquid ingredients and allow the mixture to stand while you are assembling the dry ingredients.
3. Combine the baking mix, sugar, cinnamon and salt in a medium-sized mixing bowl.
4. Using a rubber spatula, stir the wet ingredients into the dry ingredients. Stir in the nuts and dates.
5. Grease an 8-inch loaf pan and spoon the batter into the pan.
6. Bake in the preheated oven for 45 minutes, or until the top is lightly browned and a toothpick inserted in the center comes out clean.

Cook's Note: The batter for this recipe can be made into 12 muffins rather than a bread. To make muffins, preheat the oven to 350ºF and bake for 20-25 minutes, or until a toothpick inserted in the center comes out clean.

Breakfast

Toasted Coconut Almond Muffins

The combination of toasted coconut and almonds gives these gluten-free muffins a nutty flavor and delightful chewy texture.

Prep time: 20 minutes
Cook time: 20-25 minutes

Makes: 6 muffins

- ½ cup unsweetened shredded coconut
- 1¼ cup Gluten-Free Baking Mix (page 265)
- 2 teaspoons baking powder
- ¼ teaspoon sea salt
- 2 tablespoons Almond Flour (page 260)
- 2 tablespoons honey
- ¼ cup maple syrup
- 1 egg, lightly beaten*
- ⅓ cup safflower oil or Ghee (page 258)
- ½ cup Almond Milk (page 260)
- ½ teaspoon vanilla extract
- ½ teaspoon almond extract

1. Preheat the oven to 350°F.
2. Grease a 6-cup muffin pan and set aside.
3. Place the coconut on a small baking dish and toast in the preheated oven for 5 minutes, or until golden brown. Watch carefully, because coconut can burn very quickly. Allow to cool slightly.
4. Combine the baking mix, baking powder, salt and almond flour, and the cooled, toasted coconut in a medium-sized bowl.
5. Combine the wet ingredients, add them to the dry ingredients and stir.
6. Fill each muffin cup with a scant ½ cup of batter.
7. Bake in the preheated oven for 20-25 minutes, or until a toothpick inserted in the center of a muffin comes out clean.

* To make this recipe egg free, add one additional tablespoon of flaxseed meal to the dry ingredients and increase the almond milk to ⅔ cup.

Breakfast

PHASE 3

Applesauce Walnut Tea Bread

Apples and cinnamon always pair well. Cinnamon Applesauce and chopped apples give this bread intense apple flavor.

Prep time: 20 minutes
Cook time: 50-55 minutes

Makes: 1 loaf

2 cups Gluten-Free Baking Mix (page 265)
2 teaspoons baking powder
¼ teaspoon sea salt
½ cup xylitol or coconut palm sugar
2 eggs, lightly beaten*
½ cup Cinnamon Applesauce (page 96)
¾ cup Almond Milk (page 260)
1 teaspoon cinnamon
¼ teaspoon ginger
1 teaspoon vanilla
½ cup safflower oil
½ cup chopped walnuts
1 green apple, peeled and chopped

1. Preheat the oven to 350°F.
2. Combine the baking mix, baking powder, salt and xylitol or coconut palm sugar in a mixing bowl and set aside.
3. Combine the remaining ingredients, except for the walnuts and the apple.
4. Using a rubber spatula, stir the wet ingredients into the dry ingredients until just combined.
5. Stir in the walnuts and chopped apple.
6. Grease an 8-inch loaf pan. Spoon the batter into the loaf pan.
7. Bake in the preheated oven for 50-55 minutes, or until the top is nicely browned and a toothpick inserted in the center comes out clean.

* To make this recipe egg free, add one additional tablespoon of flaxseed meal to the dry ingredients and increase the almond milk to 1 cup.

Cook's Note: The batter for this recipe can be made into 12 muffins, rather than a loaf. To make muffins, preheat the oven to 350°F and fill each muffin cup with a scant ½ cup of batter. Bake for 20-25 minutes, or until a toothpick inserted in the center of a muffin comes out clean.

Breakfast

Breakfast Burritos

Make the wraps and measure out the ingredients the night before, and the next morning, you'll be eating your breakfast burritos in 20 minutes!

Prep time: 15 minutes
Cook time: 10 minutes

Makes: 4 servings

1 recipe Soft Flour Tortillas (page 177)
1 cup Tomato Salsa (page 197)
½ cup sour cream
½ cup canned black beans, drained
1 cup shredded Cheddar cheese, divided
1 tablespoon butter
8 eggs

1. Preheat the oven to 350ºF.
2. Place the wraps in foil and warm them in the preheated oven while you assemble the ingredients.
3. Remove the wraps from the oven and top each with a quarter of the salsa, sour cream and black beans, and with 2 tablespoons of the cheese.
4. Heat the butter in a medium-sized frying pan.
5. Add the eggs to the pan and cook for 30 seconds, until they are set.
6. Scatter the remaining cheese over the eggs and scramble with a fork. Cook until set.
7. Spoon equal amounts of the cooked eggs over each of the wraps.
8. Roll the wraps, place them on a baking tray and return them to the oven.
9. Heat for 5 minutes, or until warm, and serve.

Cook's Note: If you prefer corn tortillas to the flour type, you can substitute the Traditional Soft Corn Tortillas (page 206) in this recipe. They are smaller so fill them less and make one or two more.

Soups/Salads/Sides/Snacks

PHASE 3

Soft Flour Tortillas

Have you been missing flour tortillas? Well, now you can make a gluten-free version that is easy to make and tastes great.

Prep time: 10 minutes
Cook time: 8-12 minutes

Makes: 4 (9-inch) tortillas

1¼ cup Gluten-Free Baking Mix (page 265)
¼ cup tapioca flour
1 teaspoon xanthan gum
½ teaspoon each sea salt and baking powder
2 teaspoons coconut palm sugar
¼ cup coconut palm shortening
½ teaspoon apple cider vinegar
⅓ to ½ cup cold filtered water
Additional tapioca flour for rolling
1 teaspoon extra virgin olive oil

1. Add the dry ingredients and the shortening to the bowl of a food processor. Pulse on and off 5 or 6 times or just until the shortening is incorporated.

2. Add the vinegar to the water and slowly pour it down the feed tube with the motor running constantly. The dough will form a ball. You might not need all the water. Stop processing when the dough ball has formed.

3. Generously dust a cutting board, preferably plastic, with some of the additional tapioca starch. Cut the dough into quarters. Place one of the dough balls on the starch and press down with your hand. Sprinkle a generous amount of starch on top of the dough and roll it out into 8-9 inch circles.

4. Heat a large frying pan, griddle (preferably cast iron), or another type of heavy-bottomed pan, over medium-high heat, for 2-3 minutes or until hot. It should not be too hot or the tortilla will burn or become too brittle to roll.

5. Before making the first tortilla wipe the frying pan or griddle with a folded paper towel dipped in the oil. Lower the heat to medium.

6. Using a large metal spatula loosen the tortilla on the board and slide it into the heated frying pan. Cook the tortilla for 1 to 1½ minutes per side or until just starting to color. Repeat steps 3-6 with the remaining 3 dough balls.*

7. Stack the cooked tortillas on a tray.

*A tortilla press can be used to make the tortillas. Follow the instructions provided by the manufacturer.

Bonus Recipe: Tortilla Chips – Preheat the oven to 350°F. Brush both sides of the tortillas with oil and sprinkle with salt, if desired. Stack the tortillas and cut them into eighths. Spread the chips on a large baking sheet in one layer and bake for 12-14 minutes, or until crisp. Turn the chips once during baking.

recipes for Repair

Soups/Salads/Sides/Snacks

PHASE 3

Broccoli, Red Cabbage and Quinoa

This extremely nutritious side dish is as beautiful as it is tasty.

Soak time: 8 hours or overnight
Prep time: 10 minutes
Cook time: 20 minutes

Makes: 4 servings

- 1 cup quinoa
- 1½ cups Vegetable Broth (page 259)
- 4 ounces broccoli florets
- 4 ounces red cabbage, cut into 1-inch pieces
- ¼ cup Ghee (page 258)
- 1 teaspoon raw apple cider vinegar
- ½ teaspoon dry mustard
- ½ teaspoon each garlic powder and onion powder
- ½ teaspoon sea salt
- ¼ teaspoon freshly ground black pepper

1. Place the quinoa in a large bowl of room temperature water and soak for 8 hours or overnight.
2. Bring the vegetable broth to a boil in a small saucepot over medium heat.
3. While the broth is coming to a boil, rinse the quinoa in a small mesh strainer for 3 minutes.
4. Add the quinoa to the broth and cook for about 10-15 minutes, or until the quinoa resembles small beads and the broth has evaporated.
5. While the quinoa cooks, steam the broccoli and red cabbage together for about 6 minutes, or until tender.
6. While the broccoli and cabbage steam, combine the ghee, vinegar, mustard, garlic and onion powders and salt and pepper in a small frying pan and heat for 1 minute.
7. Combine the vegetables and the quinoa in a serving bowl.
8. Pour the ghee mixture over the vegetables and quinoa and toss well to coat.

Nutrition Note: The World Health Organization has rated the quality of protein in quinoa as at least equivalent to that in milk. Quinoa offers more iron than other grains and contains high levels of potassium and riboflavin, as well as vitamin B6, niacin and thiamin. It is also a good source of magnesium, zinc, copper and manganese, and has some folic acid.

Soups/Salads/Sides/Snacks

PHASE 3

Chicken with Wild Rice and Vegetable Soup

Chicken soup is the ultimate comfort food. In this version, brown and wild rice add texture. Served with one of the many salads found in this book, this soup is ideal for lunch or a light supper.

Prep time: 20 minutes
Cook time: about 1 hour 20 minutes

Makes: about 3½ quarts

- 2 tablespoons extra virgin olive oil
- 1 onion, cut into 1-inch pieces
- 3 cloves garlic, chopped
- 3 carrots, peeled and diced
- 1 medium zucchini, diced
- 3 stalks celery, sliced
- 1 can (28 ounces) diced tomatoes, with liquid
- 2 quarts Chicken Bone Broth (page 264)
- 1 cup uncooked brown and wild rice mix
- ½ teaspoon sea salt
- ¼ teaspoon freshly ground black pepper
- 1½ cups cooked chicken, cut into ½-inch pieces

1. Heat the oil in a 4-quart saucepot over medium heat for 1-2 minutes, or until hot.
2. Sauté the onion over medium heat for about 3 minutes, or until limp.
3. Add the garlic, carrots and zucchini and sauté for 5 minutes.
4. Add the remaining ingredients, except for the chicken, and stir well to combine.
5. Bring the soup to a boil over medium-high heat. Lower the heat to medium and simmer for 45 minutes.
6. Add the chicken and cook for 30 minutes.
7. Refrigerate or freeze any leftover soup.

Cook's Note: You can make beef and vegetable soup by substituting beef broth and cooked beef for the chicken, or you can make minestrone by substituting cooked beans for the rice and eliminating the chicken.

Soups/Salads/Sides/Snacks

PHASE 3

Red Pepper Hummus

Take some of this delicious hummus to work for a great afternoon protein pick-me-up when your energy is waning.

Prep time: 15 minutes
Stand time: 2 hours

Makes: 2 cups

- 1 can (15.5 ounces) chickpeas, rinsed and drained
- 2 large red peppers, roasted (one hand chopped and reserved)
- 3 tablespoons tahini
- 3 tablespoons apple cider vinegar
- 1½ teaspoons each garlic powder and onion powder
- 1 teaspoon sea salt
- 3 tablespoons extra virgin olive oil
- 1-2 tablespoon filtered water (if needed)
- ½ tablespoon freshly chopped parsley, basil and chives
- 1 teaspoon freshly chopped lemon thyme

1. Combine all of the ingredients, except for the roasted red pepper that you hand chopped, in the bowl of a food processor. Pulse several times to chop, and then turn on and process continually until the hummus is a smooth consistency.
2. If the hummus is too thick, add 1 tablespoon of water at a time until you reach the desired consistency.
3. Stir in the reserved chopped red pepper.
4. Spoon the hummus into a serving bowl and refrigerate for at least 2 hours before serving to allow the flavors to meld.

Cook's Note: Use this hummus as a template to make a variety of different types of hummus, such as pesto or horseradish. Let your imagination be your guide.

Soups/Salads/Sides/Snacks   PHASE 3

White Bean and Sun-Dried Tomato Spread

Keep some of this versatile spread in your fridge. Spread it on a sandwich to add some zest, or serve it with crackers and vegetables as a snack.

Prep time: 15 minutes
Stand time: 2 hours

Makes: 1¼ cups

- 1 can (15.5 ounces) cannellini beans, rinsed and drained
- 2 tablespoons chopped sun-dried tomatoes, packed in olive oil
- 1 small clove garlic
- 4 sprigs parsley
- 1 sprig lemon thyme, stripped
- 2 basil leaves
- 3 tablespoons extra virgin olive oil
- 1 tablespoon lemon juice
- 1 tablespoon tomato paste
- ½ teaspoon onion powder
- ½ teaspoon sea salt
- ¼ teaspoon freshly ground black pepper

1. Place all the ingredients in the bowl of a food processor and run for about 1 minute or until smooth.
2. Spoon the spread into a serving bowl and refrigerate at least 2 hours to allow the flavors to meld.
3. Serve with assorted raw vegetables or your favorite gluten-free cracker.

Cook's Note: Spread some on fish or chicken before broiling to add a Mediterranean flavor.

Soups/Salads/Sides/Snacks   PALEO   PHASE 3

Butternut Squash and Apple Soup

Butternut squash and apples are staples of the fall harvest. Here, they combine to make a warm, tasty soup with a spicy, nutty flavor.

Prep time: 30 minutes
Cook time: 50 minutes

Makes: 6 servings

- 1 large shallot, minced
- 1 clove garlic, chopped
- 1 butternut squash (about 2-2½ pounds), peeled, seeded and cut into 1-inch pieces
- 2 tart apples, peeled, seeded and cut into 1-inch pieces
- 1 teaspoon curry powder
- ½ teaspoon cumin
- ¼ teaspoon allspice
- ¼ teaspoon nutmeg
- ½ teaspoon freshly chopped rosemary (optional)
- 1 teaspoon sea salt
- ¼ teaspoon freshly ground black pepper
- 2 tablespoons extra virgin olive oil
- 2 tablespoons honey
- 3-3½ cups Chicken Bone Broth (page 264) or Vegetable Broth* (page 259)
- 1 tablespoon Coconut Milk (page 261) or plain yogurt* (optional)

1. Preheat the oven to 425°F.
2. Place the shallot, garlic, squash and apples on a baking sheet that has sides.
3. Combine all the spices and the salt and pepper and sprinkle them over the vegetables in the pan.
4. Pour the oil and honey over the vegetables, toss well to coat and bake in the preheated oven for 40 minutes, or until they start to caramelize.
5. Place the roasted vegetables in a food processor or blender with 1 cup of the broth. Purée until smooth.
6. Pour the puréed mixture into a saucepan and add the remaining stock. Stir well and cook for 10 minutes. Use more stock, if needed.
7. Serve hot, with the coconut milk or a dollop of yogurt if desired.

   No longer a dairy-free recipe if the optional plain yogurt is added.

   **Use Vegetable Broth in place of Chicken Bone Broth for a vegetarian version.*

Cook's Note: This soup can be made a day in advance and reheated. It also freezes very well, so if you have extra squash and apples to use up, why not make a double batch and freeze it for future use?

Soups/Salads/Sides/Snacks   PHASE 3

Corn Fritters

Corn fresh from the farm is a special treat. There's no need to cook it – just cut it from the cob and add it to your recipes. When corn is out of season, substitute defrosted frozen corn.

Prep time: 10 minutes
Cook time: 6 minutes

Makes: 8 fritters

- 1½ cups corn, fresh and uncooked, or defrosted frozen
- 1 egg*
- ½ cup Almond Milk (page 260)
- ¾ cup Gluten-Free Baking Mix (page 265)
- 1 teaspoon baking powder
- ½ teaspoon each onion and garlic powder
- ¼ teaspoon sea salt
- ⅛ teaspoon freshly ground black pepper
- 2-4 tablespoons extra virgin olive oil or Ghee,** divided (page 258)

Substitute 1/4 cup of applesauce for the egg.

**For dairy-free use the oil in place of the ghee.*

1. Combine all the ingredients, except for the oil, in a mixing bowl.
2. Heat 2 tablespoons of the oil or ghee in a frying pan for 1-2 minutes, or until hot.
3. Ladle about ¼ cup of batter per fritter into the hot oil. Cook the fritter for about 2-3 minutes per side, or until golden brown.
4. Add more oil as needed and continue until all the fritters are cooked.

Cook's Note: Cook only 3-4 fritters at a time, so as not to overcrowd the pan. Place the cooked fritters on a baking tray and keep them warm in a 250ºF oven while you make the remaining fritters.

Soups/Salads/Sides/Snacks   PALEO   PHASE 3

Roasted Vegetables

These colorful vegetables are a great side to serve with Seared Peppered London Broil (page 213).

Prep time: 15 minutes
Cook time: 40 minutes

Makes: 6 servings

- 1 medium-sized (1 pound) eggplant, unpeeled
- 1 large (12 ounce) zucchini
- 2 red, yellow or green peppers, seeded and cut in half lengthwise
- 1 red onion, peeled
- 2 carrots peeled, cut into 1-inch pieces
- 2 dozen whole cherry tomatoes
- 2 tablespoons tomato paste
- 1 tablespoon Mixed Herb Pesto (page 153) *
- ½ teaspoon sea salt
- ½ teaspoon freshly ground black pepper
- 1 teaspoon each garlic powder and onion powder
- ¼ cup extra virgin olive oil

1. Preheat the oven to 425ºF.
2. Cut all the vegetables, except for the tomatoes, into equal-sized pieces (about 1-inch pieces).
3. Place the vegetables, including the tomatoes, in a single layer on one large or two small baking sheets.
4. Combine the salt, pepper, garlic powder and onion powder and sprinkle the mixture evenly over the vegetables. Toss well to coat.
5. Drizzle the oil evenly over the vegetables and toss again.
6. Place the tray in the preheated oven and cook for 40 minutes, or until the vegetables begin to caramelize on the edges. Midway through cooking, carefully remove the tray from the oven and turn the vegetables with a large spoon.

If you don't have the pesto prepared, substitute 1 tablespoon chopped basil and 2 tablespoons chopped parsley and stir into the vegetables midway through cooking.

Cook's Note: Serve with the Seared Peppered London Broil (page 213) or over pasta for a beautiful, healthy, vegetarian meal.

Soups/Salads/Sides/Snacks PHASE 3

Summer Vegetable Medley Salad

Summer is when vegetables are at their freshest and most flavorful, so it's the ideal time of year to serve this steamed and raw salad tossed with a sweet citrus dressing.

Prep time: 20 minutes
Cook time: 5 minutes
Stand time: 1 hour

Makes: 6 servings

1 cup fresh corn kernels
4 ounces snow peas
1 cup julienned green beans
1 cup finely shredded red cabbage
1 cup julienned carrots

Citrus Dressing
⅓ cup extra virgin olive oil
1 lemon, zested and juiced
½ orange, zested and juiced
1 teaspoon each garlic powder and onion powder
2 teaspoons freshly chopped chives
1 teaspoon freshly chopped thyme
1 teaspoon mustard
½ teaspoon sea salt
⅛ teaspoon freshly ground black pepper
1 tablespoon raw honey

1. Steam the corn, snow peas and green beans together for 5 minutes, or until they are tender but still crisp.
2. Cool the steamed vegetables in a bowl filled with cold water and ice.
3. Drain the cooked vegetables and combine with the remaining raw vegetables in a serving bowl.
4. Combine the dressing ingredients and whisk thoroughly.
5. When you are ready to serve, pour the dressing over the vegetables. Toss well to coat.

Soups/Salads/Sides/Snacks

PHASE 3

Slow Cooked Baked Beans

Slow cooking gives these tangy baked beans a barbecued flavor.

Prep time: 4 hours and 20 minutes (including soaking the beans)

Cook time: 12 hours

Makes: about 5 cups

- ½ pound dried navy beans
- Filtered water
- 1 tablespoon extra virgin olive oil
- 1 medium onion, chopped
- 2 cloves garlic, finely chopped
- 1 cup Easy Spicy Ketchup (page 287)
- ½ cup maple syrup
- 1½ cups filtered water
- 1 tablespoon mustard
- 1 (2-inch) strip of kombu (optional)
- ½ teaspoon freshly ground black pepper

1. Rinse the dried beans and place them in a 3-quart saucepot. Cover them with several inches of water. Bring the water to a boil over medium-high heat and cook uncovered for 4 minutes.
2. Remove from the heat and allow the beans to soak in the covered pot for 4 hours.
3. Drain the beans and place them in the slow cooker.
4. Heat the oil in a small frying pan over medium heat for 1-2 minutes, or until hot.
5. Sauté the onion for 3 minutes, or until lightly browned.
6. Add the garlic and sauté for 30 seconds.
7. Add the onion and garlic and the remaining ingredients to the slow cooker, and stir well to combine.
8. Cover the cooker and set it to cook on Low for 12 hours, or until the beans are tender.

Nutrition Note: Kombu is a sea vegetable that is frequently used in Asian cuisine. It is high in vitamins A, B2 and C, calcium and iodine. A member of the kelp family, kombu is used when cooking beans because it helps to make them more digestible. It is usually sold in dried, nearly black strips that soften when immersed in water.

Recipes for Repair

Soups/Salads/Sides/Snacks   PHASE 3

Zucchini Corn Bake

You can also serve with a salad for a light supper.

Prep time: 20 minutes

Cook time: 50-60 minutes

Makes: 4-6 servings

2 cups diced, unpeeled zucchini

1½ cups (about 3 ears) fresh corn, cut from the cob

1 medium onion, finely chopped

1 teaspoon each freshly chopped parsley and basil

½ teaspoon freshly chopped thyme

4 eggs

2 tablespoons extra virgin olive oil

½ cup Almond Milk (page 260)

¾ cup Gluten-Free Baking Mix (page 265)

1 teaspoon garlic powder

½ teaspoon sea salt

¼ teaspoon freshly ground black pepper

½ cup grated Parmesan cheese

1 cup grated Cheddar cheese

1. Preheat the oven to 400°F.
2. Grease an 8-inch square baking dish.
3. Combine all the ingredients in a large bowl. Stir well to mix completely.
4. Pour the mixture into the prepared baking dish.
5. Bake in the preheated oven for 50-60 minutes, or until a toothpick inserted in the center comes out clean.

Cook's Note: This recipe can be prepped in advance by cooking only partially. Cook for 30 minutes and refrigerate. When you are ready to serve, cover the dish with foil and bake in a 350°F oven for 25-30 minutes, or until hot.

Soups/Salads/Sides/Snacks PALEO   PHASE 3

Kale Chips

Kale chips are surprisingly delicious and incredibly nutritious. Buy a small bag at a health food store and you'll spend upwards of $7 for a two-ounce bag! Make them yourself for big savings!

Soaking time: 4 hours
Prep time: 20 minutes
Dehydration time: 12-14 hours

Makes: 12 servings (about 8 ounces)

- ½ cup each raw sunflower seed and raw cashews
- 2⅔ cups filtered water, divided
- 2 peeled carrots, cut into 2-inch pieces
- 2 cloves garlic, cut in half
- 2 tablespoons raw apple cider vinegar
- 1 large red pepper, seeded and cut into 2-inch pieces
- ½ medium onion, cut into 2-inch pieces
- ½ cup nutritional yeast (optional)
- 1 teaspoon sea salt
- 1 bunch kale leaves, around 10 ounces

1. Place sunflower seeds, cashews and 1 teaspoon of salt into a blender container. Add 2 cups of water, cover and soak for 4 hours.
2. Pour sunflower seeds and cashews into a sieve and rinse well.
3. Return the nut mixture to the blender container and add ⅔ cup of water and the all the remaining ingredients, except for the kale, to the blender container. Process for 1-2 minutes or until completely smooth.
4. Tear the kale leaves from the rib and then rip into bite size pieces and add to a large bowl.
5. Pour the blended mixture over the kale and stir well to ensure each piece is coated well.
6. Place coated kale pieces in a single layer on parchment paper-lined trays and dehydrate at 125°F for 12-14 hours or until crunchy. Store in a glass container.

Cook's Note: This recipe calls for a lot of time, but most of it is down time. The actual time you spend preparing the kale chips is only 10-15 minutes. If you have a large enough dehydrator, consider doubling the recipe as these chips will store for several weeks!

Sauces and Condiments  PALEO   PHASE 3

Fruit Salsa

This blend of summer fruits makes a perfect salsa to serve with broiled fish or chicken.

Prep time: 15 minutes
Stand time: 30 minutes

Makes: about 2 cups

- 2 scallions, white part only, chopped (1 cup)
- 1 large peach, peeled and chopped (1 cup)
- ½ cup freshly chopped pineapple
- ½ ripe mango, peeled and chopped (about ¾ cup)
- 2 teaspoons chopped jalapeño pepper
- ¼ teaspoon garlic powder
- ¼ teaspoon sea salt
- ¼ teaspoon pepper
- 1 teaspoon extra virgin olive oil
- ¼ lime, juiced
- 1 1-inch slice of ginger, finely chopped
- ¼ teaspoon raw honey

1. Combine all the ingredients in a mixing bowl.
2. Allow the salsa to stand at room temperature for 30 minutes, to allow the flavors to blend.

Cook's Note: When these summer fruits are not available, you can substitute an orange for the peach, and a peeled and sliced pear for the mango.

Sauces and Condiments   PALEO   PHASE 3

Tomato Salsa

Everyone loves salsa. Enjoy it as a dip, or as a topping for Sloppy Joes (page 205). Serve the Sloppy Joes on Traditional Soft Corn Tortillas (page 206) for an easy Mexican meal.

Prep time: 20 minutes
Stand time: 30 minutes

Makes: 2 cups

- 1½ pounds cherry or Roma tomatoes, chopped
- 1 stalk celery, chopped
- 1 tablespoon chopped jalapeño pepper
- 2 chopped scallions, white part only
- 1 clove garlic, crushed
- ½ lime, juiced
- 1 teaspoon cumin
- ½ teaspoon sea salt
- ¼ teaspoon freshly ground black pepper
- ¼ teaspoon raw honey
- 2 tablespoons chopped cilantro or parsley
- 1 tablespoon freshly chopped basil

1. About 1 hour before serving time, combine all the ingredients in a small mixing bowl.
2. Allow the salsa to stand at room temperature for about 30 minutes before serving. Refrigerate any leftover salsa.

Cook's Note: This versatile salsa can be made with fresh tomatoes when they are at the height of their season, or with chopped, canned tomatoes during the rest of the year. Be sure to remove the seeds from the jalapeño pepper, and *never* touch your eyes or skin after handling these or any hot peppers. If possible, wear disposable gloves while chopping peppers.

Tomato Salsa, page 197

Soups/Salads/Sides/Snacks   PHASE 3

Guacamole

Guacamole is usually served as a dip, but here are a few off-beat serving ideas: put some guacamole on your eggs in the morning, over fresh garden tomatoes for lunch, or on the side of your Sloppy Joes (page 205) for dinner.

Prep time: 15 minutes
Stand time: 1 hour

Makes: about 1½ cups

- 2 small, ripe avocados
- ½ lime, juiced
- 1½ teaspoons sea salt
- ¼ teaspoon cumin
- 1 small clove garlic, minced
- 1 tablespoon chopped jalapeño pepper
- 2 tablespoons chopped red onion
- 2 ripe Roma or cherry tomatoes, seeded and chopped
- 2 teaspoons chopped cilantro or parsley

1. Cut the avocados in half and scoop out the pulp. Add some of the lime juice and toss until the pulp is coated, so the avocado won't darken in color.
2. Add the salt and cumin, and mash the avocado with a fork.
3. Combine the rest of the lime juice and the remaining ingredients, and stir them into the avocado.
4. Allow the guacamole to sit at room temperature for about an hour before serving, to allow the flavors to blend.

Nutrition Note: Avocado is a rich source of vitamins B6 and E, potassium and healthy essential fatty acids and glutathione. It also contains both monounsaturated and polyunsaturated fats, and it acts as a "nutrient booster" by enabling the body to absorb more fat-soluble nutrients, such as alpha- and beta-carotene and lutein, in other foods that are ingested along with the avocado.

Soups/Salads/Sides/Snacks   PHASE 3

Cream of Tomato Bisque

Whether you have a bumper crop of tomatoes in your garden, or you get them from your farm share or farmers' market, nothing beats tomatoes at the peak of their season. Have this soup for lunch, or with salad for a light dinner on a cool night.

Prep time: 20 minutes
Cook time: 35 minutes

Makes: 6 servings (about 5 cups)

- 1 tablespoon extra virgin olive oil
- 2 tablespoons chopped shallots (about 1 large shallot)
- 2 cloves garlic, chopped
- 2 pounds fresh ripe tomatoes, chopped
- 2 tablespoons tomato paste
- 1 tablespoon freshly chopped parsley
- 1 tablespoon freshly chopped basil
- 1 teaspoon sea salt
- 1 teaspoon honey
- 1 teaspoon dried Herbes de Provence or Italian seasoning
- ½ teaspoon freshly ground black pepper
- 1¼ cups Chicken Bone Broth (page 264)
- ¾ cup heavy cream
- 1 tablespoon freshly chopped basil (for garnish)

1. Heat the oil in a 3-quart saucepot over medium heat for 1-2 minutes, or until hot.
2. Sauté the shallot over medium heat for 2 minutes, or until it starts to brown.
3. Add the garlic and sauté for 30 seconds.
4. Add all the remaining ingredients, except for the heavy cream and the basil. Bring the soup to a boil, then lower the heat to medium and simmer for 20 minutes.
5. Strain the soup into a bowl and reserve the liquid.
6. Place the contents of the strainer in a blender container or the bowl of a food processor, and blend or purée until smooth.
7. Return the reserved tomato liquid to the saucepot, and add the puréed solids and heavy cream.
8. Bring the soup to a simmer over medium heat.
9. As soon as the soup simmers, it is ready to serve. Sprinkle with chopped basil if desired.

Veggie Burgers

Want a healthier alternative to a beef burger? These veggie burgers are just what you are looking for. The best thing about them is that you won't be giving up flavor for health.

Prep time: 20 minutes
Cook time: 12 minutes

Makes: 6 burgers

- 2½ tablespoons extra virgin olive oil, divided
- 1 large onion, chopped
- 2 cloves garlic, chopped
- ¾ cup celery, chopped
- 2 carrots, peeled and chopped
- 1 cup kale, packed, chopped
- 1 can (15.5 ounces) black, pinto, or kidney beans, drained and rinsed
- 4 sprigs parsley, leaves only
- 2 large basil leaves
- 1 tablespoon each chia seeds, sesame seeds and flaxseed meal
- ⅓ cup sunflower seeds
- 2 tablespoons mustard
- ¾ cup Almond Flour (page 260) or chickpea flour
- 1 teaspoon sea salt
- ¼ teaspoon freshly ground black pepper

1. Heat 2 tablespoons of the oil in a large frying pan over medium heat for 1-2 minutes, or until hot.
2. Add the onions and sauté for 2 minutes, or until limp. Add the garlic, celery, carrot and kale and sauté for 3 minutes. Remove the vegetables to a bowl and reserve.
3. Place the remaining ingredients in the bowl of a food processor. Pulse on and off several times, just until the beans are chopped and the mixture is combined.
4. Place the contents of the food processor into the bowl containing the reserved vegetables. Stir well to combine.
5. Add the remaining oil to the frying pan and heat for 1 minute or until hot.
6. Form the mixture into 6 patties and place them into the frying pan. Cook 2-3 minutes per side, or until nicely browned.
7. Serve immediately.

Cook's Note: When you reach Phase 4 you may add 1 tablespoon of hemp seeds. They will add an additional protein boost, and they contain all nine of the essential amino acids. With an excellent 3-1 balance of Omega 3 and Omega 6 fatty acids they promote cardiovascular health. Since they are so good for you, why not add them to your smoothies and baked goods?

Entrees PALEO   PHASE 3

Stir-Fried Chicken with Red Peppers and Cashews

Prep time: 25 minutes
Cook time: 10 minutes

Makes: 4 servings

Marinade
3 cloves garlic, crushed
½ cup Easy Spicy Ketchup (page 287)
¼ cup organic tamari*

Chicken
1 pound skinless, boneless, white meat chicken breasts cut into thin strips
3-4 tablespoons grapeseed or extra virgin olive oil, divided
2 red peppers, seeded, cut in half lengthwise and sliced into ½-inch slices
4 scallions, including the white part and 1 inch of the green part, thinly sliced on the diagonal
½-¾ cup filtered water
1 cup cashews

* Substitute coconut aminos (see resources section) for tamari for Paleo.

1. Combine the marinade ingredients in a gallon-sized resealable plastic storage bag. Add the chicken and seal well. Allow the chicken to marinate for several hours in the refrigerator.
2. When you are ready to cook the chicken, remove it from the marinade, reserving the marinade for later use. Blot the chicken with a paper towel to remove any excess marinade.
3. Heat half the oil in a heavy duty frying pan until it is very hot and starts to sizzle.
4. Lower the heat to medium-high, add about half of the chicken and stir fry for about 1½-2 minutes, or until it is nicely browned. Remove from the frying pan.
5. Add the remaining chicken, stir fry for 1½-2 minutes and remove.
6. Add the remaining oil. Stir fry the red peppers and the scallions for 2 minutes, or until they are slightly charred.
7. Return the chicken to the frying pan.
8. Add the water to the bag with the remaining marinade and pour the liquid into the pan with the chicken. Stir and cook for 1 minute.
9. Add the cashews and stir well.
10. Serve over cooked brown rice, if desired (and you can tolerate grains).

Sloppy Joes (page 205) on Traditional Soft Corn Tortillas (page 206)

Entrees   PALEO   PHASE 3

Sloppy Joes

This easy-to-make, Mexican-inspired recipe will be a family favorite. You can make it the night before and reheat to serve – in fact, it tastes even better the second day.

Prep time: 15 minutes
Cook time: 20 minutes

Makes: 4 servings

- 2 teaspoons extra virgin olive oil
- 1 small onion, chopped
- 1 pound ground beef
- 1 tablespoon chili powder
- 1 teaspoon garlic powder
- 1 teaspoon paprika
- ½ teaspoon cumin
- ½ teaspoon sea salt
- ¼ teaspoon celery salt
- ⅛ teaspoon freshly ground black pepper
- 1 can (6 ounces) tomato paste
- 1 cup filtered water

1. Heat the oil in a medium-sized frying pan over medium heat for 1-2 minutes, or until hot.
2. Add the onion and sauté for about 2 minutes, or until limp.
3. Add the meat and cook for 5 minutes, or until it loses its red color.
4. Combine the spices, salt and pepper and stir them into the meat mixture.
5. Stir in the tomato paste and water.
6. Lower the heat and simmer for 10 minutes, stirring occasionally.
7. Serve in Traditional Soft Corn Tortillas (page 206). Top with Tomato Salsa (page 197) or Guacamole (page 199) and/or grated cheese, if desired.

Bonus Recipe: Burrito – This recipe can also be made into a burrito by following these instructions: Wrap Traditional Soft Corn Tortillas (Page 206) or the Soft Flour Tortillas (page 177) in foil and heat them for 5 minutes in a 400°F oven. Spread each of the warmed tortillas with 2 tablespoons of salsa and 1 tablespoon of sour cream. Add 1 piece of Boston lettuce and top with 2 tablespoons of black beans, 2 tablespoons of grated Cheddar cheese and ¼ of the Sloppy Joes recipe. Roll each finished burrito and keep it warm on a tray in the oven while you prepare the remaining burritos. Warm all the finished burritos for a few minutes before serving. You may also use the chicken from the Chicken Fajita recipe (page 219), if preferred.

Traditional Soft Corn Tortillas

Corn tortillas and Sloppy Joes make a meal everyone in the family will love. You can also use fully cooled tortillas as sandwich wraps.

Prep time: 15 minutes
Stand time: 30 minutes
Cook time: 20 minutes

Makes: 8 (6-inch) tortillas

1½ cups corn masa harina flour
½ teaspoon sea salt
1 cup hot filtered water
2 tablespoons extra virgin olive oil
Additional masa harina flour for dusting

1. Combine the flour and salt in a small bowl.
2. Combine the oil and water and add to the flour mixture. Stir to combine.
3. Form the dough into a ball and then divide into 8 equal-sized balls.
4. Generously dust a cutting board, preferably plastic, with some of the additional masa harina. Place one of the dough balls on the masa and press down with your hand. Sprinkle a small amount of masa on the top of the dough and continue to press down with the palm of your hand until the dough becomes a 6-inch circle.
5. Heat a large frying pan, griddle (preferably cast iron), or another type of heavy-bottomed pan, over medium-high heat, for 2-3 minutes or until hot. It should not be too hot or the tortilla will burn or become too brittle to roll.
6. Before making the first tortilla, wipe the frying pan or griddle with a folded paper towel dipped in the oil. Lower the heat to medium.
7. Using a large metal spatula, loosen the tortilla on the board and slide it into the heated frying pan. Cook the tortilla for 1 to 1½ minutes per side or until just starting to color. Repeat steps 4-6 with the remaining dough balls.*
8. Stack the tortillas on a plate lightly covered with foil to keep warm. Serve immediately with Sloppy Joes (page 205).

A tortilla press can be used to make the tortillas. Follow the instructions provided by the manufacturer..

Cook's Note: The dough can be made and the tortillas formed in advance and stored in the refrigerator until you are ready to use them.

Entrees  PALEO

Slow Cooked Pulled Chicken

Slow cooking is every working person's best friend. After a long, hard day, what could be more pleasing than to walk into a house filled with the delicious aroma of BBQ?

Prep time: 15 minutes
Cook time: 9 hours 20 minutes

Makes: about 2 quarts

- 2 tablespoons extra virgin olive oil
- 6 large chicken thighs with skin (4 pounds)
- 1 large onion, chopped
- 4 cloves garlic, pressed
- 3 cups Easy Spicy Ketchup (page 287)
- 1 tablespoon chili powder
- 1-2 tablespoons raw apple cider vinegar
- ¼ cup honey or 3 tablespoons coconut palm sugar
- 2 tablespoons mustard
- 1 teaspoon ground cumin
- ½ teaspoon sea salt
- 1 teaspoon celery salt
- 1 teaspoon paprika

1. Heat the oil in a large frying pan over high heat for 3 minutes, or until hot.
2. Lower the heat to medium-high, add the chicken, and brown it on the skin side for 8-10 minutes, or until well browned. Turn the chicken thighs and cook for 5 minutes.
3. Remove the chicken from the pan to cool.
4. Add the onion and garlic to the pan and sauté for about 3 minutes, or until limp and just starting to brown.
5. Remove the skin from the chicken and discard.
6. Place the sautéed onions and the remaining ingredients in a slow cooker and stir well.
7. Add the skinned chicken. Cover the cooker, and set it to Cook on Low for 7-9 hours.
8. Remove the chicken from the cooker and, using 2 forks, shred the meat and discard the bones.
9. Return the chicken to the pot and stir well.

Cook's Note: Brown the chicken with the skin on, because the rendered fat from the skin adds lots of flavor. Remove the skin before adding the chicken to the slow cooker, because the added fat is not desirable in the finished dish. You can do all the prep for this recipe the night before and store the ingredients in the refrigerator. Then, all that's left to do in the morning is to add the ingredients to the slow cooker and turn it on. You can't overcook this recipe – the longer it cooks, the better it tastes! The recipe makes a lot by design; it's a great choice for a party, or a "pot luck supper," or even just an everyday meal. Leftovers reheat well, and can even be frozen for future use.

Spinach and Sun-Dried Tomato Quiche

This mildly flavored gluten-free, whole grain crust compliments the bold taste of the spinach and sun-dried tomatoes.

Prep time: 30 minutes
Stand time: 30 minutes
Cook time: 50 minutes

Makes: 6-8 servings

Crust
- 1½ cups All-Purpose Gluten-Free Baking Mix (page 265, bonus recipe)
- ⅛ teaspoon sea salt
- ⅓ cup coconut palm shortening
- 3-4 tablespoons ice-cold filtered water

Filling
- 2 tablespoons extra virgin olive oil
- 1 large shallot, finely chopped
- 2 cloves garlic, finely chopped
- ⅓ cup chopped sun-dried tomatoes, packed in olive oil
- 1 bag (6 ounces) baby spinach, finely chopped (about 3 cups)
- ½ teaspoon sea salt
- ¼ teaspoon freshly ground black pepper
- 1 cup Almond Milk (page 260)
- 4 eggs
- 1 cup grated sharp Cheddar cheese
- ½ cup grated Parmesan cheese

1. Combine the baking mix and the salt into the bowl of a food processor. Add the shortening and cover. Pulse on and off 5 or 6 times, or until the shortening is cut into the mix.
2. With the food processor running, pour the ice water down the feed tube and process the dough just until it starts to form a ball. Add the water slowly, so as not to add too much.
3. Form the dough into a ball and wrap it in plastic warp. Refrigerate for about 30 minutes.
4. Preheat the oven to 400ºF.
5. Line a board with parchment paper and lightly dust the paper with flour. Place the dough on the paper, lightly flour the top of the dough and roll it into a 10-inch circle.
6. Fit the rolled out dough into a 9-inch quiche dish or pie plate. Bake the crust in the preheated oven for 8 minutes.
7. Meanwhile, heat the oil in a large frying pan over medium heat for 1-2 minutes, or until hot.
8. Add the shallot and sauté for 1½ minutes. Add the garlic and sauté for 30 more seconds.
9. Add the sun-dried tomatoes and sauté for 1 minute.
10. Add the spinach, salt and pepper and sauté for 1 minute, or until just limp. Allow the mixture to cool slightly.
11. Combine the milk, eggs and cheeses in a large bowl and mix well.
12. Add the spinach mixture to the milk and egg mixture and stir well.
13. Pour the filling into the pre-baked crust and bake for 35 minutes, or until the top is nicely browned and a knife inserted 1 inch from the center of the quiche comes out clean.

Entrees

PHASE 3

Chicken Tamaki

Tamaki is a type of hand-rolled, cone-shaped sushi that's easy for a sushi beginner to make and eat. This version is comprised of cooked brown rice, stir-fried chicken, carrot and cucumber, with a tasty dipping sauce.

Prep time: 15 minutes
Cook time: 5 minutes

Makes: 8 rolls

Marinade/Dipping Sauce
¼ cup tamari
¼ cup Easy Spicy Ketchup (page 287)
2 tablespoons filtered water
1 teaspoon mustard
½ teaspoon sesame oil
2 teaspoons honey
½ teaspoon wasabi (optional)
8 ounces skinless chicken breast, cut into thin strips
2 tablespoons safflower oil

Rolls
4 sheets nori (dried seaweed), cut in half horizontally
⅓ cup cooked brown rice
1 carrot, peeled and cut into thin strips
1 cucumber, cut into thin strips

1. Combine all the marinade/dipping sauce ingredients, except for the chicken and the oil, and divide the mixture in half.
2. Pour half the sauce into a quart-sized resealable plastic bag. Pour the remaining sauce into a small serving bowl for dipping, and set aside. Add the chicken to the bag with the marinade. Seal the bag and refrigerate it for up to an hour.
3. Heat the oil in a medium-sized frying pan for 3 minutes, or until hot.
4. Remove the chicken from the plastic bag. Stir fry the chicken in the hot oil for 2-3 minutes, or until nicely browned.
5. Lay a piece of nori on a cutting board. Spread 1 tablespoon of cooked rice over the nori. Place a piece of the cooked chicken, a carrot stick and a cucumber spear on top of the rice. Starting at one end, roll the nori so that it makes a cone-shaped roll with the filling inside.
6. Repeat the above step to make the remainder of the rolls.
7. Serve with the dipping sauce on the side.

Nutrition Note: Wasabi is a plant best known for its spicy root. Grated wasabi root tastes like strong horseradish and is commonly served with sushi. It is very low in cholesterol and sodium and is a good source of vitamins B6 and C, calcium, magnesium, potassium, manganese and dietary fiber.

Entrees PALEO   PHASE 3

Shepherd's Pie

Make this "comfort food" recipe on a cold winter's night and freeze the leftovers. Or divide it in half before baking and freeze it for a night when you are running short on time.

Prep time: 20 minutes
Cook time: 1 hour

Makes: 8 servings

Topping
2 recipes Mashed Cauliflower (page 96)

Filling
2 tablespoons extra virgin olive oil
1 large onion, chopped
3 cloves garlic, chopped
2 large carrots peeled, and chopped
6 ounces green beans, chopped
2 pounds ground beef or ground turkey
1 cup Easy Spicy Ketchup (page 287)
1 tablespoon mustard
2 teaspoons Italian seasonings
1 teaspoon sea salt
¼ teaspoon pepper
1 cup grated Cheddar cheese (optional)

1. Prepare a double recipe of the Mashed Cauliflower and reserve for later use.
2. Heat the oil in a large frying pan over medium heat for 1-2 minutes, or until hot.
3. Add the onions and sauté for 2 minutes or until limp. Add the garlic and sauté for 30 seconds.
4. Add the meat and cook for 7 minutes or until it's starting to brown. Drain off the fat and liquid.
5. Preheat the oven to 375ºF.
6. Stir in all the remaining ingredients except the cheese and simmer for 10 minutes.
7. Spoon the mixture into one or two casserole dishes and top with the reserved Mashed Cauliflower.
8. Place the casserole into the preheated oven and bake for 45 minutes. Top with grated cheese, if desired, and bake for an additional 15 minutes.
9. Serve immediately.

Cook's Note: You can use ground beef, turkey, chicken or lamb in this dish. For a little variety, add corn or peas in place of the green beans.

Entrees

Seared Peppered London Broil

Prep time: 10 minutes
Cook time: 18-24 minutes

Makes: 6 servings

1½-2 teaspoons whole black peppercorns
¼ teaspoon each garlic salt and onion powder
½ teaspoon sea salt
½ teaspoon Herbes de Provence
1 teaspoon mustard
½ teaspoon honey
2 pounds top round, cut for London broil, cut 1-inch thick
1 teaspoon grapeseed oil

1. Preheat the oven to 500°F.
2. Place the peppercorns on a small tray lined with plastic wrap. Cover the peppercorns with a second piece of plastic wrap. Crack the peppercorns with a meat mallet or rolling pin. Remove the top layer of plastic wrap.
3. Combine the pepper, garlic salt, onion powder, salt and Herbs de Provence on a flat plate.
4. Combine the mustard and honey.
5. Paint the top of the steak with half the honey mustard.
6. Place the painted side of the steak on the peppercorn mixture and paint the other side of the steak with the remaining honey mustard.
7. Turn the steak over to coat the second side with the peppercorn mixture. The steak should be sparsely coated on both sides with the mixture.
8. Heat a cast iron or heavy-bottomed frying pan over medium-high heat for 8 minutes, or until very hot.
9. Add the oil and tilt the pan so that the oil coats the bottom of the pan.
10. Place the steak in the pan. Cook for 5 minutes to sear one side; then, turn the meat and cook for 5 minutes on the other side.
11. Place the pan in the preheated oven for 10 minutes.*
12. Allow the steak to stand for 5 minutes before slicing. Slice in thin slices on the diagonal, against the grain.

   The cook time given is for medium-rare meat. If you prefer rare meat, reduce the cook time to 8 minutes. If you prefer well-done meat, cook for 12-14 minutes.

Cook's Note: Serve with Roasted Vegetables (page 187), if desired.

Entrees PALEO   PHASE 3

Mediterranean Chicken

Add some brown rice or a side salad to this colorful and flavor-packed recipe and you have a meal that friends and family alike will savor.

Prep time: 20 minutes
Cook time: 20 minutes

Makes: 4 servings

- 3 tablespoons corn meal*
- 1 teaspoon each garlic powder and onion powder
- ½ teaspoon sea salt
- ¼ teaspoon freshly ground black pepper
- 1 pound skinless, boneless white meat chicken breasts, cut in 2-inch strips
- 3 tablespoons extra virgin olive oil, divided
- 1 medium onion, chopped
- 1 clove garlic, chopped
- 1½ cups Chicken Bone Broth (page 264)
- 1½ tablespoons tomato paste
- 8 sun-dried tomatoes, packed in olive oil, chopped
- 1 (12 ounce) jar or can artichoke hearts, drained
- 12 pitted Greek olives (green), cut in half
- 1 teaspoon lemon juice
- 2 tablespoons each of parsley and basil, chopped
- 1 lemon, cut in slices
- 2 teaspoons additional chopped parsley

1. Combine the corn meal, garlic and onion powders, salt and pepper on a flat plate. Coat the chicken with the mixture.
2. Heat 1 tablespoon of the oil in a large frying pan over medium heat for 1-2 minutes, or until hot.
3. Brown the chicken on both sides, about 3 minutes per side. Remove the chicken from the pan and reserve for later use.
4. Add the remaining oil to the frying pan and heat for 1 minute, or until hot. Sauté the onions for 2 minutes or until they are just beginning to brown. Add the garlic and sauté for 30 seconds.
5. Add the remaining ingredients except for the lemon slices and additional parsley. Stir well to combine.
6. Simmer the sauce for 7 minutes. Add the lemon slices and cook 2 more minutes.
7. Return the chicken to the frying pan and cook for 3 minutes.
8. Sprinkle the remaining parsley over the chicken and serve.

*You may omit the corn meal, which is not suitable for Paleo.

Recipes for Repair

Multicolored Stuffed Peppers

These stuffed peppers are rich in color and flavor. Use any color of peppers you like, or try the colorful quartet shown in the picture.

Prep time: 20 minutes
Cook time: 35-40 minutes

Makes: 4 servings

- 4 whole peppers, tops and seeds removed
- 2 tablespoons grapeseed or safflower oil
- 1 medium onion, chopped
- 3 cloves garlic, crushed
- 1 pound sweet Italian turkey sausage, removed from the casing
- ¼ cup tomato paste
- 1 tablespoon freshly chopped parsley
- ½ teaspoon each freshly chopped thyme and oregano
- ½ teaspoon sea salt
- ¼ teaspoon freshly ground pepper
- 1½ cups fresh or frozen corn kernels
- 2½ cups tomato sauce

1. Preheat the oven to 400ºF.
2. Place the peppers in an 8-inch square baking dish and bake in the pre-heated over for 20 minutes, while you prepare the filling.
3. Heat the oil in a large frying pan over medium heat for 1-2 minutes, or until hot.
4. Sauté the onion for about 3 minutes, or until it starts to brown.
5. Add the garlic and sauté for 30 seconds.
6. Add the sausage meat and cook for about 5 minutes, or until it loses its color.
7. Add the tomato paste and cook for 5 minutes.
8. Add the herbs, salt, pepper and corn, and stir well to combine. Cook for 3 minutes.
9. Remove the peppers from the oven. Stuff each pepper with the filling mixture.
10. Pour half the tomato sauce into the pan around the peppers. Reserve the rest for later use.
11. Return the peppers to the preheated oven and bake for 15-20 minutes.
12. Reheat the remaining sauce and spoon a little over each pepper. Serve any remaining sauce with the peppers.

Cook's Note: Easy Oven-Roasted Marinara Sauce (page 280) is perfect for this recipe, and you can save time by making it while you are prepping the pepper stuffing. In fact, double the recipe and freeze it for future use.

Entrees   PHASE 3

Greek Ground Lamb Crumble

Serve this lamb crumble on a Soft Flour Tortilla topped with Tzatziki Sauce.

Prep time: 20 minutes
Cook time: 12 minutes

Makes: 4 servings

2 tablespoons extra virgin olive oil
1 medium onion, chopped
1 clove garlic, finely chopped
1 pound ground lamb*
½ teaspoon sea salt
¼ teaspoon freshly ground black pepper
½ teaspoon paprika
½ teaspoon dried oregano
½ teaspoon dried thyme
½ teaspoon dry mustard
1 can (6 ounces) tomato paste
1 cup filtered water
1 recipe Tzatziki Sauce (page 278)**
1 recipe Soft Flour Tortilla* (page 177)**

1. Heat the oil in a medium-sized frying pan over medium heat for 1-2 minutes, or until hot.
2. Sauté the onion for 2 minutes, or until it starts to brown.
3. Add the garlic and sauté for 30 seconds.
4. Raise the heat to high and add the lamb. Break up the lamb with a wooden spoon and allow it to cook undisturbed for a few minutes so that it starts to brown; then, cook for 5 minutes.
5. Combine the salt, pepper, paprika, oregano, thyme and dry mustard and sprinkle over the lamb.
6. Stir in the tomato paste and the water and cook for 5 minutes, stirring several times during cooking. If the heat seems to be too high, lower it to medium-high.
7. Spoon the browned meat into the wraps and top each with a dollop of tzatziki.

* Substitute ground turkey or beef if you prefer.
** Omit for dairy-free and/or Paleo.
*** Omit for Paleo.

Cook's Note: Unless you have a lot of time to prepare this dish, it is highly recommended that you prepare the tzatziki sauce and tortillas in advance. You can even prepare the meat in advance, and reheat it in a frying pan when you are ready to serve (add a little water while reheating, if needed). If you prepare everything in advance, you can assemble this meal in less than 15 minutes, and everything will taste as good as or better than if you had made it all to order.

Entrees   PALEO

Chicken Fajitas

This recipe will be a family favorite. Easy to make and delicious to eat. How can you beat that?

Prep time: 15 minutes
Stand time: 2 hours
Cook time: 15 minutes

Makes: 4 servings

Marinade
3 cloves garlic, crushed
½ teaspoon onion powder
¼ cup lemon juice
¼ cup filtered water
2 tablespoons extra virgin olive oil
2 teaspoons chili powder
½ teaspoon ground cumin
2 teaspoons paprika
1 teaspoon sea salt
¼ teaspoon freshly ground black pepper
1 pound white meat chicken breast, cut into thin strips

Fajitas
2-3 tablespoons extra virgin olive oil, divided
1 large onion, cut into strips
1 each yellow, red, orange and green bell pepper, cut into 1-inch strips
1 recipe Soft Flour Tortillas (page 177) *

* Not suitable for Paleo. Serve on lettuce instead.

1. Combine all the marinade ingredients in a large plastic storage bag.
2. Add the chicken to the bag and seal. Massage the bag to distribute the marinade, and coat the chicken. Refrigerate for several hours.
3. Heat 1 tablespoon of the oil in a large frying pan for 1-2 minutes or until hot. Add the onions and cook for 2-3 minutes or until lightly browned.
4. Add a little more oil and the peppers to the frying pan and sauté for 3 minutes or until they begin to soften.
5. Remove the peppers and onions from the frying pan and reserve.
6. Add the remaining oil. Remove the chicken from the bag and reserve the marinade. Add the chicken to the pan and cook for 5 minutes or until nicely browned. Return the pepper and onions to the pan along with the reserved marinade and stir well to combine. Cook for 1 minute.
7. Serve immediately wrapped in Soft Flour Tortillas.

Cook's Note: If you prefer beef fajitas, substitute thinly sliced flank or hanger steak for the chicken.

Meatballs and Spaghetti Squash

If you have never had spaghetti squash, you are in for a surprise. It isn't pasta, but it sure looks and tastes like it! Topped with meatballs and Garden Fresh Tomato Sauce, it's a great substitute for the real thing.

Prep time: 20 minutes
Cook time: 1 hour and 10 minutes

Makes: 6 servings and 12 meatballs

1 recipe Garden Fresh Tomato Sauce (page 281)

Meatballs
1 pound ground beef
2 tablespoons cooked quinoa
1 teaspoon onion powder
½ teaspoon garlic powder
½ teaspoon sea salt
¼ teaspoon freshly ground black pepper
2 tablespoons extra virgin olive oil

Squash
1 (4-5 pound) spaghetti squash, halved lengthwise and with seeds removed
2 cups hot filtered water

1. If you have not already made the Garden Fresh Tomato Sauce, do so now.
2. Combine all the meatball ingredients, except for the tomato sauce and the oil, in a medium-sized bowl. Form the meat mixture into 12 (2-inch) meatballs.
3. Heat the oil in a medium-sized frying pan over medium heat for 1-2 minutes, or until hot.
4. Add the meatballs to the frying pan and cook for 8-10 minutes, or until well-browned on all sides.
5. Place the tomato sauce in a saucepot to simmer over medium heat. Add the meatballs to the tomato sauce and allow them to cook for at least 1 hour.
6. When you begin cooking the meatballs in the sauce, preheat the oven to 350ºF.
7. Place the squash, cut side down, in a dish with sides that is large enough to hold both pieces.
8. Pour 2 cups of hot water into the dish.
9. Bake in the preheated oven for 40-50 minutes, or until a knife inserted in the center of the squash passes easily through the skin.
10. Remove the squash from the pan and allow it to sit for 5 minutes, or until it is cool enough to handle.
11. Using a fork, separate the stringy pulp into spaghetti-like strands and spoon it into a serving bowl.
12. Top with some sauce and meatballs, and serve the extra sauce and meatballs on the side.

Cook's Note: The texture of the cooked squash will be similar to angel hair pasta. If you prefer the texture to be more vegetable-like, take 10 minutes off the cook time.

Entrees PALEO

Honey Battered Chicken

The sauce on this battered chicken has an Asian flavor and can be enjoyed with a stir-fried medley of your favorite vegetables.

Prep time: 10 minutes
Cook time: 15 minutes

Makes: 6 servings

Battered Chicken
2 eggs
1½ pounds of chicken, cut into 1½-inch chunks
1½ cups Almond Flour (page 260)
1½ teaspoons onion powder
1½ teaspoons garlic powder
1½ teaspoons paprika
½ teaspoon freshly ground black pepper
¼-⅓ cup grapeseed* or safflower oil,* divided

Sauce
3 tablespoons raw honey
1 tablespoon Coconut Milk (page 261)
2 tablespoons mustard
1 teaspoon tamari**

*Not suitable for Paleo. Substitute extra virgin olive oil instead.
**Substitute coconut aminos (page 38) for tamari for Paleo.

1. Beat the eggs in a large bowl.
2. Add the chicken to the beaten eggs.
3. Mix the almond flour, onion powder, garlic powder, paprika and pepper together on a flat plate or tray.
4. Dredge the egged chicken cubes in the flour mixture until they are nicely coated.
5. Heat ¼ cup of the oil in a medium-sized frying pan over medium heat for 1-2 minutes, or until hot.
6. Add half the chicken pieces and cook for 3 minutes per side and reserve.
7. Add the remaining oil, if needed. Add the remaining chicken to the pan and cook for 3 minutes.
8. Remove the chicken from the frying pan, draining off any fat that remains and wipe the pan with a paper towel.
9. Mix the honey, coconut milk, mustard and tamari in the pan and add the reserved chicken and cook for 30 more seconds.
10. Serve immediately.

Slow Cooked Vegetarian Tempeh Chili

Prep time: 20 minutes
Stand time: 1 hour
Cook time: 12-14 hours

Makes: about 3 quarts

- 1 pound red kidney beans, rinsed
- 3 tablespoons grapeseed oil, divided
- 1 large onion, chopped
- 3 large garlic cloves, chopped
- 1 red or green pepper, chopped
- 2 stalks celery, sliced
- 1 carrot, peeled and chopped
- 1 (8 ounce) package tempeh
- 2-3 tablespoons chili powder
- 1 teaspoon ground cumin
- 1 teaspoon ground coriander
- 1 (2-inch) strip of kombu (optional)
- 1 can (28 ounces) diced tomatoes
- 3 cups Vegetable Broth (page 259)
- 1 cup raw fresh corn kernels
- ½ cup sour cream*, optional
- 1 cup Cheddar cheese*, optional

1. Place the beans in a 4-quart saucepot and fill the pot with water to a level of at least 3 inches above the beans. Bring to a boil over medium-high heat. Turn the heat off and allow the beans to soak for 1 hour.
2. While the beans are soaking, heat 2 tablespoons of the oil in a large frying pan over medium heat for 1-2 minutes, or until hot.
3. Sauté the onion for 3 minutes, or until it starts to brown.
4. Add the garlic and sauté for 30 seconds.
5. Add the pepper, celery and carrot and sauté for 3 minutes.
6. Spoon the sautéed vegetables into the bowl of a slow cooker.
7. Heat the remaining oil in the frying pan over medium heat for 1-2 minutes, or until hot.
8. Add the tempeh to the frying pan and sauté for 3 minutes, or until browned.
9. Add the sautéed tempeh and all the remaining ingredients, except for the corn, to the slow cooker. Drain the water from the soaked beans and rinse well. Stir them into the slow cooker.
10. Cover the cooker and set it to Cook on Low for 12-14 hours. Stir the corn into the cooker for the last 2 hours of cooking.
11. Serve topped with sour cream and grated Cheddar cheese, if desired.

Omit for dairy-free.

Nutrition Note: Tempeh has a firm texture and strong flavor. Like tofu, tempeh is made from soybeans, but it has different nutritional characteristics and textural qualities. It's made by a natural culturing and controlled fermentation process that binds the soybeans into a cake form. This process gives tempeh a higher protein, dietary fiber and vitamin content than tofu.

Entrees   PHASE 3

Red and Green Pepper Frittata

A frittata is the Italian version of an omelet. It is partially cooked on the stovetop and then finished in the oven.

Prep time: 10 minutes
Cook time: 50 minutes

Makes: 2-3 servings

- 1 red pepper, seeded and thinly sliced
- 1 green pepper, seeded and thinly sliced
- 1 medium red skinned potato, thinly sliced
- 2 tablespoons extra virgin olive oil, divided
- ½ teaspoon sea salt
- 1 teaspoon garlic powder
- ¼ teaspoon freshly ground black pepper
- 4 eggs, lightly beaten
- 1 teaspoon Herbes de Provence
- 2 tablespoons grated Parmesan, or your favorite permitted cheese

1. Preheat the oven to 400°F.
2. Place the peppers and potato in a single layer on a baking sheet.
3. Pour 1 tablespoon of the oil over the vegetables.
4. Combine the salt, garlic powder and pepper and sprinkle evenly over the vegetables.
5. Toss the vegetables well to coat.
6. Bake in the preheated oven for 40 minutes (stirring once after 20 minutes), or until the potatoes and the edges of the peppers begin to brown.
7. Remove the vegetables from the oven, but leave the oven on.
8. Whisk the eggs, Herbes de Provence and cheese together.
9. Heat the remaining oil in an oven-proof 10-inch frying pan over medium heat for 1-2 minutes, or until hot.
10. Pour the eggs into the hot pan and cook for about 1 minute to allow them to set.
11. Spoon the vegetables over the eggs and cook for 1 minute.
12. Place the frying pan in the hot oven and cook for 7 minutes, or until the top is browned and the eggs are set.
13. Serve the frittata directly in the frying pan, or turn it out onto a large plate.

Cook's Note: Frittatas are a great way to use leftover vegetables. Use this recipe as a template and substitute your favorite cooked vegetables. You can even add cooked turkey sausage, leftover salmon or chicken to the vegetables.

Entrees

PHASE 3

Homemade Pasta

Who doesn't love homemade pasta? This easy-to-make gluten-free version will become a family favorite.

Prep time: 35 minutes
Cook time: 2-3 minutes

Makes: 1 pound

¾ cup tapioca flour
¼ cup potato starch (not potato flour)
½ cup brown rice flour
¼ cup oat flour
½ teaspoon sea salt
2 tablespoons xanthan gum
3 eggs
2 tablespoons extra virgin olive oil
2 tablespoons filtered water
2 tablespoons corn meal (for dusting)

1. Combine the dry ingredients in the bowl of a food processor, and pulse 2 or 3 times to mix.
2. Combine the eggs, oil and water, and add to the food processor. Pulse several times until the dough forms a ball.
3. Cut the dough ball in half, then cut each half into quarters, yielding 8 small pieces.
4. Flatten each dough ball with a rolling pin, and roll them out into 10x5 inch ovals or until they are the thickness of standard lasagna noodles. If the dough is sticky, dust them lightly with additional brown rice flour.
5. Cut each piece of rolled out dough into ¼- to ½-inch strips.
6. Place the cut pasta on a cookie sheet and dust with a small amount of corn meal. Cover the cookie sheet with plastic wrap and refrigerate until ready to use.
7. To cook the pasta, boil a large pot of water. Add 1 teaspoon of sea salt. Shake each piece of pasta to knock off any excess corn meal, and drop the pasta into the boiling water. Cook until al dente. Fresh pasta takes about 1½-2 minutes to cook, so take care not to overcook.
8. Top with your favorite sauce, or Easy Oven-Roasted Marinara Sauce (page 280) or Garden Fresh Tomato Sauce (page 281).

Cook's Note: This recipe can also be made using a stand mixer with a pasta attachment instead of a food processor. Follow the mixer's manufacturer's instructions to make the pasta dough, and use the fettuccine cutter to cut the noodles.

Desserts/Drinks PALEO

PHASE 3

Mixed Berries with Crème Patisserie (Vanilla Pastry Cream)

Your family and friends will be impressed when you serve this fancy-sounding dessert. No one has to know just how simple it is to make.

Prep time: 10 minutes
Cook time: 8 minutes

Makes: 4 servings

1¼ cup Almond Milk (page 260)
4 egg yolks
3 tablespoons tapioca flour
1½ tablespoons honey
1½ tablespoons maple syrup
2 teaspoons vanilla
2-3 cups assorted berries

1. Heat the almond milk in a small saucepan over medium heat for about 5 minutes, until it scalds, at which time small bubbles will rim the edge of the pan. Remove from the heat.
2. Combine the egg yolks, tapioca flour, honey and maple syrup in another small saucepan.
3. Pour 2 tablespoons of the scalded milk into the egg mixture and whisk constantly until combined.
4. Pour in the remaining milk and whisk until combined.
5. Cook over medium heat until the mixture thickens, whisking occasionally.
6. Remove from the heat and stir in the vanilla.
7. Spoon the crème into a bowl and cover with plastic wrap, so that the plastic wrap lies directly on top of the crème.
8. Refrigerate until ready to use. Spoon into a glass and top with berries.

Bonus Recipe: Mixed Berry Tart – Make this recipe into a delicious tart using the pie crust found in the Spinach and Sun-Dried Tomato Quiche recipe (page 209). Bake the crust in a 9½x1½ tart pan or pie plate as directed for 10 minutes and allow it to cool completely. Fill the crust with a fully cooled recipe of Crème Patisserie (above) and top with 4 cups of assorted berries. Refrigerate the pie for several hours before serving.

Desserts/Drinks

PHASE 3

Lime Ice

This is as simple a recipe as can be, but be sure to begin making the ice early in the day, so that it will be ready when you want to eat it.

Prep time: 5 minutes
Cook time: 7 minutes
Cool time: 2½ hours

Makes: 2 cups

1½ cups filtered water
¾ cup xylitol
¼ cup lime (or lemon) juice

1. Combine the water and the xylitol in a small saucepan and cook over high heat for about 7 minutes, or until it comes to a boil.
2. Remove from the heat and stir in the juice.
3. Allow to cool over a water bath, or place the mixture in the freezer for 15 minutes to cool.
4. Pour the cooled mixture into a 13x9-inch pan and place it in the freezer.
5. After about 1½ hours, remove the pan from the freezer and scrape the ice with a fork, mixing the more softly-frozen center with the harder edges.
6. Return the pan to the freezer. Repeat the forking process every half hour for about 2 hours, or until the ice is set.

Cook's Note: Substitute lemon juice for lime to make Lemon Ice, or 2 tablespoons of lemon juice and 2 tablespoons of orange juice to make Citrus Ice.

Desserts/Drinks  PALEO   PHASE 3

Strawberry Ice Cream

Nothing is quite as satisfying as homemade ice cream on a beautiful summer day. Make this delicious ice cream when strawberries are at the peak of their season.

Prep time: 10 minutes
Freeze time: Varies from machine to machine

Makes: about 1 quart

- 1 can (14 to 16.6 ounces) full fat coconut milk
- 1 pound ripe strawberries, chopped and divided
- 6 pitted Medjool dates, soaked
- ½ teaspoon vanilla
- 10-15 drops liquid stevia* (to taste)

* Not suitable for Paleo. Use 9 dates instead, if omitted.

1. Place the coconut milk, all but 1 cup of the strawberries (reserve those for later use), and the remaining ingredients into a blender container.
2. Blend on high until smooth, about 1 minute.
3. Pour the mixture into the bowl of an electric ice cream maker. Stir in the reserved strawberries. Follow the instructions that came with the ice cream maker to freeze the ice cream.
4. Serve immediately and store leftovers in the freezer.

Cook's Note: This ice cream is best when eaten the day it's made, so make it the day you want to serve it, if possible. If you don't like strawberry ice cream, or you want a change, substitute a different type of berry or 2 cups of peaches for the strawberries and continue as directed. You may have to adjust the amount of sweetener according to the ripeness and sweetness of the fruit.

Desserts/Drinks  PALEO   PHASE 3

Watermelon Lime Cooler

This drink could not be easier to make, but it will have everyone asking you for the recipe!

Prep time: 10 minutes

Makes: about 2 cups

2 cups watermelon chunks, seeds removed
1 lime, juiced
1 cup ice cubes

1. Place the ingredients in a blender container. Cover, and blend on High, or on a frozen drink setting.

Cook's Note: This drink is great to serve at a summer barbecue. Blend the watermelon and lime in batches ahead of time. When you are ready to serve, fill a pitcher with crushed ice, pour the juice over the ice and stir.

Raspberry Lemonade Slushie

Serve this lemonade over crushed ice to make slushies, or as traditional lemonade in tall glasses over cubed ice. Either way, it's a cooling, delicious drink.

Prep time: 10 minutes
Cook time: 10 minutes

Makes: 1 quart

1 quart filtered water
½ cup xylitol
1 cup raspberries
½ cup lemon juice (juice of 2 lemons)
Finely crushed ice

1. Combine the water, xylitol and raspberries in a saucepan. Bring the water to a boil and boil for 10 minutes, or until the raspberries are reduced to pulp.
2. Remove the saucepan from the heat and strain the liquid through a sieve to remove all the seeds. Discard the seeds.
3. Stir in the lemon juice and refrigerate the drink until ready to serve.
4. Using a blender or ice crusher, crush the ice and scoop it into glasses. Pour the lemonade over the ice and serve.

Cook's Note: Blueberries, blackberries, strawberries or even sliced peaches or mango can be substituted for the raspberries in this recipe.

Recipes for Repair

Desserts/Drinks

PHASE 3

Maple Walnut Shortbread Cookies

These cookies, sweetened with maple syrup and made with ground walnuts and gluten-free flours, taste every bit as buttery and decadent as traditional shortbread cookies.

Prep time: 10 minutes
Stand time: 1 hour
Cook time: 15 minutes

Makes: 12 cookies

- ½ cup butter or Ghee (page 258), at room temperature
- 2 tablespoons maple syrup
- 1 teaspoon vanilla
- ¼ cup very finely chopped walnuts
- ¼ cup oat flour
- 2 tablespoons sorghum flour
- 2 tablespoons tapioca flour
- 3 tablespoons potato starch (not potato flour)
- ¼ teaspoon xanthan gum
- ⅛ teaspoon sea salt

1. Combine the butter, syrup and vanilla in a mixing bowl. Using an electric mixer, mix on High for 2 minutes.
2. Place the remaining ingredients into a container and cover. Shake well to ensure ingredients are mixed thoroughly.
3. Add the dry mixture to the mixing bowl and mix on Low until combined, about 1 minute.
4. Using a rubber spatula, mix well to ensure that all the ingredients are thoroughly combined.
5. Spoon the dough onto a sheet of parchment paper, making a straight line of dough about 8 inches long. Fold the paper over the dough and form into an 8-inch long by 2-inch wide log.
6. Refrigerate the dough log for about 30 minutes, or until firm.
7. Slice the log into ½-inch slices and place them on a large cookie sheet, leaving 1 inch of space around each cookie.
8. Refrigerate the cookies for at least 30 minutes.
9. Preheat the oven to 350ºF.
10. Bake the cookies in the preheated oven for 13-15 minutes, or until the edges begin to brown.
11. Allow the cookies to cool for a few minutes on the baking sheet, and then transfer them to a cooling rack to cool completely.
12. Store the cookies in a tin or cookie jar.

Cook's Note: This dessert is not only delicious, but it's suitable for people with egg and gluten intolerances.

Desserts/Drinks   PHASE 3

Oatmeal Craisin Cookies

Try this oatmeal cookie with a twist.

Prep time: 15 minutes
Cook time: 13-15 minutes

Makes: 10 (3-inch) cookies

- ¼ cup coconut palm shortening or organic butter*, cut into 4 pieces
- ⅓ cup coconut palm sugar
- 8-10 drops liquid stevia
- 1 egg**
- 1 teaspoon vanilla
- 1 cup certified gluten-free old-fashioned oats
- ⅔ cup Gluten-Free Baking Mix (page 265)
- 1 teaspoon baking powder
- ½ teaspoon baking soda
- ⅛ teaspoon sea salt
- 1 teaspoon cinnamon
- ½ cup craisins

1. Preheat the oven to 350°F.
2. Place the shortening or butter, palm sugar, stevia, egg or applesauce, and vanilla in a mixing bowl. Using an electric mixer, mix on High for 2 minutes.
3. Combine the remaining ingredients, except for the craisins, and add them to the mixing bowl, mixing on Low until just combined.
4. Stir in the craisins. Using a standard ice cream scoop, measure 10 portions of batter onto a large baking sheet, leaving at least 1 inch of space around each cookie.
5. Using your palm, press the cookies lightly, to slightly flatten them into 3-inch rounds.
6. Bake in the preheated oven for 13-15 minutes, or until the cookies are lightly browned.
7. Allow the cookies to cool for a few minutes on the baking sheet and then transfer them to a cooling rack to cool completely. Store the cookies in a tin or cookie jar.

* For dairy-free use shortening in place of butter.

** To make this recipe egg free, substitute 3 tablespoons Cinnamon Applesauce (page 96) for the egg.

Cook's Note: By craisins, we mean fruit-juice sweetened dried cranberries. You may substitute raisins instead once you reach Phase 4.

Phase 4 Contents

Banana Raisin Bread	237
Mango Pineapple Smoothie	238
Gluten-Free Italian Loaf	239
Classic Sandwich Bread	241
Classic Meatloaf	242
Chicken Croquettes	243
Broiled Shrimp with Shallots and Tomatoes and Herbs	245
Slow Cooked Pot Roast with Root Vegetables	246
Maryland Crab Cakes	247
Chicken Milanese	249
Chocolate Banana Ice Cream	250
Chocolate Coconut Macaroons	251
Rice Pudding	253
Black Bean Brownies	255

A Note About Gluten

If you are familiar with the Lyme Inflammation Diet, you may remember that gluten-containing grains were once an allowable food. While some people can tolerate gluten, Dr. Singleton finds it to be mostly a pro-inflammatory food and felt it would be best to eliminate it from the diet. Each person is unique, however, and some have no problem with gluten.

Dr. Singleton is a good example. Since his recovery from Lyme disease, he can now tolerate gluten. He has also found that some of his patients are able to introduce gluten-containing grains back into their diet, which is why they were originally part of the diet.

If at some point in the future you are feeling well and would like to try to introduce gluten-containing grains into your diet proceed with caution. It would be best to start with a whole grain that has a lower gluten level, such as barley (see related chart below). It would also be advisable to follow the soaking guidelines on page 42.

Gluten Level in Certain Grains

None	Low	High
Amaranth, Brown Rice, Buckwheat, Corn, Millet, Quinoa, Sorghum, Teff, Wild Rice	Barley, Faro, Kamut, Oats*, Rye, Spelt	Durum, Wheat, Einkorn, Semolina

*If you are gluten intolerant, be sure the package says gluten-free.

Phase 4: The Maintenance Phase (6 months to indefinite)

Phase 4 begins eight weeks after you began Phase 1. Although Phase 4 provides you with more food choice options than do Phases 1-3, your goal in Phase 4 is to continue to consume only foods and beverages that are healthy. Should you still be experiencing symptoms of chronic inflammation, remain on the earlier Phases of the diet until your symptoms subside before moving on to Phase 4. Once you do begin this Phase, strictly abide by the diet's guidelines for at least six months to ensure that you obtain the most benefit.

After you reintroduce the foods in this Phase, you should be able to determine which healthy foods you can enjoy without triggering inflammation, and which foods you should permanently avoid. After six months of following Phase 4, you may begin to occasionally reintroduce some of the foods to which you were previously sensitive (not allergy-triggering foods, which should only ever be added after clearance from your physician), but these foods should still only be consumed once a week or less, if at all. A good rule of thumb is, "If in doubt, leave it out." You should strive to permanently avoid poor quality foods, such as fried foods and refined sugar.

Phase 4 includes all the foods and beverages you safely consumed during the first three Phases. Be sure to continue to follow the General Food Guidelines and Food Choices for Detoxification on pages 28-30 as you progress into Phase 4.

Foods Allowed During Phase 4

Fruits
Grapes (purple) [1]
Kiwi [1]
Papaya [1]
Raisins [1] NEW

Nuts/Seeds
Hemp seeds

Vegetables
All other pickles NEW
Parsnips NEW
Radishes
Red potatoes
Turnips
Watercress
Yams

Grains
Possibility of gluten-containing grains (see note on page 234)

Protein Sources
Cod NEW
Grouper NEW
Pork [2] NEW
Shellfish [2] NEW

Herbs/Spices
Horseradish NEW

Dairy
Feta
Unsweetened kefir

Fats
Peanut oil

Other
Chocolate (unsweetened, with 70% or greater cocoa content)
Gelatin NEW
Yeast NEW

NEW: Foods added or shifted to earlier Phases of the diet, since the original version of the diet.

[1] Use sparingly, as they are very high in sugar.

[2] These are not ideal foods and should be eaten rarely – no more than once a week.

Breakfast *PHASE 4*

Banana Raisin Bread

Prep time: 20 minutes
Stand time: 10 minutes
Cook time: about 1 hour (including roasting bananas)

Makes: 1 loaf

- 2 large ripe bananas
- ½ cup certified gluten-free old-fashioned oats
- 2 eggs, lightly beaten*
- 1 teaspoon vanilla
- ¼ cup honey or xylitol
- ½ cup safflower oil or Ghee** (page 258)
- ¼ cup Almond Milk (page 260)
- 1 cup Gluten-Free Baking Mix (page 265)
- ¼ cup Almond Flour (page 260)
- 1 teaspoon baking powder
- 1 teaspoon baking soda
- ¼ teaspoon sea salt
- ½ cup raisins or chopped walnuts

1. Preheat the oven to 425°F.
2. Grease an 8-inch loaf pan.
3. Place the bananas, with skins on, on a baking sheet and bake in the preheated oven for 20 minutes.
4. Remove the bananas from the oven and allow to cool slightly. Lower the oven to 350°F.
5. Remove the skins and mash the bananas. Place the mashed bananas, along with any liquid that accumulated on the baking tray, into a bowl.
6. Add the oats, eggs, vanilla, honey or xylitol and oil or ghee and mix well. Allow the mixture to stand for about 10 minutes, to soften the oats.
7. Meanwhile, combine the baking mix, almond flour, baking powder, baking soda and salt, and stir into the banana mixture.
8. Stir in the raisins or nuts and spoon the batter into the greased pan.
9. Bake in the preheated oven for 45-50 minutes, or until a toothpick inserted in the center comes out clean.

* To make this recipe egg free, add one additional tablespoon of flaxseed meal to the dry ingredients and increase the almond milk to ½ cup.

** For dairy-free use the oil in place of the ghee.

Cook's Note: The batter for this recipe can be made into 12 muffins, rather than a loaf. To make muffins, preheat the oven to 350°F and fill each muffin cup with a scant ½ cup of batter. Bake for 20-25 minutes, or until a toothpick inserted in the center of a muffin comes out clean.

Breakfast  PHASE 4

Mango Pineapple Smoothie

Kefir has a similar flavor to plain yogurt, and is a pleasant way to get some probiotics while you are taking antibiotics. Drink this smoothie for dessert or breakfast, or even take it to work for lunch.

Prep time: 5 minutes

Makes: 2 cups

½ cup cows' milk kefir* or Coconut Milk (page 261)
1 tablespoon orange juice
1 cup chopped mango (½ mango)
½ cup chopped fresh pineapple
2 teaspoons raw honey
½ teaspoon vanilla
½ cup ice cubes

For dairy-free and Paleo, use coconut milk in place of the kefir.

1. Place all the ingredients in a blender container. Cover, and blend on High, or on a frozen drink setting, until smooth.
2. Pour into a tall glass and serve immediately.

Cook's Note: Use these recipes as a template, and substitute fruits or berries that are in season, or that you especially like.

Soups/Salads/Sides/Snacks

PHASE 4

Gluten-Free Italian Loaf

No disclaimer is needed for this delicious gluten-free bread. Serve it to family and friends. They may be shocked to find out it's dairy-, egg- and gluten-free!

Prep time: 20 minutes
Rise time: 60 minutes
Cook time: 50-55 minutes

Makes: 1 loaf

1 cup Millet Flour (page 266)
¾ cup sorghum flour
¾ cup corn starch
¾ cup potato starch (not potato flour)
¾ cup tapioca starch
2¼ teaspoons xanthan gum
2 teaspoons salt
1½ tablespoon coconut palm sugar
1½ tablespoons active dry yeast (not quick rising)
1½ tablespoons extra virgin olive oil
2 cups warm filtered water (105°F)

Topping

2 tablespoons sesame seeds
1 teaspoon coarse sea salt
¼ teaspoon garlic powder
½ teaspoon filtered water

1. Combine all of the dry ingredients except for the yeast in a large mixing bowl and stir very well to combine. Add the yeast and stir again. (When salt touches yeast directly, it can kill the yeast.)

2. Combine the oil and warm water and add to the mixing bowl.

3. Mix at a low speed for 30 seconds, or until the flour and liquids are combined.

4. Scrape the bowl with a rubber spatula to incorporate all the flour, and then mix at high speed for 4 minutes. The mixture will be thick (similar to pound cake batter).

5. Lightly grease an 8-inch loaf pan with oil. Spoon the mixture into the greased pan.

6. Combine the dry topping ingredients. Brush the loaf with the water and sprinkle the topping evenly over the dough. Press the seeds in lightly with your fingertips.

7. Allow the dough to rise in a warm (about 80°F) draft-free place for one hour, or until the bread has risen to nearly the top of the pan. The top will crack slightly.

8. While the bread is rising, place the oven rack in the middle position and preheat the oven to 350°F.

9. Bake the risen dough for 50-55 minutes or until an instant read thermometer reads 205°F, or until tapping the top of the bread makes a hollow sound.

10. Remove the bread and allow it to cool for 5 minutes before turning it out onto a rack to cool completely.

Cook's Note: Use leftover bread for Italian Breadcrumbs (page 267) or Croutons (page 268).

Cran-Raspberry Sauce, page 275

Soups/Salads/Sides/Snacks

PHASE 4

Classic Sandwich Bread

Who doesn't remember fondly eating peanut butter on soft white bread? Thought those days where gone forever, now that you are eating gluten-free? Well, you thought wrong.

Prep time: 20 minutes
Rise time: 50 minutes
Cook time: 45-50 minutes

Makes: 1 loaf

- 2 eggs, at room temperature
- 2 tablespoons safflower oil
- 2 tablespoon honey
- 1 cup warm filtered water, 110° F
- 2½ cups brown rice flour
- ½ cup tapioca starch
- ½ cup potato starch (not flour)
- 1 tablespoon xanthan gum
- 1 teaspoon sea salt
- 2¼ teaspoons active dry yeast (not quick rising)

1. Beat the eggs in a large mixing bowl at medium speed for 2 minutes.
2. Combine the remaining wet ingredients, add to the beaten eggs and beat 1 minute.
3. Combine all of the dry ingredients except for the yeast in a large mixing bowl and stir very well to combine. Add the yeast and stir again. (When salt touches yeast directly, it can kill the yeast.)
4. Add the flour mixture to the wet ingredients in the mixing bowl. Mix at low speed for 30 seconds, or until the flour and the liquids are combined.
5. Scrape the bowl with a rubber spatula to incorporate all the flour, and then mix at high speed for 4 minutes. The mixture will be thick (similar to pound cake batter). Brush the loaf with the water
6. Lightly grease an 8-inch loaf pan with oil. Spoon the mixture into the greased pan.
7. Allow the dough to rise in a warm (about 80°F) draft-free place for 50 minutes, or until the bread has risen to nearly the top of the pan.
8. While the bread is rising, place the oven rack in the middle position and preheat the oven to 350°F.
9. Bake the risen dough for one 45-50 minutes or until an instant read thermometer reads 205 °F or until tapping the top of the bread makes a hollow sound.
10. Remove the bread and allow it to cool for 5 minutes before turning it out onto a rack to cool completely.

Cook's Note: Gluten-free breads are best eaten the day they are baked. After the bread has cooled slice the loaf and freeze any slices that you will not be eating in the next day or so. Toasting this bread helps bring out the nutty flavor of the grains.

Entrees   PHASE 4

Classic Meatloaf

Meatloaf is the ultimate comfort food. Now you can enjoy this gluten-, dairy- and egg-free version!

Prep time: 20 minutes
Cook time: 1¼-1½ hours

Makes: 6 servings

Meatloaf
1 tablespoon extra virgin olive oil
1 large onion, chopped
1 clove garlic, crushed
1½ pounds chopped beef or ground turkey
⅔ cup Easy Spicy Ketchup (page 287)
1 teaspoon mustard
2 tablespoons applesauce or 1 egg
2 tablespoons filtered water
¾ cup Italian Breadcrumbs (page 267) or certified gluten-free old-fashioned oats
1 teaspoon sea salt
¼ teaspoon freshly ground black pepper

Vegetables
2 carrots, peeled and cut into 1-inch pieces
6 small red potatoes, unpeeled and cut into quarters
1 large onion, cut into wedges
Sea salt and pepper

1. Preheat the oven to 375ºF.
2. Heat the oil in a frying pan over medium heat for 1-2 minutes, or until hot.
3. Add the onion and sauté for 2 minutes, or until limp.
4. Add the garlic and sauté for 30 seconds.
5. Allow the onions to cool for a few minutes. Then, place them, along with the remaining ingredients, in a large mixing bowl and mix well.
6. Place the mixture on a large baking pan and form the mixture into an oval.
7. Surround the meatloaf with the carrots, potatoes and onions. Season with salt and pepper.
8. Bake the meatloaf and vegetables in the preheated oven for 1¼-1½ hours, or until it is nicely browned.

Cook's Note: Make two meatloafs at once. Serve one for dinner and put the other uncooked loaf in the freezer for another night. Serve the leftovers on a sandwich, which is delicious when topped with lettuce and tomato and served on the Classic Sandwich Bread (page 241).

Entrees　　　　　　　　　　　　　　　　　　　　　　　　PHASE 4

Chicken Croquettes

These croquettes are a tasty way to use up leftover chicken or turkey. Serve them with Cran-Raspberry Sauce (page 275).

Prep time: 20 minutes
Cook time: 15 minutes

Makes: 8 croquettes

12 ounces cooked chicken or turkey, cut into 2-inch pieces
1 small onion, quartered
1 small carrot, peeled and quartered
4 mushrooms, quartered
1 stalk celery, quartered
2 sprigs parsley
1 clove garlic
½ Chicken Bone Broth (page 264)
1 egg, beaten
1 large potato, peeled, boiled and mashed
½ teaspoon sea salt
¼ teaspoon freshly ground black pepper
1 tablespoon grated Parmesan cheese
1 cup Italian Breadcrumbs (page 267), divided
2 tablespoons grapeseed or extra virgin olive oil

1. Place the chicken in the bowl of a food processor and pulse 5-6 times, until the chicken is chopped, but not puréed. Remove the chopped chicken to a large mixing bowl.
2. Place the onion, carrot, mushrooms, celery, parsley and garlic in the food processor and pulse until the vegetables are finely chopped.
3. Remove the chopped vegetables to the mixing bowl with the chicken and stir well.
4. Combine the chicken broth, egg, potato, salt, pepper, cheese and ⅓ of the breadcrumbs, and stir the mixture into the chicken and vegetables.
5. Pour the remaining breadcrumbs on a flat plate.
6. Form the mixture into eight 4-inch ovals and roll them in the breadcrumbs.
7. Heat the oil in a large frying pan over medium-high heat for 1-2 minutes, or until hot.
8. Cook the croquettes for about 8-10 minutes, turning them so that they brown on both sides and all edges.

Cook's Note: You can prepare the croquettes in advance, and cook them later. This will save you time on a busy work day.

Entrees

PHASE 4

Broiled Shrimp with Shallots and Tomatoes and Herbs

This recipe is a cross between Scampi and Veracruz. It has shallots, lemon, garlic, tomatoes and herbs. Sounds yummy, doesn't it?

Prep time: 20 minutes
Cook time: 10 minutes

Makes: 4 servings

1 small shallot

8 grape tomatoes

1 large clove garlic

4 sprigs parsley, leaves only

3 chives, cut in 2-inch pieces

1 sprig lemon thyme, leaves only

1 teaspoon sea salt

¼ teaspoon freshly ground black pepper

1 pound jumbo shrimp, cleaned, deveined, butterflied, skins removed, tails left on

1 lemon cut in wedges

Topping

1 (2 ounce) slice Classic Sandwich Bread (page 241), grated

¼ teaspoon sea salt

⅛ teaspoon freshly ground black pepper

1 tablespoon grated Parmesan Cheese

1. Place the first 8 ingredients into the bowl of a food processor. Cover and pulse on and off about 10 times just until the tomatoes and herbs are finely chopped.

2. Place the cleaned shrimp on a baking sheet. Top each shrimp with about 1 teaspoon of the tomato mixture.

3. Place the oven rack 4 inches from the broiler. Preheat to broil.

4. Combine the topping ingredients and sprinkle over the shrimp.

5. Place the shrimp in the oven and broil for 5 minutes or until the crumbs are browned.

6. Serve immediately, with lemon wedges.

Cook's Note: If you prefer, you may substitute scallops for shrimp.

Entrees   PHASE 4

Slow Cooked Pot Roast with Root Vegetables

Never had parsnips and turnips or don't think you like them? Give this recipe a try! You just might be surprised what a wonderful flavor they lend to the delicious gravy in this recipe.

Prep time: 40 minutes
Cook time: 9-10 hours

Makes: 4-6 servings

2 tablespoon brown rice flour*

¼ teaspoon each garlic and onion powder

1 teaspoon sea salt

½ teaspoon freshly ground black pepper

1 (3-pound) beef chuck roast

2 tablespoons extra virgin olive oil, divided

3 medium carrots, chopped

3 stalks celery, chopped

1 small turnip, peeled and chopped

1 medium parsnip, chopped

1 medium onion, chopped

3 medium potatoes*, quartered

3 cloves garlic, chopped

1 cup Beef Broth (page 264 in the note at the bottom)

2 tablespoons Easy Spicy Ketchup (page 287)

1. Combine the flour, garlic, onion powder, salt and pepper on a flat plate.
2. Coat the meat on both sides with the flour mixture.
3. Heat 1 tablespoon oil in a large frying pan over medium-high heat for 1-2 minutes, or until hot.
4. Brown the meat until well browned on each side, about 5 minutes per side. Remove and reserve.
5. Add the remaining oil to the pan. Add all the vegetables, salt and pepper and sauté for 10 minutes or until they are starting to brown.
6. Transfer the sautéed vegetables to a slow cooker. Place the meat on top of the vegetables.
7. Combine the broth and ketchup and add it to the cooker.
8. Cover the cooker and set it to Cook on Low for 9-10 hours.
9. Remove the meat from the cooker. Slice or cut into chunks and serve with the vegetables and gravy.

For Paleo, eliminate the brown rice flour and potatoes.

Cook's Note: This pot roast can be made in the oven. Brown the meat and vegetables in a Dutch oven. Add all the remaining ingredients and increase the broth to 3 cups. Cover and cook in a preheated 300ºF oven for 3 hours or until tender.

Entrees

PHASE 4

Maryland Crab Cakes

Make this recipe the next time you are having company, and get ready for the compliments!

Prep time: 20 minutes
Stand time: 1 hour
Cook time: 12 minutes

Makes: 8 cakes

¼ cup extra virgin olive oil, divided
1 medium onion, chopped
1 large clove garlic, finely chopped
1 small red pepper, chopped
1 small yellow or orange pepper, chopped
2 stalks celery, chopped
½ cup Homemade Mayonnaise (page 270)
1 egg
1 teaspoon sea salt
1 teaspoon garlic powder
1 teaspoon Old Bay seasoning
¼ teaspoon freshly ground black pepper
¾ cup Italian Breadcrumbs (page 267), divided
1 teaspoon lemon juice
1 tablespoon parsley, chopped
1 teaspoon basil, chopped
1 can (1 pound) lump crabmeat

1. Heat 2 tablespoons of the oil in a medium-sized frying pan over medium heat for 1-2 minutes, or until hot.
2. Add the onions, garlic, peppers and celery to the frying pan and sauté for 10 minutes, or until the vegetables are very soft and starting to brown.
3. While the vegetables are cooking combine the mayonnaise, egg, salt, garlic powder, Old Bay seasoning, black pepper, ¼ cup breadcrumbs, lemon juice, parsley and basil in a medium-sized mixing bowl and mix well.
4. Remove the frying pan from the heat and allow the sautéed vegetables to cool for about 5 minutes before adding them to the bowl.
5. Stir the vegetables into the mixture in the bowl and then carefully fold in the crabmeat, trying not to break up the chunks. Cover the bowl and refrigerate for at least 30 minutes.
6. Spread the remaining ½ cup of breadcrumbs on a flat plate. Using a ⅓ cup measuring cup, divide the mixture into 8 portions.
7. Form the mixture into cakes and dredge them in the breadcrumbs.
8. Place the cakes on a tray and refrigerate for at least 30 minutes before cooking.
9. Heat the remaining 2 tablespoons of oil in the frying pan over medium heat for 1-2 minutes or until hot.
10. Cook 4 cakes at a time in the hot oil for 3 minutes per side or until nicely browned. You can keep the cooked cakes warm in a 250ºF oven until they are all ready to serve.
11. Serve with Tartar Sauce (page 289) or Horseradish Mustard (page 289), if desired.

Cook's Note: Don't skimp on the quality of the crab when making this recipe. Be sure to buy lump crabmeat. It is quite expensive, but the results are well worth the price.

Chicken Milanese

Make the dressing ahead of time and all that is left to do is bread and cook the chicken. In less than 15 minutes you have a beautiful dinner that is perfect for a warm summer night.

Prep time: 15 minutes
Cook time: 12 minutes

Makes: 4 servings

Dressing
- ¼ cup lemon juice
- 2 teaspoons Dijon mustard
- ½ teaspoon each sea salt, garlic powder and onion powder
- ¼ teaspoon freshly ground black pepper
- 2 teaspoons each freshly chopped, parsley, basil and chives
- ½ teaspoon lemon thyme
- ½ cup extra virgin olive oil

Chicken
- 2 tablespoons Homemade Mayonnaise (page 270)
- 2 teaspoons Dijon mustard
- 1 teaspoon ground horseradish
- 2 tablespoons extra virgin olive oil
- 4 (6 ounce) skinless boneless chicken breasts, pounded very thin
- 1 cup Italian Breadcrumbs (page 267)
- 2-4 tablespoons extra virgin olive oil

Salad
- 4 cups assorted greens
- Parmesan cheese*, shaved or grated (optional)

1. Combine all the dressing ingredients in a small jar and shake well. Reserve for later use.
2. Combine the mayonnaise, mustard and horseradish in a small bowl. Using a pastry brush coat the chicken pieces on both sides with the mixture.
3. Spread the breadcrumbs on a large plate. Dredge the chicken in the crumbs and coat both sides.
4. Heat 2 tablespoons of the oil in a large frying pan over medium heat for 1-2 minutes, or until hot.
5. Place 2 of the coated chicken pieces into the hot oil and cook for 3 minutes per side or until well browned. Remove and keep warm.
6. Add the remaining oil, if needed, and cook the remaining pieces.
7. While the last two pieces of chicken are cooking, toss the greens with 4 tablespoons of the reserved dressing.
8. Divide the dressed greens equally on 4 dinner plates. Place a piece of chicken on top of each. Drizzle 1 tablespoon of the remaining dressing over each piece of chicken. Top with shaved or grated Parmesan cheese, if desired, and serve immediately.

Eliminate for dairy-free.

Desserts/Drinks

PHASE 4

Chocolate Banana Ice Cream

There are plenty of commercially available, non-dairy ice cream options on the market. But most have cane sugar and additives not allowed on this diet. We've come up with an alternative that tastes like real ice cream, and we know you will love it!

Prep time: 10 minutes
Freezing time: varies from machine to machine

Makes: about 1 quart

1 can (14 to 16.6 ounces) full fat coconut milk
1 large banana, cubed, divided
6 large pitted Medjool dates, soaked
½ teaspoon vanilla
5 tablespoons unsweetened cocoa powder
10-15 drops stevia (to taste)

1. Place the coconut milk, half of the bananas (reserve the other half for later use) and the remaining ingredients into a blender container.
2. Blend on High until smooth, about 1 minute.
3. Pour the mixture into the bowl of an electric ice cream maker. Stir in the reserved banana. Follow the instructions that came with the ice cream maker to freeze the ice cream.
4. Serve immediately. Store leftovers in the freezer.

Cook's Note: This recipe was developed using Medjool dates. If they are not available substitute another variety. The sweetness might vary, so taste the mixture before freezing and alter by adding more dates, as needed. The ice cream will be the consistency of soft serve when it comes out of the ice cream maker. If you prefer it to be harder, place it in the freezer for about a half hour before serving.

If you are storing leftover ice cream in your freezer, you might need to allow it to soften for a few minutes before serving. Some freezers are colder than others, so use your judgment.

Desserts/Drinks  PHASE 4

Chocolate Coconut Macaroons

You'll have a hard time believing that these spectacular treats are gluten-free, dairy-free, egg-free, vegan. They don't require any cooking, so they are a raw food delight. What more can you ask for?

Prep time: 10 minutes
Chill time: 30 minutes

Makes: 10 macaroons

- 2 tablespoons cocoa powder, unsweetened
- ¼ cup extra virgin coconut oil, softened
- 1 teaspoon pure vanilla extract
- 2 tablespoons maple syrup or coconut palm nectar
- Pinch of salt
- ¾ cup unsweetened shredded coconut
- ⅔ cup very finely chopped pecans, or nut of your choice

1. Combine the cocoa, coconut oil, vanilla, syrup and salt. Stir well to combine completely. The mixture will have the appearance of melted chocolate.
2. Add the coconut and stir with a spoon until it's well incorporated into the chocolate mixture.
3. Line a cookie sheet with parchment paper.
4. Scoop the mixture into balls using a small ice cream scoop or serving spoon.
5. Place the chopped nuts on a flat plate. Roll each ball in the nuts until well coated.
6. Place each macaroon on the parchment-lined tray and refrigerate.
7. Once chilled, about 30 minute, the treats are ready to eat.

Cook's Note: Coconut oil is a liquid at temperatures above 76°. For this recipe it's best if the oil is soft, but not liquid. If yours is not soft, put the jar in a pot of water and warm on the stove top for 5-10 minutes (do not allow water to boil). You want to be sure that the temperature of the oil does not go above 95°, in order for this recipe to comply with a raw foods diet.

Desserts/Drinks

PHASE 4

Rice Pudding

Rice pudding is the ultimate comfort dessert. This version uses leftover brown rice, which gives the pudding a nutty flavor and chewy texture.

Prep time: 10 minutes
Cook time: 30 minutes

Makes: 4 servings

- 1½ cups cooked brown rice
- 2 cups Almond Milk (page 260)
- ⅓ cup xylitol
- 2 tablespoons melted butter or Ghee (page 258)
- ⅓ cup raisins
- 1 teaspoon vanilla extract
- 1 teaspoon cinnamon

1. Combine the rice, almond milk, xylitol, butter or ghee and raisins in a medium-sized saucepan. Cook the mixture over medium-high heat for about 10 minutes, or until it starts to bubble.
2. Stir the pudding, lower the heat to medium and cook for 20 minutes, or until most of the liquid is absorbed.
3. Remove from the heat and stir in the vanilla and half of the cinnamon.
4. Spoon the pudding into serving dishes and dust with the remaining cinnamon.

Cook's Note: If you like runnier rice pudding, stir in a little more almond milk before serving.

Desserts/Drinks

PHASE 4

Black Bean Brownies

The words "black beans" and "brownie" don't seem to go together, do they? Make these "fudgy brownies," serve them to your family and friends and then tell them that they are made with beans. I bet you will get quite a surprised reaction from them all!

Prep time: 20 minutes
Cook time: 45-50 minutes

Makes: 9 brownies

- 8-9 ounces pitted Medjool dates, soaked
- 2 tablespoons Cinnamon Applesauce (page 96)
- 4 ounces unsweetened chocolate, melted
- 1 teaspoon vanilla
- ¼ teaspoon sea salt
- 1 (15.5 ounces) can black beans, rinsed and drained
- ½ cup chopped pecans, optional

1. Preheat the oven 350°F.
2. Place the dates in a small bowl and cover with water. Soak them while the oven is preheating and you are assembling the ingredients.
3. Drain the dates and place them in the bowl of a food processor. Add the applesauce, melted chocolate, vanilla and salt. Cover and pulse on and off 8 to 10 times, or until the dates are ground and the mixture is combined.
4. Add the beans and process for 1-2 minutes, or until completely smooth. Scrape down the sides of the bowl, once or twice if needed. The mixture will be very thick.
5. Grease the bottom of an 8-inch square baking pan. Spread the mixture evenly over the bottom of the pan using a wet rubber spatula. Top with pecans, if desired, and press them lightly into the batter.
6. Bake in the preheated oven for 45 to 55 minutes or until a toothpick inserted two inches from the center comes out clean.
7. Remove the pan from the oven and allow the brownies to cool completely in the pan before cutting. Store in a container in the refrigerator.

Cook's Note: The weight of canned beans includes the liquid, which is discarded in this case. If you use cooked beans, rather than canned, use 8 ounces of black beans.

The center of the cooked brownies will be soft. This is what gives the them their fudgy texture.

Pantry Contents

Ghee		258
Vegetable Broth		259
Almond Flour		260
Almond Milk		260
Coconut Milk		261
Brown Rice Milk		261
Almond Butter		262
Homemade Baking Powder		262
Cashew Honey Butter		263
Tahini		263
Chicken Bone Broth		264
Beef Broth		264
Gluten-Free Baking Mix		265
All-Purpose Gluten-Free Baking Mix		265
Spicy Rub		266
Millet Flour		266
Italian Breadcrumbs		267
Croutons		268

Homemade Baking Powder, page 262   Millet Flour, page 266   Spicy Rub, page 266

Italian Breadcrumbs, page 267   Ghee, page 258   Almond Butter, page 262

Pantry  PHASE 1

Ghee

Ghee is another name for clarified butter. Clarified butter is the clear yellow liquid that is left after the milk solids have been removed from butter.

Prep time: 5 minutes
Cook time: 45 minutes

Makes: about 1½ cups

1 pound unsalted organic butter

1. Preheat the oven to 250ºF.
2. Place the butter in an oven-proof dish[A].
3. Bake in the preheated oven for 45 minutes. Foam will form on the surface[B], and the milk solids will sink to the bottom of the dish.
4. Remove the pan from the oven and carefully skim off and discard the foam[C].
5. Ladle the clear liquid into a container[D]. Cover and refrigerate for future use.
6. Discard the milk solids[E].

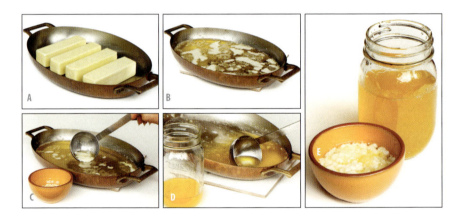

Safety Note: Although pure clarified butter/ghee does not need to be refrigerated, we recommend you store your ghee in the refrigerator because some milk solids may still be present, which can cause the ghee to become rancid. Use ghee in recipes as you would use regular butter (tablespoon for tablespoon).

Nutrition Note: During the clarification process, the milk proteins are removed, making the ghee virtually free of lactose. This makes it a relatively safe alternative for those who are lactose intolerant.

Pantry · PALEO · PHASE 1

Vegetable Broth

Use this broth as a base for vegetarian soups or in other recipes that call for broth, such as Lentil Soup (page 137). Vegetable broth can always be substituted for chicken or beef stock. Broth can also be substituted for wine in many recipes.

Prep time: 15 minutes
Cook time: 1 hour and 30 minutes

Makes: 1½ quarts

- 2 tablespoons extra virgin olive oil, divided
- 1 large onion, chopped
- 6 cloves garlic, chopped
- 2 leeks, well rinsed and chopped
- 4 carrots, peeled and chopped
- 4 stalks celery, chopped
- 4 ounces fresh baby spinach
- 3 ounces cremini mushrooms, cut in quarters
- 2 tablespoons chives, chopped
- 4 ounces green beans
- 12 sprigs parsley
- 2 sprigs thyme
- 2 teaspoons sea salt
- 1 teaspoon garlic powder
- 3 quarts filtered water

1. Heat the oil in a 6-quart saucepot or stockpot over medium heat for 1-2 minutes, or until hot.
2. Sauté the onion, garlic and leeks in the oil for 5 minutes.
3. Add the remaining ingredients, and bring the broth to a boil. Reduce the heat and simmer for 1 hour and 30 minutes.
4. Place a strainer or colander in a 5-quart pot or bowl. Pour the broth and vegetables into the strainer. Press the vegetables with the back of a large spoon, mashing them into purée. Scrape the purée from the sieve into the bowl of stock. This will thicken the broth and add flavor to the broth.

PHASE 3 Variation: Once you reach Phase 3, you may add 2 large, chopped tomatoes to the recipe for an even more complex flavor.

Pantry   PALEO   PHASE 1

Almond Flour

Making your own nut flours is easy and can save you money.

Prep time: 5 minutes

Makes: 1 cup

1 cup blanched almonds

1. Using a food processor or coffee grinder, process the nuts until they reach a flour-like consistency Be careful not to process the almonds too long, or you will end up with nut butter.
2. Refrigerate any unused portions, as it could become rancid if left out.

Cook's Note: If you use almonds with the skins still on, the result will be almond meal, which is similar, but won't give you the exact results as almond flour. You may substitute hazelnuts, pecans or walnuts to make alternate flours.

Almond Milk

Once you taste a few of the recipes that use almond or coconut milk in place of cow's milk, you will discover that you can easily live without dairy.

Prep time: 5 minutes
Soaking time: 8-12 hours
Cook time: 5 minutes

Makes: 3½ cups

7½ cups filtered water, divided
1½ cups almonds

1. Place the almonds in a blender container. Add 4 cups of water and soak overnight or for 8-12 hours.
2. Rinse nuts well, return to the blender container and cover with 3½ cups of fresh water. Put the cover on and blend for 2-3 minutes.
3. Line a colander or a sieve with cheesecloth. Pour the almond mixture into the cheesecloth to strain out the milk. Squeeze out all of the liquid from the pulp into the bowl.
4. Save pulp for another use or discard and store almond milk in the refrigerator for up to 5 days.

Pantry  PALEO   PHASE 1

Coconut Milk

Prep time: 5 minutes
Soaking time: 8 hours

Makes: 1½ cups

3½ cups filtered water, divided
1½ cups unsweetened shredded coconut

1. Place the coconut in a medium bowl. Add 2 cups of water and soak overnight (about 8 hours).
2. Drain the water and add the coconut to a blender container and cover with 1½ cups of water. Put the cover on and blend for 2-3 minutes.
3. Line a colander or a sieve with cheesecloth. Pour the coconut mixture into the cheesecloth to strain out the milk. Squeeze out all of the liquid from the pulp into the bowl.
4. Save pulp for another use or discard and store coconut milk in the refrigerator for up to 5 days.

Brown Rice Milk

Prep time: 5 minutes
Soaking time: overnight or 8 hours

Makes: 2 cups

½ cup brown rice
4 cups filtered water, divided

1. Place the rice in a medium bowl. Add 2 cups of water and soak overnight (about 8 hours).
2. Drain the water and add the rice to a blender container and cover with 2 cups of water. Put the cover on and blend for 2-3 minutes.
3. The rice will be pulverized and settle at the bottom of the blender container.
4. Line a colander or a sieve with cheesecloth. Pour the liquid into the cheesecloth to strain out the milk. Squeeze out all the of the liquid from the pulp into the bowl.
5. Discard the rice pulp.
6. Store the rice milk in a sealed container in the refrigerator for up to two days or freeze the excess.

Cook's Note: Fresh homemade milks have no preservatives but will last for about five days in a sealed container in the refrigerator, with the exception of the brown rice milk, which only stores well in the refrigerator for up to two days.

Phase variations: If you are using these dairy-free milks for a bowl of granola or to drink, try adding the following when you reach the appropriate Phase of the diet for some extra flavor: 3 pitted Medjool dates, 1 tablespoon maple syrup or 1 tablespoon raw honey, plus 1½ teaspoon vanilla extract.

Pantry | PALEO | PHASE 1

Almond Butter

Nothing could be easier to make than nut butter. All you need is a cup of nuts and a food processor or coffee grinder.*

Prep time: 5 minutes

Makes: ½ cup

1 cup roasted almonds
¼ teaspoon sea salt

1. Place the almonds and salt in the bowl of a food processor. Pulse 10 times, or until the nuts are chopped.
2. Process continually for 2 minutes.
3. Turn off the processor, scrape the sides, and continue to process until the mixture is the consistency of butter.
4. Refrigerate.

If you are using a coffee grinder, grind no more than ½ cup at a time.

Cook's Note: If the butter is not quite smooth enough for you, add 1 tablespoon of extra virgin olive oil or avocado oil to the mixture, and continue to process for a couple of minutes until the mixture is smoother.

Homemade Baking Powder

Most commercial baking powders contain cornstarch, which is not permitted in the first two Phases of this diet. Making your own baking powder enables you to make the recipes for baked goods found in Phase 2.

Prep time: 2 minutes

Makes: 1 teaspoon

¾ teaspoon cream of tartar
¼ teaspoon baking soda

1. Combine the ingredients.

Cook's Note: Use in recipes that call for baking powder. This recipe makes 1 teaspoon; if you need more, double the amounts.

Pantry  PALEO   PHASE 2

Cashew Honey Butter

Adding honey to the nuts in this recipe makes a sweet spread. Put it on bananas, apples or pears for an enjoyable and nutritious snack.

Prep time: 5 minutes

Makes: ½ cup

1 cup lightly salted cashews
½-1 tablespoon raw honey
1 tablespoon extra virgin olive oil

1. Place all the ingredients in the bowl of a food processor. Pulse 10 times, or until the nuts are chopped.
2. Process continually for 2 minutes.
3. Turn off the processor, scrape the sides, and continue to process until the mixture is the consistency of butter.
4. Refrigerate.

Cook's Note: Use this recipe as a template and substitute any permitted nut to make your favorite nut butter.

Tahini

Tahini is so expensive to buy, yet is so easy to make.

Prep time: 2 minutes
Cook time: 15 minutes
Cool time: 30 minutes

Makes: 2½ cups

1 pound sesame seeds
⅓-½ cup safflower oil

1. Preheat the oven to 350ºF.
2. Spread the sesame seeds in a thin layer on a cookie sheet. Cook 8-10 minutes shaking twice during the cooking. Do not allow seeds to brown. They should be a tan color.
3. Allow the toasted sesame seeds to cool completely (about 30 minutes).
4. Put the seeds into a blender or food processor. Add ¼ cup of oil and process or blend for 5 minutes or until smooth. Add the remaining oil as needed.
5. Store the cooled tahini in covered container in the refrigerator for up to three months.

recipes for Repair

Pantry   PHASE 3

Chicken Bone Broth

You may wonder why this recipe advises roasting the chicken and vegetables before adding them to the stockpot. Roasting intensifies the flavors, and more flavorful broth makes for more flavorful recipes.

Prep time: 15 minutes
Cook time: 4 hours
Cool time: 30 minutes

Makes: 4½ quarts

- **4 pounds chicken thighs**
- **4 stalks celery, cut into 3-inch pieces**
- **4 carrots, cut into quarters**
- **4 leeks, cleaned, and with green tops removed, cut into 1-inch pieces**
- **1 onion, cut into quarters**
- **1 head garlic, cut in half**
- **6 ripe plum tomatoes, cut in quarters**
- **1 teaspoon sea salt**
- **½ teaspoon freshly ground black pepper**
- **6 quarts filtered water**
- **4 sprigs thyme**
- **8 sprigs parsley**
- **4 sprigs oregano**

1. Preheat the oven to 350°F.
2. Place all the ingredients, except for the herbs and water, in a roasting pan. Roast in the preheated oven for 1½-2 hours.
3. Transfer the roasted chicken and vegetables to an 8-quart saucepot or stockpot. Add the water and herbs, and bring the broth to a boil over high heat. Reduce the heat to medium, and simmer for 2 hours.
4. Allow the broth to cool for about 30 minutes. Remove the chicken from the bones, and save for future use.
5. Place a strainer or colander in a 5-quart pot or bowl. Pour the broth and vegetables into the strainer. Press the vegetables with the back of a large spoon, mashing them into purée. Scrape the purée from the bottom of the sieve into the bowl of stock. This will thicken the broth and add flavor to the stock.
6. Refrigerate the stock, and/or freeze any unused portions in small containers for future use.

Bonus Recipe: Beef Broth – To make beef bone broth, substitute 4 pounds of beef bones for the chicken.

Nutrition Note: Ever wonder why so many moms give chicken soup to their sick children? Soups made from stocks not only facilitate the growth of cells in the gut lining, but can also aid in decreasing inflammation.

Pantry   PHASE 3

Gluten-Free Baking Mix

This versatile gluten-free baking mix is used in many of the baked goods recipes in this book. You can also use it in your own recipes as a one-for-one substitution for all-purpose white flour.

Prep time: 5 minutes

Makes: about 5¼ cups

1 cup brown rice flour
1 cup sorghum flour
¼ cup flaxseed meal
1 cup tapioca starch
1 cup potato starch (not flour)*
1 cup corn starch*
1 tablespoon xanthan gum
1 teaspoon sea salt

1. Combine all the ingredients in a large container or resealable container and shake or mix well to combine.
2. Keep refrigerated.

If you can't tolerate corn or potatoes substitute arrowroot starch for either, but not both.

Bonus Recipe: All-Purpose Gluten-Free Baking Mix: 2 cups brown rice flour, ⅔ cup potato starch (not flour), ⅓ cup tapioca starch, 1 teaspoon xanthan gum and ½ teaspoon sea salt. This is this recipe we use when we make the pie crust on page 209. If you run out of any of the flours for the above mix, try this less complex version in place of any recipe that calls for the baking mix above.

Cook's Note: If you plan to do a lot of gluten-free baking, you may double or triple this recipe and keep the extra in a container in the freezer. Label the container to keep track of how long the mix is being stored. This mix can also be used as a one-for-one substitution for all-purpose white flour in recipes (not in this book) that you want to convert to gluten-free. Read page 34 for information on gluten-free grains and substitutions and page 167 for Gluten-Free Baking Tips.

Spicy Rub

Rubs can be used on chicken and fish, as well as on steaks and chops. This spicy version will add zip to any grilled, roasted or broiled meat.

Prep time: 5 minutes

Makes: ½ cup

¼ cup paprika

2 tablespoons chili powder

2 teaspoons each dry mustard, ground cumin, coarse sea salt and xylitol*

½ teaspoon each dried oregano and dried thyme

½ teaspoon freshly ground black pepper

1. Combine all the ingredients in a small jar or covered container.

* You may substitute coconut palm sugar for the xylitol.

This rub will keep for 3 months when stored in a covered jar or container in your pantry. The recipe can be halved or doubled.

Millet Flour

Millet is used in this recipe, but you could just as easily grind amaranth, oat groats or any other grain by following the same instructions. Just substitute the grain of your choice, and follow these very easy directions.

Prep time: 5 minutes

Makes: ½ cup

½ cup millet

1. Place the millet* in an electric coffee grinder. Grind continuously until all the grain is reduced to a fine flour.
2. Refrigerate any leftover flour in an airtight container.

* Depending on which grain is ground, this recipe may be appropriate for Phase 2, 3 and/or 4, so be sure to consult the allowable foods in the beginning of each Phase.

Cook's Note: If your recipe calls for a larger amount of flour, grind more in ½ cup portions; do not put more than ½ cup of grain in the coffee grinder at a time.

Pantry

Italian Breadcrumbs

Use leftover Classic Sandwich Bread (page 241) or Gluten-Free Italian Loaf (page 239) to make these delicious breadcrumbs. Store them in an airtight container, and use in any recipe that calls for breadcrumbs.

Prep time: 10 minutes
Cook time: 45 minutes

Makes: ¾ cup

- 6 ounces gluten-free bread, cut into 1-inch cubes
- 1 teaspoon each garlic powder, onion powder and Italian seasonings
- ½ teaspoon sea salt
- ¼ teaspoon freshly ground black pepper
- 1 tablespoon grated Parmesan cheese* (optional)

Eliminate for dairy-free.

1. Preheat the oven to 250°F.
2. Place the bread cubes in the bowl of a food processor. Pulse until the bread is reduced to fine crumbs.
3. Spread the crumbs in a thin layer on a sheet pan. Bake for 45 minutes, or until the crumbs are dry.
4. Return the crumbs to the food processor and process until they are evenly, finely ground.
5. Remove to a bowl and combine with the remaining ingredients.
6. Cool completely before using or storing.

Cook's Note: This recipe can be doubled or tripled if you have a large amount of leftover bread to use up. The breadcrumbs will keep for over a month if stored in an airtight container.

Pantry

PHASE 4

Croutons

Leftover Classic Sandwich Bread (page 241) or Gluten-Free Italian Loaf (page 239) can be used to make these croutons. Allow them to cool, and then store them in an airtight container.

Prep time: 5 minutes
Cook time: 35 minutes

Makes: about 3 cups

- ½ teaspoon each, onion and garlic powder
- ½ teaspoon Herbes de Provence
- 8 ounces allowable bread, cut into ¾-inch cubes
- 3 tablespoons extra virgin olive oil
- 1 tablespoon grated Parmesan cheese

1. Preheat the oven to 350ºF.
2. Combine the onion powder, garlic powder and Herbes de Provence in a medium bowl.
3. Toss the bread cubes in the herbs and cheese until coated.
4. Add the oil to the bowl and toss until the bread cubes are coated. Toss in the herbs and cheese again, if needed.
5. Place the bread cubes on a small baking sheet and bake in the preheated oven for 35 minutes. Carefully turn them midway through cooking to ensure even baking.
6. Cool completely before serving or storing.

Cook's Note: Croutons make a great addition to any salad and can also be added to soup.

Sauces & Condiments Contents

Homemade Mayonnaise 270
Herb Mayonnaise 270
Curried Mayonnaise 270
Pesto Mayonnaise 270
Mustard Mayonnaise Dressing 270
Garlic-Shallot Mayonnaise (Aioli) 271
Sun-Dried Tomato Aioli 271
Zabaglione Sauce 272
Béarnaise Sauce 273
Berry Pear Sauce 274
Cran-Raspberry Sauce 275
Mango Dressing 276
Blueberry Syrup 277
Tzatziki Sauce 278
Peachy Barbecue Sauce 279
Easy Oven-Roasted Marinara Sauce 280
Garden Fresh Tomato Sauce 281
Miso Barbecue Sauce 282
Mustard Ranch Dressing 283
Orange Herb Dressing 284
Peach and Pineapple Dipping Sauce 285
Peach and Blackberry Chutney 286
Easy Spicy Ketchup 287
Fruity Glaze 288
Horseradish Mustard Sauce 289
Tartar Sauce 289
Thousand Island dressing 289

Sauces and Condiments PALEO PHASE 1

Homemade Mayonnaise

Basic mayonnaise can be turned into a flavorful spread with the addition of some simple ingredients. As indicated, most of the Variations are permitted in Phase 1.

Prep time: 15 minutes

Makes: about 1 cup

1 egg and 1 egg yolk, room temperature

½ teaspoon sea salt

1½ tablespoons raw apple cider vinegar

¾ cup extra virgin olive oil or virgin olive oil
(see Cook's Note on page 271)

1. Place the eggs, salt and vinegar in a blender container. Cover, and blend on High for 30 seconds.
2. With the blender running, remove the center of the lid. Very slowly (this should take about 1½-2 minutes), drizzle the oil in a steady stream into the opening until the sauce forms an emulsion and thickens.
3. Remove the mayonnaise from the blender. Keep refrigerated.

PHASE 1 Variations:

Herb Mayonnaise: Stir 1-2 tablespoons of your favorite freshly chopped herbs, such as basil, oregano, rosemary, dill, chives or any combination, into the Homemade Mayonnaise.

Curried Mayonnaise: Stir ½-1 teaspoon of curry powder into the Homemade Mayonnaise.

Pesto Mayonnaise: Stir 1-2 tablespoons of Mixed Herb Pesto (page 153) into the Homemade Mayonnaise.

PHASE 2 Variation:

Mustard Mayonnaise Dressing: Stir 1 tablespoon of mustard into the Homemade Mayonnaise.

Cook's Note: Mayonnaise can be made in a food processor, but it will be thinner than commercial mayonnaise. However, it will thicken somewhat when refrigerated.

 Egg-Free Suggestion: There has been a recent discovery that the brine from beans, called aquafaba, is a promising egg substitute. We have yet to try it, but there are egg-free mayonnaise recipes online with this substitute. If you can not tolerate eggs do an internet search for "aquafaba mayonnaise recipe" and try it for yourself!

Sauces and Condiments PALEO   PHASE 1

Garlic-Shallot Mayonnaise (Aioli)

Prep time: 20 minutes

Makes: about 1 cup

- 1 egg and 1 egg yolk, room temperature
- 1 small clove garlic
- ½ small shallot, cut in half
- ½ teaspoon sea salt
- ½ teaspoon raw honey
- 1½ tablespoons raw apple cider vinegar
- ¾ cup extra virgin olive oil or virgin olive oil

1. Place all the ingredients, except for the oil, in a blender container. Cover, and blend on High for 30 seconds.
2. With the blender running, remove the center of the lid. Very slowly (this should take about 2 minutes), drizzle the oil in a steady stream into the opening until the sauce forms an emulsion and thickens.
3. Remove the mayonnaise from the blender. Keep refrigerated.

PHASE 3 Variation: To make Sun-Dried Tomato Aioli, add 2 tablespoons of sun-dried tomatoes to the blender with the shallots and garlic, and proceed as directed above.

Cook's Note: Extra virgin olive oil has a strong flavor. When you reach Phase 3, experiment with some of the more neutral-flavored oils, such as sunflower seed oil or safflower oil. All oils are a one-to-one substitution. If using these oils, be sure to check their labels for "expeller pressed," which ensures that no chemicals were used in pressing the seeds to make the oil.

Sauces and Condiments PHASE 1

Zabaglione Sauce

If company is coming and you have no idea what to serve for dessert, make this easy sauce and serve it over berries or any seasonal fruit. You can even make it in advance to save time.

Prep time: 5 minutes
Cook time: 10 minutes

Makes: about ¾ cup

4 egg yolks
1 tablespoon xylitol* or raw honey
2 tablespoons Almond Milk (page 260)
½ teaspoon vanilla extract

* Not suitable for Paleo.

1. Whisk all the ingredients in the top section of a double boiler (see Cook's Note).
2. Fill the bottom section of the boiler with about 1 inch of hot water. Heat for about 5 minutes or until it simmers, over medium heat. Do not allow the water to boil.
3. Place the top section of the boiler over the simmering water. Be careful not to let the water in the bottom section touch the top section in which the sauce is being cooked. If the water touches the top section, the egg will curdle or scramble.
4. Cook, whisking constantly, for about 3 minutes, or until the sauce thickens to a pudding-like consistency. Remove the top section of the double boiler from the heat and remove the sauce to a bowl to cool.

PHASE 3 Variation: Once you reach Phase 3, you may add some lemon juice and lemon zest to the recipe.

Cook's Note: If you do not have a double boiler, use a saucepan and a bowl that fits over the pan without touching the contents.

Warning: If you see small lumps forming while you whisk the sauce, remove the top section from the heat immediately and whisk the sauce vigorously. Lumps can form if the water is too hot, or if it touches the bottom of the top section. You will be able to save your sauce if you catch it in time and whisk constantly until it is smooth. Remove the finished sauce from the top section as soon as you finish whisking, as the heat stays in the metal and can cause the sauce to curdle.

Sauces and Condiments PALEO   PHASE 1

Béarnaise Sauce

See the recipe for Poached Eggs Florentine with Béarnaise Sauce on page 79.

Prep time: 10 minutes

Makes: about ¾ cup

- 2 egg yolks
- ¾ teaspoon chopped tarragon or lemon thyme
- 1/8 teaspoon sea salt
- ½ tablespoon raw apple cider vinegar
- ⅓ cup Ghee (page 258)

1. Place all the ingredients, except for the ghee, in a blender container and blend on High for 30 seconds.
2. With the blender running, slowly drizzle the ghee into the container until it forms an emulsion.
3. Remove the sauce from the container and use immediately, or refrigerate until ready to use.

Cook's Note: Béarnaise sauce, like mayonnaise, can be made in a food processor rather than a blender, but it will be thinner than Béarnaise sauce made from commercial mayonnaise. However, it will thicken somewhat when refrigerated.

Sauces and Condiments

PHASE 2

Berry Pear Sauce

This sauce is very versatile. Use it to top pancakes or crepes, or serve it alongside roast chicken.

Prep time: 10 minutes
Cook time: 10 minutes

Makes: 4 servings

- 1 ripe pear, peeled and cut into thin slices
- ½ cup raspberries
- ½ cup blackberries
- ⅓ cup filtered water
- 2 teaspoons xylitol* or coconut palm sugar

* Not suitable for Paleo.

1. Combine all the ingredients in a small saucepan. Cook over medium heat for 5 minutes.
2. Remove the fruit to a serving bowl. Raise the heat, and bring the syrup to a boil. Cook for 5 minutes, or until the liquid is the consistency of maple syrup.
3. Serve over Oat Crepes (page 128).

PHASE 3 Variation: Once you reach Phase 3, you may substitute peaches for the pears and/or strawberries for the raspberries.

Cook's Note: You can substitute apples for pears. If fresh berries are not available, substitute frozen.

Sauces and Condiments   PALEO

Cran-Raspberry Sauce

Make plenty of this tasty sauce when you reach Phase 2 you will find it in several recipes in Phase 2 and 3. In addition to the recipes that call for it, this sauce will also be a great accompaniment to poultry dishes.

Prep time: 5 minutes
Cook time: 30 minutes

Makes: about 3½ cups

- 1 cup filtered water
- 1 bag (12 ounces) fresh or frozen cranberries
- 1 cup frozen raspberries
- ½-¾ cup xylitol* or coconut palm sugar
- 10-12 drops liquid stevia* (optional)

Not suitable for Paleo.

1. Place all the ingredients in a 3-quart saucepan. Cook over medium- high heat until the liquid begins to boil.
2. Cover. Lower the heat to medium-low and simmer for 10-15 minutes.
3. Stir with a wooden spoon, once or twice during the last 5 minutes. Pressing the berries against the side of the pan to crush.
4. Remove the pan from the cook-top and cool before refrigerating. Store in a jar or a covered container.

Cook's Note: Cranberries are seasonal, but they freeze very well, so buy a few bags to freeze and use year-round. Leave them in their original, unopened bags, and place each bag in a freezer zip-top bag for extra protection against freezer burn.

Sauces and Condiments — VG | PALEO — PHASE 2

Mango Dressing

This salad dressing is perfect over salad topped with broiled, blackened or grilled fish, such as Cran-Raspberry Glazed Salmon (page 149). It can also dress any mixed fruit salad.

Prep time: 5 minutes

Makes: 1 cup

- 1 ripe mango, peeled and diced
- 2 tablespoons raw apple cider vinegar
- 1 tablespoon raw honey
- 2 teaspoons maple syrup
- 1 tablespoon pineapple juice
- ¼ teaspoon sea salt
- ⅛ teaspoon freshly ground black pepper
- ⅛ teaspoon each onion and garlic powder
- ¼ cup extra virgin olive oil

1. Place all the ingredients, except for the oil, in the bowl of a food processor. Cover the processor, and process until the mango is completely liquefied.
2. Pour the oil down the feed tube and process for 30 seconds.
3. Refrigerate.

PHASE 3 variation: Once you reach Phase 3, you may add ½ lemon, juiced and zested. Place the lemon in the food processor along with the other ingredients in Step 1. You may also substitute orange juice for the pineapple juice once you reach Phase 3.

Cook's Note: When you zest a lemon, be careful not to include any of the white layer (pith) on the underside of the lemon's skin, as it is very bitter. A lemon's zest has more flavor than its juice because all the essential oils are in the skin.

Sauces and Condiments   PALEO   PHASE 2

Blueberry Syrup

Most commercial syrups are made with corn syrup and other additives, but this syrup is mostly blueberries. The result is a syrup so pure, it tastes like eating liquid blueberries. Pour it over pancakes, waffles or even ice cream.

Prep time: 10 minutes
Cook time: 20 minutes
Cool time: 30 minutes

Makes: about ½ cup

1 pint fresh blueberries, rinsed and with stems removed
½ cup filtered water
⅓ to ½ cup xylitol* or coconut palm sugar
1 teaspoon raw apple cider vinegar
½ teaspoon vanilla

Not suitable for Paleo.

1. Place all the ingredients, except for the vanilla, in a blender container. Blend on High until liquefied.
2. Pour the mixture into a 3-quart or larger saucepot. (If you use a smaller pot, the syrup might boil over while it is cooking.)
3. Heat the mixture over high heat for about 1 minute, or until it comes to a boil. Lower the heat to medium and simmer for 10 minutes. The mixture will begin to bubble and form a layer of foam during the last 10 minutes of cooking.
4. Skim all the foam off the surface and discard. You will be left with clear syrup.
5. Remove the syrup from the heat and stir in the vanilla.
6. Allow the syrup to cool for about 30 minutes before using or storing. Store any unused portions in a glass jar or container, and refrigerate for up to 3 weeks.

Cook's Note: This recipe can be doubled, but be sure to use a 5- to 6-quart saucepot to avoid boil over.

To make Raspberry Syrup, substitute raspberries for blueberries and reduce the water to ¼ cup. Continue as directed above. When using raspberries, you must strain the cooked syrup through a sieve to remove the seeds. If the syrup seems too thin after removing the seeds, return it to the saucepot, bring it to a boil over high heat and cook for 2 minutes, or until it thickens slightly. The syrup will thicken a bit more as it cools.

Sauces and Condiments

Tzatziki Sauce

This yogurt cucumber sauce is a perfect side dish, salad dressing, or topping for Greek Ground Lamb Crumble (page 218) with Soft Flour Tortillas (page 177).

Prep time: 20 minutes
Stand time: 1 hour and 30 minutes

Makes: about 1½ cup

- **2 cups peeled, seeded and finely chopped cucumbers (1 large or 2 medium cucumbers)**
- **½ teaspoon sea salt**
- **¼ teaspoon freshly ground black pepper**
- **½ teaspoon extra virgin olive oil**
- **½ teaspoon raw apple cider vinegar**
- **½ small garlic clove, crushed**
- **1 teaspoon dried onion flakes or ½ teaspoon onion powder**
- **1 teaspoon freshly chopped mint (optional)**
- **1 (6 ounce) container plain Greek yogurt**

1. Place the cucumbers in a bowl, sprinkle them with the salt and toss well to coat.
2. Place the salted cucumbers in a strainer positioned over a bowl. Allow the cucumbers to stand for about 30 minutes. Rinse and drain.
3. Place the cucumbers between some paper towels, or in a clean dish towel, and squeeze out any remaining liquid.
4. Combine the remaining ingredients and stir well.
5. Add the cucumbers to the mixture, and allow to stand in the refrigerator for at least 1 hour before using.

Cook's Note: If you can make the tzatziki the night before, or even several hours before you plan to serve it, the flavors will have time to blend together.

Sauces and Condiments   PALEO   PHASE 3

Peachy Barbecue Sauce

Sweet peaches, spicy ketchup and a kick of chili powder make this barbecue sauce great for broiled meats, or as a burger topping. Try mixing it with some Herb Mayonnaise (page 270) for a sandwich spread.

Prep time: 15 minutes
Cook time: 17 minutes

Makes: about 1½ cups

- 4 ripe peaches, peeled and cubed
- 1 cup Easy Spicy Ketchup (page 287)
- 1 tablespoon raw apple cider vinegar
- 1 teaspoon lemon juice
- 1 tablespoon orange juice
- 1 teaspoon mustard
- 1 teapoon onion powder
- ½ teaspoon paprika
- ½ teaspoon sea salt
- ½-1 teaspoon chili powder
- ¼ teaspoon freshly ground black pepper
- 1-2 tablespoons raw honey

1. Combine all the ingredients, except for the honey, in a food processor, and process until smooth.
2. Pour the mixture into a saucepot. Cover the pot, and cook over high heat for about 2 minutes, or until the sauce just boils. Lower the heat to medium, and cook for about 15 minutes, or until the sauce thickens.
3. Allow the sauce to cool to 115°F before stirring in the honey.
4. Refrigerate any leftover sauce for future use.

Cook's Note: If you like your sauces spicy hot, add a full tablespoon of chili powder (or ½ teaspoon cayenne pepper). You can also intensify the heat after cooking by adding extra chili powder and simmering for 15 more minutes.

Sauces and Condiments

Easy Oven-Roasted Marinara Sauce

Cooking marinara sauce in the oven might sound strange, but it works, and it saves you the trouble of sautéing onions and garlic (not to mention cleaning up a messy stove-top).

Prep time: 10 minutes
Cook time: 45 minutes

Makes: about 2 cups

- 1 can (28 ounces) whole tomatoes, chopped, or 2 pounds vine-ripened tomatoes, chopped
- 2 tablespoons extra virgin olive oil
- 2 tablespoons tomato paste
- 1 tablespoon Mixed Herb Pesto (page 153) *
- 1 teaspoon each of dried oregano, onion powder and garlic powder
- ½ teaspoon sea salt
- ¼ teaspoon freshly ground black pepper
- 1-2 teaspoons honey
- 2 teaspoons balsamic vinegar

1. Preheat the oven to 425ºF.
2. Place the chopped tomatoes on a baking sheet. Add all the remaining ingredients and stir well to combine. Spread the mixture out into a thin layer.
3. Put the baking sheet in the preheated oven and roast for 30-45 minutes, or until the tomatoes begin to caramelize and most of the liquid has cooked off.
4. The sauce will be very thick and chunky. If thinner, smoother sauce is desired, add ¼-½ cup water and purée the mixture in a food processor.
5. Serve the sauce immediately over pasta (add a little pasta water to thin, if desired) or refrigerate it for future use.

* If you don't have the pesto prepared, substitute 1 tablespoon chopped basil and 2 tablespoons chopped parsley and stir into the tomato sauce during the last 10 minutes of cooking.

Sauces and Condiments

PHASE 3

Garden Fresh Tomato Sauce

Tomatoes fresh from the garden or farm stand can't be beat. This recipe makes a large batch of sauce, so one session in the kitchen will give you enough for several meals. The sauce also freezes very well.

Prep time: 20 minutes
Cook time: 1-2 hours

Makes: about 3 quarts

- 1 large or 2 medium onions, quartered
- 6 cloves garlic, peeled
- 2 tablespoons extra virgin olive oil
- 6 pounds fresh ripe tomatoes
- 2 tablespoons freshly chopped parsley
- 2 tablespoons freshly chopped basil
- 2 teaspoons dried oregano
- 1 teaspoon sea salt
- ½ teaspoon freshly ground black pepper
- 1-2 tablespoons raw honey

1. Place the onions and garlic in a food processor and pulse about 8 times, or until the onion is finely chopped.
2. Heat the oil in a 5-quart saucepot over medium heat for 1-2 minutes, or until hot.
3. Sauté the onions for 5 minutes, or until they start to brown.
4. While the onions cook, process the tomatoes in batches in a food processor, pulsing about 10 times for each batch, or until the tomatoes are puréed.
5. Pour the puréed tomatoes into the saucepot.
6. Add all the remaining ingredients, except for the honey. Bring the mixture to a boil over medium-high heat. Reduce the heat to medium and simmer for 1-2 hours.
7. Remove from the heat and allow the sauce to cool before stirring in the honey.
8. Store the sauce in the refrigerator until ready to use, or freeze it in serving-sized containers for future use.

Nutrition Note: Tomatoes are rich in the powerful antioxidant, Lycopene. Cooking them releases the Lycopene from the plant's cells and increases the body's ability to absorb it.

Sauces and Condiments

PHASE 3

Miso Barbecue Sauce

Miso is a fermented soy product that can be used in soups and sauces. This sauce has a distinctly Asian flavor and can be used as a marinade or barbecue sauce.

Prep time: 15 minutes

Makes: ¾ cup

- 2 tablespoons miso
- ¼ cup filtered water
- 1 1-inch piece ginger, cut into quarters
- 1 clove garlic, cut in half
- 3 scallions, white part only, cut into 3 pieces each
- ¼ teaspoon pepper
- 1 tablespoon raw apple cider vinegar
- 1 teaspoon sesame oil
- 2 tablespoons Easy Spicy Ketchup (page 287)
- 2 tablespoons raw honey
- 1 tablespoon safflower oil
- 1 tablespoon tamari

1. Place all the ingredients in a blender container. Cover, and blend on High until smooth.
2. Use as a marinade for chicken, turkey or fish.

Cook's Note: Never reuse a marinade, or pour it over cooked food. If you want to baste your cooked dish with the marinade, marinate your dish in ½ cup of the marinade and reserve the rest for basting, or for serving as a sauce with the meal. Also, if you do serve marinade as a sauce with the meal, heat it to boiling before serving.

Sauces and Condiments   PHASE 3

Mustard Ranch Dressing

Use this dressing for salad, as a dip for fresh cut vegetables or spread it on chicken or fish before broiling or baking.

Prep time: 5 minutes

Makes: ½ cup

½ cup Herb Mayonnaise (page 270)
2 tablespoons cows' milk kefir
½ teaspoon mustard
¼ teaspoon garlic powder
¼ teaspoon sea salt
¼ teaspoon freshly ground black pepper

1. Combine all the ingredients in a small bowl.
2. Refrigerate any leftover portion.

Cook's Note: This recipe can be doubled. The dressing can be refrigerated for up to 3 weeks.

Sauces and Condiments  PALEO PHASE 3

Orange Herb Dressing

Orange is a delightful flavor variation on a classic vinaigrette dressing. Toss with your favorite greens and top with dried fruits, such as chopped figs, dates or cranberries, and nuts.

Prep time: 10 minutes

Makes: about ½ cup

- 2 tablespoons raw apple cider vinegar
- 1 tablespoon raw honey
- ¼ cup orange juice
- 1 small clove garlic, crushed
- 1½ teaspoons mustard
- ½ teaspoon Herbes de Provence
- ¼ teaspoon sea salt
- ⅛ teaspoon pepper
- ⅓ cup extra virgin olive oil

1. Combine all the ingredients in a jar or container with a lid. Cover, and shake for 30 seconds, or until the oil thoroughly combines with the other ingredients.
2. Serve over your favorite salads, or use as a marinade for chicken or fish.

Cook's Note: For a change of pace, marinate chicken or firm flesh fish in this dressing for up to 30 minutes before broiling.

Sauces and Condiments

PHASE 3

Peach and Pineapple Dipping Sauce

Once you reach Phase 3, serve this sauce with Coconut Chicken Tenders (page 150), or with any other poultry dish.

Prep time: 10 minutes
Cook time: 30 minutes

Makes: about 1½ cups

- 2 large peaches, peeled and chopped (about 2 cups)
- 1 cup fresh, chopped pineapple
- ⅓ cup orange juice or orange mango juice
- ¼ teaspoon garlic powder
- ⅛ teaspoon sea salt
- 1 tablespoon raw honey

1. Place all the ingredients, except for the honey, in a small saucepan. Cook over high heat for about 5 minutes, or until the mixture comes to a boil. Cover the pan, and lower the heat to medium. Cook for about 15 minutes, or until the fruit breaks down and the mixture thickens.
2. Break up the fruit with a large spoon and continue to cook, stirring occasionally, for about 15 minutes or until the fruit begins to brown.
3. Pour the mixture into the bowl of a food processor and pulse several times, until the sauce is smooth.
4. Allow the sauce to cool to 115°F before adding the honey.
5. Serve warm or cold. Refrigerate any remaining sauce for future use.

Cook's Note: When peaches are not in season, use sliced frozen peaches with no added sugar. Peaches frozen at the height of the season are flavorful, and make a very good substitute for fresh peaches. Fresh pineapples are generally available year-round, but if they are too pricey in the colder months, substitute canned, crushed pineapple with no added sugar.

Peach and Blackberry Chutney

Dress up broiled meats and poultry with this chutney made from summer fruits. It tastes sweet, tart and spicy – three flavors all rolled into one.

Prep time: 15 minutes
Cook time: 28 minutes

Makes: about 1½ cups

- 1 tablespoon extra virgin olive oil
- 3 scallions, white part only, chopped
- 1 clove garlic, crushed
- 1 teaspoon freshly chopped ginger
- 3 ripe peaches, peeled and chopped
- 1 cup blackberries
- ⅓ cup raisins
- ¼ cup orange juice
- ½ teaspoon sea salt
- ¼ teaspoon freshly ground black pepper
- 1 tablespoon raw honey

1. Heat the oil in a small saucepan over medium heat for 1-2 minutes, or until hot.
2. Sauté the scallions for about 2 minutes, or until they are limp.
3. Add the garlic and ginger, and sauté for 1 minute.
4. Add all the remaining ingredients, except for the honey, and bring the mixture to a boil. Cover the pan, lower the heat, and simmer for 20 minutes.
5. Allow the chutney to cool to 115°F before adding the honey.
6. Refrigerate and serve cold.

Cook's Note: Chutney can be made with dried fruits when fresh are not in season. Substitute dried apricots for the peaches and fresh or dried apples for the blackberries.

Sauces and Condiments  PALEO

Easy Spicy Ketchup

Tomatoes are part of the nightshade family of vegetables, so introduce them into your diet slowly, because they can cause inflammation (page 165 for more information). If you have no problem with tomatoes, try this ketchup, which is easy to make and has no preservatives or additives.

Prep time: 5 minutes, plus 20 minutes soaking time

Makes: 4 cups

- 12 pitted Medjool dates
- 1⅓ cups filtered water
- ¾ cup apple cider vinegar
- 3 jars or cans (6 ounces each) tomato paste
- 8-10 drops liquid stevia*
- 1-2 teaspoons chili powder
- 1¼ teaspoons sea salt
- 1½ teaspoons onion powder
- 1½ teaspoons garlic powder
- 1½ teaspoons paprika
- 1 teaspoon celery salt
- ¼-½ teaspoon ground cumin
- ¼ teaspoon freshly ground black pepper (optional)
- ¼ teaspoon cayenne pepper (optional)

Omit for Paleo and increase the quantity of dates from 12 to 14

1. Place the dates in a blender container and add the water and vinegar and soak the dates until soft, about 20 minutes.
2. Add the remaining ingredients.
3. Cover and blend on high until the dates are ground up and the ingredients are well blended. The mixture will be very thick so it may be necessary to scrape the sides of the blender container with a rubber spatula once or twice during the blending process.
4. Place the ketchup in a jar and refrigerate.

Cook's Note: Prepare this recipe at the beginning of Phase 3, as there are several recipes that call for it, and if you have some already made, it will save you time. If you prefer milder ketchup, eliminate the cayenne pepper and use half the amount of black pepper specified.

Sauces and Condiments   PALEO PHASE 3

Fruity Glaze

This sweet, tart glaze livens up any chicken dish. Try painting some on broiled or baked chicken about 10 minutes before the chicken is done cooking.

Prep time: 10 minutes
Cook time: 7 minutes

Makes: about ½ cup

- ½ cup Raspberry Syrup (page 277) or Cran-Raspberry Sauce (page 275)
- 2 teaspoons mustard
- 1½ tablespoons tamari*
- 2 tablespoons orange juice or pineapple juice
- ½ teaspoon garlic powder
- 1 teaspoon onion powder
- ¼ teaspoon sea salt
- ¼ teaspoon freshly ground black pepper

Substitute coconut aminos (page 38) for tamari for Paleo.

1. Combine all the ingredients in a small saucepan. Cook over high heat for about 2 minutes, or until the sauce comes to a boil. Lower the heat to medium and simmer for 5 minutes, or until the sauce thickens.

2. Paint the glaze on broiled, baked or grilled chicken during the last 5 minutes of cooking.

Cook's Note: Cooking with fruit adds nutrition, flavor and variety to your dishes. Use this basic glaze as is, or replace the raspberry syrup with puréed peaches or cooked, puréed cherries.

Sauces and Condiments   PHASE 4

Horseradish Mustard Sauce

Use this sauce on sandwiches, or with broiled beef.

Prep time: 15 minutes

Makes: 1 cup

½ cup freshly grated or bottled horseradish root
2 tablespoons stone ground mustard
1 teaspoon onion powder
1 teaspoon garlic powder
½ teaspoon sea salt
½ cup Homemade Mayonnaise (page 270)
¼ teaspoon freshly ground black pepper
1½ teaspoons raw apple cider vinegar
1 teaspoon raw honey

1. Combine all the ingredients in a bowl.
2. Refrigerate for several hours before using.
3. Refrigerate any leftover sauce.

Cook's Note: Either buy pre-ground horseradish in a jar, or grind it yourself. To grind it in a food processor, cut the root into small pieces to make the processing easier. The fumes are very strong, so be careful not to inhale as you remove the cover from the processor. Leftover ground horseradish freezes very well.

Tartar Sauce

If you have leftover fish, why not make a sandwich topped with lettuce, a slice of tomato and a dollop of tartar sauce?

Prep time: 5 minutes

Makes: about 1 cup

1 recipe's worth Homemade Mayonnaise (page 270)
3 tablespoons chopped pickles
½ teaspoon mustard

1. Combine all the ingredients and stir well.
2. Refrigerate.

> **PHASE 4 variation:** You can add a tablespoon or two of Easy Spicy Ketchup (page 287) to make Thousand Island dressing.

Recipes for Repair

Resources

Healthy Eating

Below we have listed some of our favorite websites, stores and books that will help you locate and/or learn about some of the foods we discuss in the book. For an up-to-date list go to the resources section on our website, www.recipesforrepair.com, as we are always adding to it as we find new ones.

Online Vendors for Purchasing High Quality Foods

Amazon sells a lot more than just books. Many organic food and grocery products can be found here. Just do a search and see if one of their independent sellers has what you are looking for.
www.amazon.com

Apitherapy raw honey is unheated and unfiltered and can be bought in bulk.
www.honeygardens.com

Blue Mountain Organics is a premier provider of certified organic raw and sprouted nuts, nut butters, flours, grains, dried fruits, and superfoods and have wonderful prices.
www.bluemountainorganics.com

Bob's Red Mill Natural Foods produces more than 400 products, including a full line of certified gluten-free products and an extensive line of certified organic products. Products can be found in grocery and natural foods stores, closeout stores or online.
www.bobsredmill.com

ButcherBox delivers 100% grass-fed beef, organic chicken, and heritage pork directly to your home. While they are a monthly membership service, you can adjust your frequency. Sign up using promo code **recipes** and they will give you $10 off your first box.
www.getbutcherbox.com

Culture's for Health is your one-stop online storefront for all products needed for fermentation, as well as a great resource to learn more about cultured foods. Sign up for their mailing list and receive 10% off your first order.
www.culturesforhealth.com

Donna Gate's, proprietor of Body Ecology, sells cow and goat milk, coconut water culture starter kits and many other wonderful products. Already fermented coconut water (coconut kefir) can be bought on this site, as well the sweeteners Lakanto and stevia.
www.bodyecology.com

Eden Foods makes a variety of mustards using raw apple cider vinegar. They also have a large line of wonderful organic foods that can be found in many natural food stores.
www.edenfoods.com

Lucky Vitamin offers wholesale prices on vitamins and supplements, and also on a large selection of organic food and grocery items, such as herbs, honey, xylitol, nut butters, beans and much more. They often have additional sales so be sure to sign up for their mailing list.
www.luckyvitamin.com

Mountain Rose Herbs has a wide variety of bulk organic foods, including herbs, spices, extracts, teas and more. Check out the monthly specials tab for extra savings.
www.mountainroseherbs.com

Thrive Market is an online store that sells natural and organic products at wholesale prices. They charge an annual membership, but their savings are so great that you make that back in savings very quickly. The site is easy to navigate and has so many wonderful products.
www.thrivemarket.com

Vitacost.com offers wholesale prices on vitamins and supplements, and also on a large selection of organic food and grocery items, such as herbs, honey, xylitol and much more. Some of the

best prices can be found on this site.
www.vitacost.com

Vital Choice is a good resource for wild Alaskan seafood and organic fare. Food is packed in dry ice before shipping, to keep it frozen and fresh during delivery.
www.vitalchoice.com

Vitamin Shoppe is a storefront, but can also be shopped online. They run a lot of great promotions on organic foods and have very good prices all around.
www.vitaminshoppe.com

Online Resources for Locating High-Quality Food

Local Harvest and Food Routes are two nation-wide organizations that provide directories to assist in finding local community supported agricultures (CSAs), sources for organic foods, food co-ops, natural food stores, sources of raw honey and dairy, grass-fed meats and much more.
www.localharvest.org
www.foodroutes.org

Northeast Organic Farming Association, New Hampshire Chapter (NOFA-NH): This organization provides support for and education in all aspects of organic agriculture.
www.nofanh.org

Organic Trade Association (OTA) works to protect organic trade, and envisions organic products becoming a significant part of everyday life, to the benefit of people's lives and the environment.
www.ota.com

The **USDA** has a comprehensive directory of farmers' markets nationwide. To find one near you, visit the following site.
www.ams.usda.gov/farmersmarkets

Weston A. Price Foundation is dedicated to "restoring nutrient-dense foods to the American diet through education, research and activism." It's a resource for whole and traditional foods and has many articles on a variety of health- and nutrition-related topics.
www.westonaprice.org

Retailers
These retailers carry mostly natural and organic foods.
Sprouts Farmers Market – www.sprouts.com
Trade Joes – www.traderjoes.com
Whole Foods – www.wholefoodsmarket.com

Closeout Stores
Closeout stores can be a great place to find organic foods at a highly discounted price.
Big Lots – www.biglots.com
Home Goods – www.homegoods.com
Ocean State Job Lot – www.oceanstatejoblot.com
TJ Maxx – www.tjmaxx.com

Nutrition-Related Reading
All New Square Foot Gardening, Second Edition: The Revolutionary Way to Grow More In Less Space by Mel Bartholomew

Artisan Vegan Cheese, by Miyoko Schinner

Eating on the Wild Side: The Missing Link to Optimum Health, by Jo Robinson

In Defense of Food: An Eater's Manifesto, by Michael Pollan

Nourishing Traditions: The Cookbook that Challenges Politically Correct Nutrition and the Diet Dictocrats, by Sally Fallon, with Mary G. Enig, Ph.D.

Real Food: What We Eat and Why, by Nina Plank

Wild Fermentation: The Flavor, Nutrition, and Craft of Live-Culture Foods, by Sandor Ellix Katz

Lyme Disease

Whether you have Lyme disease, know someone who does or want to learn strategies on how to keep yourself and your family safe from ticks, we have compiled the following list of resources. Lyme disease is a serious, yet often misunderstood illness, so the books and websites that we suggest are ones that we are familiar with and find to be reputable with a wealth of valuable information. We are sure there are others out there, but these are the one's that we are most familiar with. Go to www.recipesforrepair.com/lyme-disease for the most up-to-date list, as we are always adding books or websites as we become discover new ones.

Organizations

International Lyme and Associated Diseases Society (ILADS) is a nonprofit, international, multi-disciplinary medical society, dedicated to the diagnosis and appropriate treatment of Lyme disease and other tick-borne diseases.
www.ilads.org

Lyme Disease Foundation, Inc. (LDF) is a nonprofit dedicated to finding solutions for tick-borne disorders.
www.lyme.org

Lyme Disease Association (LDA) is an organization dedicated to Lyme disease education, prevention, research funding, and patient support.
www.lymediseaseassociation.org

LymeDisease.org is a non-profit organization that serves the patient community through advocacy, education and research and is an incredible resource for those looking to learn more about tick-borne illnesses.
www.lymedisease.org

CanLyme was formed to provide the public, including medical professionals, with balanced and validated information on Lyme disease and related coinfections. They also have great prevention information.
www.canlyme.com/

Lyme Disease Association of Southeastern Pennsylvania has some very valuable information on their website; most notably, the downloadable, free publication *Lyme Disease and associated tick-borne diseases: The Basics*, which is in its fifth edition.
www.lymepa.org

Movies and Books

Coping with Lyme Disease, by Denise Lang, with Kenneth Liegner, MD

Cure Unknown, by Pamela Weintraub

Everything You Need to Know About Lyme Disease and Other Tick-Borne Disorders, by Karen Vanderhoof-Forschner

Healing Lyme: Natural Healing and Prevention of Lyme Borreliosis and Its Coinfections, by Stephen Harrod Buhner

Insights into Lyme Disease Treatment, by Connie Strasheim

Out of the Woods: Healing Lyme Disease - Body, Mind, and Spirit by Katina Makris

The Lyme Disease Solution, by Kenneth B. Singleton, MD, MPH

The Lyme Survival Guide, by Connie Strasheim

Under Our Skin, produced by Open Eye Pictures, is the highly-acclaimed documentary that exposes the hidden story of Lyme disease – one of the most controversial and fastest growing epidemics of our time. It is a must-see movie!
www.openeyepictures.com

Bryan Rosner used his experience in journalism, his personal battle with Lyme disease, and his discovery that very few adequate Lyme disease resources exist for patients and physicians to publish a number of Lyme-related books and run this wonderful website that offers a large number of books (including some of his own), CDs, and DVDs on Lyme disease.
www.lymebook.com

Acknowledgments

We would like to extend a special thank you to Dr. Singleton, for caring so deeply about your patients. It is clear your devotion to helping the Lyme community inspired you to write *The Lyme Disease Solution* and to create the Lyme Inflammation Diet. We appreciate all the guidance you've given us, your support and your words of encouragement. And to Ursuline Singleton, MPH, thank you for sharing your nutritional knowledge, and for your support throughout the process.

Gail's Personal Words of Gratitude
To my parents, who were such wonderful role models: you showed me by example how to succeed in life. Your love and support were never-ending.

To my husband, Jerry: how do you thank someone for always being there when needed, for never doubting your ability and for always encouraging you to reach your potential? Without your love and encouragement, my life would not have been such a rich, happy experience. Thanks for all you've done for me, when this book consumed not only my life, but yours. Jerry, thanks for being you.

To Gina, my "doctor daughter," for always being only a phone call or email away when I need your help and advice. Your many achievements and your devotion to your family, friends and patients are things we have all come to count on.

To Laura, my "partner daughter," for all of your unending work that made this book something we can both be proud of. Your attention to detail, graphic design skills and amazing photographic talents will be apparent to anyone who looks at this book. You bring the same love and spirit to everything in your life, which makes all of our lives so much better for having you part of our family. To my son-in-law, Chris, for all the support you have given Laura. You have helped her in so many ways. Thank you for your patience and help throughout this process.

To Chris, my "director son": your unique sense of humor, wit and artistic talent will surely make you a success in your career. But it is your kind, caring good nature that makes you such a pleasure to be with. To my daughter-in-law, Sara: From the first day I met you, I knew that Chris had made the perfect choice. Welcome to the family.

To my sister, Lynn, my special friend, who has been so important to me my whole life. To my brother, Joseph: the older we get, the more I realize how important it is to have a big brother to count on.

To Julia, the newest, most precious member of our family. You stole my heart the first moment I saw you.

To my cousin, Diane, who is like a sister to me.

Laura's Personal Words of Gratitude
To my husband, Chris, for your love and unwavering support throughout the years. There is no greater comfort to me than to know that I have you on my side. I can't imagine life without you and love you more each day.

To my daughter, Julia, the light of my life. I look forward to preparing you healthy meals for many years to come. You have completed our lives and I love you more than I could ever express.

To my mother: there are no words to express my gratitude for all you've done for me throughout my life. Your selfless nature of putting your family first turned my idea for this book into a reality. I didn't think anything good could ever come from having Lyme disease, but in this instance, it's given me the opportunity to work with you. You're a true talent and I'm so lucky to be your daughter.

To my father: thank you for always being there for me and for your kind and generous nature. You have been always been so helpful and supportive. We could not have done this without you.

To my sister, Gina, and my brother, Chris: no matter how far apart we live, you are always in my thoughts. I am proud of you both, and I know we will always be there for each other. To my sister-in-law Sara: we're so happy to have you as part of our family!

To Bruce and Linda: Thank you for your support, especially while I was undergoing tight deadlines. I appreciate your watching Julia while I worked to meet them. We are grateful for all that you do for us.

To David Hunter, for your commitment to helping those in the Lyme community.

Index

Note: Page numbers in italics indicate photographs; page numbers followed by *t* indicate tables.

A

Açai and Blueberry Spritzer, 117
acai juice, 26, 117
additives, 28, 29, 31
advanced glycation end products (AGEs), 18
"Alcat Test," 69
alcohol, 29, 31
allergens, 49
allergies, 16, 18
allowable foods, 26–27
   during Phase 1, 26–27, 68, 69
   during Phase 2, 26–27, 120
   during Phase 3, 26–27, 166
   during Phase 4, 26–27, 235
allspice
   Butternut Squash and Apple Soup, 185
   Pumpkin Custard, 162
Almond and Herb Crusted Tilapia, 105
Almond Butter, 56, *257*, 262
almond extract, 27
Almond Flour, 260
   Almond and Herb Crusted Tilapia, 105
   Banana Raisin Bread, 237
   Chewy Coconut Almond Cookies, 115
   Honey Nut Bars, 159
   Savory Vegetable and Herb Biscotti, 89
   Seed Sandwich Thins, 134
   Toasted Coconut Almond Muffins, 173
Almond Milk, 26, 260
   Banana Raisin Bread, 237
   Cherry Vanilla Almond Blast, 77
   Corn Fritters, 186
   Make-Ahead Brown Rice Porridge with Mixed Berry Compote, 75
   Oat Crepes, 128
   Pumpkin Custard, 162
   Rice Pudding, 253
   Spinach and Sun-Dried Tomato Quiche, 209
   Toasted Coconut Almond Muffins, 173
   Whole Grain Waffles with Assorted Berries, 169
   Zabaglione Sauce, 272
   Zucchini Corn Bake, 193
almond oil, 27, 166
almonds, 26, 29, 39*t*
   Almond and Herb Crusted Tilapia, 105
   Carrot Almond Pancakes, 73
   Coconut Almond Custard, 116
   Granola, 121
   Green Beans with Shiitake Mushrooms and Almonds, 98
   Honey Nut Bars, 159
   Lamb with Apricots and Prunes Tagine, 147
   Mixed Herb Pesto with Brown Rice Pasta, 153
   Nutty Coconut Delight, 113
   Overnight Oatmeal with Dried Fruit and Almonds, 127
   Roast Rack of Lamb with Mustard Herb Crust, 143
   Sautéed Filet of Sole with Artichoke Pesto, 110
   Stir-Fried Brown Rice and Vegetables, 101
alpha lipoic acid, 29
amaranth, 234*t*
antibiotics, 29, 45, 57, 58
antibodies, 15
Apple and Nut Skillet, 83
Apple and Pear Salad with Honey Mustard Dressing, 133
apple juice, 26, 166
apples, 26, 56, 166
   Apple and Nut Skillet, 83
   Apple and Pear Salad with Honey Mustard Dressing, 133
   Applesauce Walnut Tea Bread, 175
   Butternut Squash and Apple Soup, 185
   Cinnamon Applesauce, 96
   green, 26
   Green Smoothie, 84
   Fruit and Nut Bars, 161
   Mango Dresing, 276
applesauce
   Applesauce Walnut Tea Bread, 175
   Classic Meatloaf, 242
Applesauce Walnut Tea Bread, *174*, 175
appliances, small, 55
Apricot Oat Muffins, *124*, 125
apricots, 26, 120
   Apricot Oat Muffins, 125
   Chicken Salad, 140
   Granola, 121
   Lamb with Apricots and Prunes Tagine, 147
   Overnight Oatmeal with Dried Fruit and Almonds, 127
aquafaba, 270
arame, 26, 37, 120
arrowroot, 27, 36, 166
Artichoke Hummus, 138
artichokes, 26
   Artichoke Hummus, 138
   Mediterranean Chicken, 215
   Sautéed Filet of Sole with Artichoke Pesto, 110
arugula, 26
   Grilled Salmon over Assorted Greens with Fresh Herb Vinaigrette, 94
asparagus, 26
   Creamy Asparagus Soup, 87
   Grilled Salmon over Assorted Greens with Fresh Herb Vinaigrette, 94
aspartame, 29
Atkins, Robert, 69
autoimmune dysfunctions, 15
Autumn Mixed Green and Roasted Butternut Squash Salad, 132
avocado oil, 27, 166
avocados, 26, 28, 56
   Green Smoothie, 84
   Guacamole, 199
   Peanut Butter Banana Smoothie, 170
   Spinach and Lentil Salad with Warm Honey Vinegar Dressing, 131

B

bacteria, 15
baked beans 191
baked goods, 28
   Applesauce Walnut Tea Bread, 175
   Apricot Oat Muffins, 125
   Banana Raisin Bread, 237
   Chewy Coconut Almond Cookies, 115
   Chocolate Coconut Macaroons, 251
   Classic Sandwich, 241
   Date Nut Bread, 171
   Gluten-Free Baking Mix, 265
   Gluten-Free Italian Loaf, 239
   Oatmeal Craisin Cookies, 233
   Pecan Cherry Cookies, 155
   Savory Vegetable and Herb Biscotti, 89
   Toasted Coconut Almond Muffins, 173
baking powder, 27, 166
baking soda, 27
baking tips, 167
balsamic vinegar, 280
Banana Raisin Bread, *236*, 237
bananas, 26, 28, 166
   Banana Raisin Bread, 237
   Chocolate Banana Ice Cream, 250
   Peanut Butter Banana Smoothie, 170
barbecue sauce, 279
   Miso Barbecue Sauce, 282
   Peachy Barbecue Sauce, 279
bars, 159
basil, 27, 182
   Chicken Milanese, 249
   Cream of Tomato Bisque, 200
   Garden Fresh Tomato Sauce, 281
   Maryland Crab Cakes, 247
   Mediterranean Chicken, 215
   Mixed Herb Pesto with Brown Rice Pasta, 153
   Sautéed Filet of Sole with Artichoke Pesto, 110
   Savory Vegetable and Herb Biscotti, 89
   Steamed Vegetables and Brown and Wild Rice with Fresh Herb Vinaigrette, 93
   Tomato Salsa, 197
   Veggie Burgers, 201
   White Bean and Sun-Dried Tomato Spread, 183
   Zucchini Corn Bake, 193
bay leaves, 27
B-complex, 29
beans, 27, 40–41, 120. *See also specific kinds of beans*
   Slow Cooked Baked Beans, 191
   Veggie Burgers, 201
Béarnaise Sauce, 79, 273
beef, 27, 28, 166
   Beef Broth, 264
   Classic Meatloaf, 242
   Meatballs and Spaghetti Squash, 221
   Seared Peppered London Broil, 213
   Shepherd's Pie, 211
   Sloppy Joes, 205
   Slow Cooked Pot Roast with Root Vegetables, 246
Beef Broth, 264
beet juice, cultured, 57
beets, 26
   Pickled Beets, 88
berries, 26. *See also specific berries*
   Berry Frozen Dessert, 111
   Berry Pear Sauce, 274
   Make-Ahead Brown Rice Porridge with Mixed Berry Compote, 75
   Mixed Berries with Crème Patisserie (Vanilla Pastry Cream), 227
   Pavlova, 157
   Whole Grain Waffles with Assorted Berries, 169
Berry Frozen Dessert, 111
Berry Pear Sauce, 274
beverages. *See* drinks
biscotti, Savory Vegetable and Herb Biscotti, 89
bison, 27, 166
black beans, 27, 41*t*, 120
   Black Bean Brownies, *254*, 255
   Breakfast Burritos, 176
   Veggie Burgers, 201
blackberries, 26
   Berry Frozen Dessert, 111
   Berry Pear Sauce, 274
   Coconut Berry Smoothie, 77
   Make-Ahead Brown Rice Porridge with Mixed Berry Compote, 75
   Peach and Blackberry Chutney, 286
   Whole Grain Waffles with Assorted Berries, 169
blackberry juice, 26
black-eyed peas, 41*t*
black pepper, 27, 120. *See also* peppercorns
blueberries, 26
   Berry Frozen Dessert, 111
   Blueberry Oatmeal Pancakes, 123
   Blueberry Syrup, 277
   Coconut Berry Smoothie, 77
   Make-Ahead Brown Rice Porridge with Mixed Berry Compote, 75
   Overnight Oatmeal with Dried Fruit and Almonds, 127
   Stir-Fried Brown Rice and Vegetables, 101
   Whole Grain Waffles with Assorted Berries, 169
blueberry juice, 26, 117
Blueberry Oatmeal Pancakes, *122*, 123
Blueberry Syrup, 277, *277*
bok choy, 26
   Steamed Vegetables and Brown and Wild Rice with Fresh Herb Vinaigrette, 93
   Stir-Fried Bok Choy, Leeks and Pine Nuts, 99
Brazil nuts, 26, 120
breakfast, 28, 56
   Apple and Nut Skillet, 83
   Applesauce Walnut Tea Bread, 175
   Apricot Oat Muffins, 125
   Banana Raisin Bread, 237
   Blueberry Oatmeal Pancakes, 123
   Breakfast Burritos, 176
   Brown Rice Pancake, 82
   Carrot Almond Pancakes, 73
   Cherry Vanilla Almond Blast, 77
   Coconut Berry Smoothie, 77
   Fruit and Nut Bars, 161
   Granola, 121
   Green Smoothie, 84
   Herb Scrambled Eggs with Shiitake Mushrooms, 81
   Make-Ahead Brown Rice Porridge with Mixed Berry Compote, 75
   Mango Pineapple Smoothie, 238
   Oat Crepes, 128
   Overnight Oatmeal with Dried Fruit

and Almonds, 127
Date Nut Bread, 171
Peanut Butter Banana Smoothie, 170
Pineapple Cherry Delight, 170
Poached Eggs Florentine with Béarnaise Sauce, 79
Whole Grain Waffles with Assorted Berries, 169
Breakfast Burritos, 176
broccoli, 26
   Broccoli, Red Cabbage and Quinoa, *178*, 179
   Stir-Fried Brown Rice and Vegetables, 101
Broiled Shrimp with Shallots and Tomatoes and Herbs, *244*, 245
Brown and Wild Rice Cauliflower and Mushroom Curry, 104
brownies, 255
brown rice, 26, 234*t*
   Brown and Wild Rice Cauliflower and Mushroom Curry, 104
   Brown Rice Milk, 261
   Brown Rice Pancake, 82
   Chicken Tamaki, 210
   Chicken Wild Rice and Vegetable Soup, 181
   Make-Ahead Brown Rice Porridge with Mixed Berry Compote, 75
   Mixed Herb Pesto with Brown Rice Pasta, 153
   Rice Pudding, 253
   Slow Cooked Brown Rice Risotto and Mushrooms, 109
   Steamed Vegetables and Brown and Wild Rice with Fresh Herb Vinaigrette, 93
   Stir-Fried Brown Rice and Vegetables, 101
brown rice cakes, 56
brown rice flour, 26, 120
   Classic Sandwich, 241
   Gluten-Free Baking Mix, 265
   Homemade Pasta, 226
   Slow Cooked Pot Roast with Root Vegetables, 246
Brown Rice Pancake, 82
Brussels sprouts, 26
buckwheat, 26, 34, 166, 234*t*
bulk, buying in, 51

burgers
   Stuffed Turkey Burger, 154
   Veggie Burgers, 201
Burrito, 205
butter, 27, 28, 56, 166
butternut squash
   Autumn Mixed Green and Roasted Butternut Squash Salad, 132
   Butternut Squash and Apple Soup, *184*, 185
buying in bulk, 51

C

cabbage, 26
   Broccoli, Red Cabbage and Quinoa, 179
   Calico Slaw, 95
   Summer Vegetable Medley Salad, 189
caffeine, 31
Calico Slaw, 58, 95
calories, 48
   empty, 18
cannellini beans, 41*t*. *See also* white beans
   White Bean and Sun-Dried Tomato Spread, 183
cantaloupes, 26, 120
caraway seeds, 26, 120, 134
carbohydrates, 28, 49
cardamom, 27
Carrot Almond Pancakes, *72*, 73
carrots, 26
   Calico Slaw, 95
   Carrot Almond Pancakes, 73
   Cauliflower Carrot Soup, 91
   Chicken Croquettes, 243
   Chicken Tamaki, 210
   Chicken Wild Rice and Vegetable Soup, 181
   Classic Meatloaf, 242
   Green Smoothie, 84
   Grilled Salmon over Assorted Greens with Fresh Herb Vinaigrette, 94
   Kale Chips, 195
   Lentil Soup, 137
   Roasted Vegetables, 187
   Savory Vegetable and Herb Biscotti, 89

Shepherd's Pie, 211
Shredded Carrot Salad, 97
Slow Cooked Pot Roast with Root Vegetables, 246
Slow Cooked Vegetarian Tempeh Chili, 223
Steamed Vegetables and Brown and Wild Rice with Fresh Herb Vinaigrette, 93
Stir-Fried Brown Rice and Vegetables, 101
Summer Vegetable Medley Salad, 189
Vegetable Broth, 259
Veggie Burgers, 201
cashew butter, 56, 263
cashews, 26, 39*t*, 120
   Cashew Honey Butter, 263
   Chicken Salad, 140
   Curried Cashews, 135
   Honey Nut Bars, 159
   Kale Chips, 195
   Stir-Fried Chicken with Red Peppers and Cashews, 203
cauliflower, 26
   Brown and Wild Rice Cauliflower and Mushroom Curry, 104
   Cauliflower Carrot Soup, *90*, 91
   Mashed Cauliflower, 96
cayenne, 26, 166
celery, 26, 56
   Chicken Croquettes, 243
   Chicken Salad, 140
   Chicken Wild Rice and Vegetable Soup, 181
   Grilled Salmon over Assorted Greens with Fresh Herb Vinaigrette, 94
   Lentil Soup, 137
   Maryland Crab Cakes, 247
   Sautéed Salmon Cakes, 107
   Slow Cooked Pot Roast with Root Vegetables, 246
   Slow Cooked Vegetarian Tempeh Chili, 223
   Stir-Fried Brown Rice and Vegetables, 101
   Vegetable Broth, 259
   Veggie Burgers, 201
celery root, 26, 120
celery salt, 287

chard, 26
cheddar cheese
   Breakfast Burritos, 176
   Spinach and Sun-Dried Tomato Quiche, 209
   Zucchini Corn Bake, 193
cheeses, 27, 166. *See also specific kinds of cheese*
   organic raw milk, 28
   from pasture-fed cows, 28
chemicals, 28, 45
cherries, 26
   Apple and Pear Salad with Honey Mustard Dressing, 133
   Cherry Vanilla Almond Blast, 77
   Overnight Oatmeal with Dried Fruit and Almonds, 127
   Pecan Cherry Cookies, 155
   Pineapple Cherry Delight, 170
cherry juice, 26
cherry tomatoes
   Guacamole, 199
   Roasted Vegetables, 187
   Tomato Salsa, 197
Cherry Vanilla Almond Blast, 77
Chewy Coconut Almond Cookies, *114*, 115
chia seeds, 26
   Seed Sandwich Thins, 134
   Veggie Burgers, 201
chicken, 27, 28, 56, 120, 166
   Chicken Bone Broth, 264
   Chicken Croquettes, 243
   Chicken Fajitas, 219
   Chicken Milanese, *248*, 249
   Chicken Salad, 140
   Chicken Tamaki, 210
   Chicken Wild Rice and Vegetable Soup, 181
   Chicken with Wild Rice and Vegetable Soup, *180*, 181
   Coconut Chicken Tenders, 150
   Grilled Chicken Souvlaki, 151
   Honey Battered Chicken, 222
   Mediterranean Chicken, 215
   rotisserie, 56
   Sesame Chicken Tenders, 141
   Slow Cooked Pulled Chicken, 207
   Stir-Fried Chicken with Red Peppers and Cashews, 203
   Sweet and Tangy Baked Chicken, 145
chickpeas, 27, 41*t*, 120
   Artichoke Hummus, 138
   Chickpea and Sweet Potato Patties, 139
   Indian Chickpea and Spinach Fritters, 129
   Red Pepper Hummus, 182
   Salted Roasted Chickpeas, 135
chili, 223
chilies, 26, 166
   Fruit Salsa, 196
   Guacamole, 199
chili powder, 26, 166
   Chicken Fajitas, 219
   Sloppy Joes, 205
   Slow Cooked Pulled Chicken, 207
   Slow Cooked Vegetarian Tempeh Chili, 223
   Spicy Rub, 266
chives, 27, 182
   Almond and Herb Crusted Tilapia, 105
   Chicken Milanese, 249
   Mixed Herb Pesto with Brown Rice Pasta, 153
   Summer Vegetable Medley Salad, 189
   Vegetable Broth, 259
chocolate, 27, 235
   Chocolate Banana Ice Cream, 250
   Chocolate Coconut Macaroons, 251
cholesterol, 49
chromium, 29
chronic inflammation
   assessing risk for, 19–21
   causes of, 15–18
   mechanisms of, 14–15
   understanding, 14–22
Chronic Inflammation Self-Assessment Tool, 19, 20–21
chutney, Peach and Blackberry Chutney, 286
cigarette smoking, 16–17
cilantro, 27, 199
cinnamon, 27
   Applesauce Walnut Tea Bread, 175
   Apricot Oat Muffins, 125
   Cinnamon Applesauce, 96
   Fruit and Nut Bars, 161
   Granola, 121
   Honey Nut Bars, 159
   Nutty Coconut Delight, 113
   Oatmeal Craisin Cookies, 233
   Pumpkin Custard, 162
   Rice Pudding, 253
   Whole Grain Waffles with Assorted Berries, 169
Cinnamon Applesauce, 96
   Applesauce Walnut Tea Bread, 175
   Black Bean Brownies, 255
circulars, 51
circulating immune complexes (CICs), 15
citrus juice, 26, 166
Classic Meatloaf, 242
Classic Sandwich, *240*, 241
closeout stores, 51
cloves, 27
cocoa powder
   Black Bean Brownies, 255
   Chocolate Banana Ice Cream, 250
   Chocolate Coconut Macaroons, 251
coconut, 26
   Carrot Almond Pancakes, 73
   Chewy Coconut Almond Cookies, 115
   Chocolate Coconut Macaroons, 251
   Coconut Almond Custard, 116
   Coconut Berry Smoothie, *76*, 77
   Coconut Chicken Tenders, 150, *150*
   Fruit and Nut Bars, 161
   Granola, 121
   Nutty Coconut Delight, 113
   Pecan Cherry Cookies, 155
   Toasted Coconut Almond Muffins, 173
coconut aminos, 27, 38
coconut extract, 27
coconut kefir, 27, 38, 120
   Coconut Chicken Tenders, 150
Coconut Milk, 26, 261
   Berry Frozen Dessert, 111
   Brown and Wild Rice Cauliflower and Mushroom Curry, 104
   Butternut Squash and Apple Soup, 185
   Cauliflower Carrot Soup, 91
   Chocolate Banana Ice Cream, 250
   Coconut Almond Custard, 116
   Coconut Berry Smoothie, 77
   Coconut Chicken Tenders, 150

Creamy Asparagus Soup, 87
Date Nut Bread, 171
Honey Battered Chicken, 222
Make-Ahead Brown Rice Porridge with Mixed Berry Compote, 75
Mango Pineapple Smoothie, 238
Mashed Cauliflower, 96
Overnight Oatmeal with Dried Fruit and Almonds, 127
Peanut Butter Banana Smoothie, 170
Pineapple Cherry Delight, 170
Strawberry Ice Cream, 229
coconut nectar, 27, 120
coconut oil, 27, 28, 34–35, 251
coconut palm sugar, 27, 35, 120, 239
    Applesauce Walnut Tea Bread, 175
    Blueberry Syrup, 277
    Cran-Raspberry Sauce, 275
    Oatmeal Craisin Cookies, 233
    Pineapple Cherry Delight, 170
cod, 27, 235
coffee, 26, 166
coffee grinders, 50
collard greens, 26
commercially packaged foods, 28
community supported agriculture (CSA), 50
compote, 75
condiments, 270–289
    Curried Mayonnaise, 270
    Easy Spicy Ketchup, 287
    Fresh Herb Vinaigrette, 93
    Fruit Salsa, 196
    Fruity Glaze, 288
    Garlic-Shallot Mayonnaise (Aioli), 271
    Guacamole, 199
    Herb Mayonnaise, 270
    Homemade Mayonnaise, 270
    Mango Dressing, 276
    mayonnaise, 270
    Mixed Berry Compote, 75
    Mustard Mayonnaise, 270
    Mustard Ranch Dressing, 283
    Orange Herb Dressing, 284
    Peach and Blackberry Chutney, 286
    Peach and Pineapple Dipping Sauce, 285
    Peachy Barbecue Sauce, 279
    Pesto Mayonnaise, 270
    Tomato Salsa, 197
cookies
    Chewy Coconut Almond Cookies, 115
    Maple Walnut Shortbread Cookies, 232
    Oatmeal Craisin Cookies, 233
    Pecan Cherry Cookies, 155
cooking terms, 59–63
cooperatives, 46
co-ops, 51
coriander, 223
corn, 26, 166, 234*t*
    Corn Fritters, 186
    Multicolored Stuffed Peppers, 217
    Slow Cooked Vegetarian Tempeh Chili, 223
    Summer Vegetable Medley Salad, 189
    Zucchini Corn Bake, 193
Corn Fritters, 186
corn masa harina flour, 206
corn oil, 28
corn starch
    Gluten-Free Baking Mix, 265
    Gluten-Free Italian Loaf, 239
cost cutting, 50–51
cottonseed oils, 28
coupons, 51
crab, Maryland Crab Cakes, 247
craisins, 233
cranberries, 26
    Apple and Pear Salad with Honey Mustard Dressing, 133
    Autumn Mixed Green and Roasted Butternut Squash Salad, 132
    Cran-Raspberry Glazed Salmon, *148*, 149
    Cran-Raspberry Sauce, 171, 275, *275*, 288
    Fruit and Nut Bars, 161
    Granola, 121
    Overnight Oatmeal with Dried Fruit and Almonds, 127
cranberry juice, 26
C-reactive protein, 19
cream, 27, 166
cream of tartar, 27
Cream of Tomato Bisque, 200
Creamy Asparagus Soup, *86*, 87
crepes, Oat Crepes, 128
Crispy Kale, 95
Croutons, 268
CRP blood test, 19
cucumbers, 26
    Chicken Tamaki, 210
    Green Smoothie, 84
    Tzatziki Sauce, 278
cultured foods, 57–58
cumin, 27
    Brown and Wild Rice Cauliflower and Mushroom Curry, 104
    Butternut Squash and Apple Soup, 185
    Chicken Fajitas, 219
    Easy Spicy Ketchup, 287
    Guacamole, 199
    Sloppy Joes, 205
    Slow Cooked Pulled Chicken, 207
    Slow Cooked Vegetarian Tempeh Chili, 223
    Spicy Rub, 266
curry powder, 27
    Brown and Wild Rice Cauliflower and Mushroom Curry, 104
    Butternut Squash and Apple Soup, 185
    Curried Cashews, 135
    Curried Mayonnaise, 270
custards
    Coconut Almond Custard, 116
    Pumpkin Custard, 162
cytokines, 14, 17

D

dairy, 27, 166, 235. *See also specific dairy products*
dates, 26, 35, 120
    Black Bean Brownies, 255
    Chocolate Banana Ice Cream, 250
    Easy Spicy Ketchup, 287
    Fruit and Nut Bars, 161
    Peanut Butter Banana Smoothie, 170
    Strawberry Ice Cream, 229
desserts, 28
    Berry Frozen Dessert, 111
    Berry Pear Sauce, 274
    Black Bean Brownies, 255
    Blueberry Syrup, 277
    Chewy Coconut Almond Cookies,

115
Chocolate Banana Ice Cream, 250
Chocolate Coconut Macaroons, 251
Coconut Almond Custard, 116
Fruit and Nut Bars, 161
Honey Nut Bars, 159
Iced Minted Raspberry Green Tea, 163
Maple Walnut Shortbread Cookies, 232
Mixed Berries with Crème Patissière (Vanilla Pastry Cream), 227
Nutty Coconut Delight, 113
Oatmeal Craisin Cookies, 233
Pavlova, 157
Pecan Cherry Cookies, 155
Pumpkin Custard, 162
Rice Pudding, 253
Strawberry Ice Cream, 229
Zabaglione Sauce, 272
detoxification, 22, 29–30
Deviled Eggs, 85, *85*
diet. *See also* Lyme Inflammation Diet
 poor, 18
 Standard American Diet (SAD), 14
dill pickles, 26, 166
dressings, 56
 Fresh Herb Vinaigrette, 93
 Mango Dressing, 276
 Mustard Ranch Dressing, 283
 Orange Herb Dressing, 284
dried fruit, 127
drinks, 26, 28, 120, 166
 Açai and Blueberry Spritzer, 117
 carbonated, 28
 Iced Minted Raspberry Green Tea, 163
 Lime Ice, 228
 Mint Tea, 117
 Raspberry Lemonade Slushie, 231
 Watermelon Lime Cooler, 231
dulse, 26, 37, 120

E

easy meal suggestions, 56
Easy Spicy Ketchup, 287
Ed, 19
eggplants, 26, 166, 187
eggs, 27, 56, 69
 Applesauce Walnut Tea Bread, 175

Apricot Oat Muffins, 125
Béarnaise Sauce, 273
Breakfast Burritos, 176
Brown Rice Pancake, 82
Chicken Croquettes, 243
Classic Meatloaf, 242
Classic Sandwich, 241
Corn Fritters, 186
Deviled Eggs, 85
egg salad, 85
Garlic-Shallot Mayonnaise (Aioli), 271
Herb Scrambled Eggs with Shiitake Mushrooms, 81
Homemade Mayonnaise, 270
Mixed Berries with Crème Patissière (Vanilla Pastry Cream), 227
Oat Crepes, 128
Pavlova, 157
Poached Eggs Florentine with Béarnaise Sauce, 79
Red and Green Pepper Frittata, 225
Spinach and Lentil Salad with Warm Honey Vinegar Dressing, 131
Spinach and Sun-Dried Tomato Quiche, 209
Toasted Coconut Almond Muffins, 173
Whole Grain Waffles with Assorted Berries, 169
Zabaglione Sauce, 272
Zucchini Corn Bake, 193
entrees
 Almond and Herb Crusted Tilapia, 105
 Broiled Shrimp with Shallots and Tomatoes and Herbs, 245
 Brown and Wild Rice Cauliflower and Mushroom Curry, 104
 Burrito, 205
 Chicken Croquettes, 243
 Chicken Fajitas, 219
 Chicken Milanese, 249
 Chicken Tamaki, 210
 Classic Meatloaf, 242
 Coconut Chicken Tenders, 150
 Cran-Raspberry Glazed Salmon, 149
 Greek Ground Lamb Crumble, 218
 Grilled Chicken Souvlaki, 151
 Homemade Pasta, 226
 Honey Battered Chicken, 222

Lamb with Apricots and Prunes Tagine, 147
Maryland Crab Cakes, 247
Meatballs and Spaghetti Squash, 221
Mediterranean Chicken, 215
Mixed Herb Pesto with Brown Rice Pasta, 153
Moroccan Spice-Rubbed Salmon, *102*
Multicolored Stuffed Peppers, 217
Olive Tapenade Baked Haddock, 142
Red and Green Pepper Frittata, 225
Roast Rack of Lamb with Mustard Herb Crust, 143
Sautéed Filet of Sole with Artichoke Pesto, 110
Sautéed Salmon Cakes, 107
Seared Peppered London Broil, 213
Sesame Chicken Tenders, 141
Shepherd's Pie, 211
Sloppy Joes, 205
Slow Cooked Brown Rice Risotto and Mushrooms, 109
Slow Cooked Pot Roast with Root Vegetables, 246
Slow Cooked Pulled Chicken, 207
Slow Cooked Vegetarian Tempeh Chili, 223
Spinach and Sun-Dried Tomato Quiche, 209
Stir-Fried Brown Rice and Vegetables, 101
Stir-Fried Chicken with Red Peppers and Cashews, 203
Stuffed Turkey Burger, 154
Sweet and Tangy Baked Chicken, 145
Traditional Soft Corn Tortilla, 206
Veggie Burgers, 201
Environmental Working Group, Clean 15 and Dirty Dozen, 47, *47*
enzymes, 22
eosinophils, 14
Even Oven-Roasted Marina Sauce, 280
exercise, lack of, 17
expeller pressed oil, 34
expiration dates, 51

F

fajitas, Chicken Fajitas, 219
Fallon, Sally, *Nourish Traditions*, 42
farmers' markets, 46, 51
farm stands, 46
fat cells, 17
fatigue, 17
fats, 27, 34–35, 43–44, 49, 120, 166, 235. *See also* oils
  good, 28
  oxidized, 18
  trans-fatty acids, 28
fennel, 26, 120
feta cheese, 27, 235
fiber, dietary, 49
figs, 26, 120, 127
fish, 27, 28, 107, 235. *See also specific fish*
fish cakes, 107
5-hydroxytryptophan, 29
flaxseed, 26, 121. *See also* flaxseed meal
flaxseed meal
  Cherry Vanilla Almond Blast, 77
  Fruit and Nut Bars, 161
  Gluten-Free Baking Mix, 265
  Peanut Butter Banana Smoothie, 170
  Sautéed Salmon Cakes, 107
  Savory Vegetable and Herb Biscotti, 89
  Seed Sandwich Thins, 134
  Veggie Burgers, 201
flounder, 27
flour. *See also specific kinds of flour*
  white, 28
food choices, detoxification and, 29–30
food co-ops, 51
food glossary, 34
food labels, 48
  non-GMO labels, 46
  Nutrition Facts labels, 48, *48–49*
  USDA Organic seal, 46
food sensitivities, 69. *See also* allergies
free radicals, 17, 18
Fresh Herb Vinaigrette, 93
  Calico Slaw, 95
  Grilled Salmon over Assorted Greens with Fresh Herb Vinaigrette, 94
fried foods, 28
frittatas, 225
fritters
  Corn Fritters, 186
  Indian Chickpea and Spinach Fritters, 129
fruits, 26, 120, 166, 235. *See also specific fruits*
  dried, 56, 127
  fresh, 28
  Fruit Salsa, 196
  Fruity Glaze, 288
  picking your own, 50
Fruit and Nut Bars, *160*, 161
fungi, 15. *See also* mushrooms

G

garam masala
  Lamb with Apricots and Prunes Tagine, 147
  Moroccan Spice-Rubbed Salmon, *102*
garbanzo beans. *See* chickpeas
Garden Fresh Tomato Sauce, 281
  Meatballs and Spaghetti Squash, 221
garlic, 27
  Chicken Bone Broth, 264
  Garlic-Shallot Mayonnaise (Aioli), 271, *271*
  Greek Ground Lamb Crumble, 218
  Spinach and Sun-Dried Tomato Quiche, 209
  Vegetable Broth, 259
garlic powder
  Easy Spicy Ketchup, 287
  Italian Breadcrumbs, 267
gelatin, 27, 235
general food guidelines, 28–29
genetically modified organisms (GMOs), 45
Ghee, 27, 35, 56, *257*, 258, *258*
ginger, 27
  Applesauce Walnut Tea Bread, 175
  Miso Barbecue Sauce, 282
  Moroccan Spice-Rubbed Salmon, *102*
  Peach and Blackberry Chutney, 286
  Pumpkin Custard, 162

glazes, 288
glutamine, 29
gluten, 234
Gluten-Free Baking Mix, 167, 265
  Applesauce Walnut Tea Bread, 175
  Corn Fritters, 186
  Date Nut Bread, 171
  Soft Flour Tortillas, 177
  Spinach and Sun-Dried Tomato Quiche, 209
  Toasted Coconut Almond Muffins, 173
gluten-free baking tips, 167
Gluten-Free Italian Loaf, 239
grains, 26, 34, 56, 120, 166, 234t, 235. *See also specific grains*
  whole grains, 28, 42–43
Granola, 121
grapefruit, 26, 166
grapes, 28
  purple, 26, 235
grapeseed oil, 27, 166
Great Northern beans, 41t. *See also* white beans
Greek Ground Lamb Crumble, 218
green beans
  Green Beans with Shiitake Mushrooms and Almonds, *53*, 98, *98*
  Shepherd's Pie, 211
  Steamed Vegetables and Brown and Wild Rice with Fresh Herb Vinaigrette, 93
  Summer Vegetable Medley Salad, 189
  Vegetable Broth, 259
green peppers, 166
  Chicken Fajitas, 219
  Red and Green Pepper Frittata, 225
  Roasted Vegetables, 187
  Slow Cooked Vegetarian Tempeh Chili, 223
greens
  Autumn Mixed Green and Roasted Butternut Squash Salad, 132
  Chicken Milanese, 249
  collard greens, 26
  Grilled Salmon over Assorted Greens with Fresh Herb Vinaigrette, 94
  mustard greens, 26

Green Smoothie, 84
green tea, 26, 120, 163
Grilled Chicken Souvlaki, 151
Grilled Salmon over Assorted Greens with Fresh Herb Vinaigrette, 94
groats, 26, 34, 166
grocery stores, 46
grouper, 27, 235
growth hormones, 45
Guacamole, *198*, 199
guar gum, 27, 37, 166

H

haddock, 27, 142
halibut, 27
Hazelnuts
    Fruit and Nut Bars, 161
headaches, special dietary considerations for, 31
help, recruiting, 55
hemp seeds, 26, 235
Herbes de Provence, 38
    Cream of Tomato Bisque, 200
    Croutons, 268
    Orange Herb Dressing, 284
    Red and Green Pepper Frittata, 225
    Savory Vegetable and Herb Biscotti, 89
    Seared Peppered London Broil, 213
herbs, 27, 56, 120, 235. *See also specific herbs*
    Almond and Herb Crusted Tilapia, 105
    Broiled Shrimp with Shallots and Tomatoes and Herbs, 245
    growing your own, 50
    Herb Mayonnaise, 85, 105, 107, 270, 283
    Herb Scrambled Eggs with Shiitake Mushrooms, 81
    Mixed Herb Pesto with Brown Rice Pasta, 153
    Roast Rack of Lamb with Mustard Herb Crust, 143
    Savory Vegetable and Herb Biscotti, 89
    Steamed Vegetables and Brown and Wild Rice with Fresh Herb Vinaigrette, 93
hijiki, 26, 37, 120

Homemade Baking Powder, *256*, 262
Homemade Mayonnaise, 270
Homemade Pasta, 226
honey, 120
    Cashew Honey Butter, 263
    Chewy Coconut Almond Cookies, 115
    Chicken Tamaki, 210
    Classic Sandwich, 241
    Coconut Almond Custard, 116
    Even Oven-Roasted Marina Sauce, 280
    Garden Fresh Tomato Sauce, 281
    Garlic-Shallot Mayonnaise (Aioli), 271
    Honey Battered Chicken, 222
    Honey Nut Bars, *158*, 159
    Mango Dressing, 276
    Mango Pineapple Smoothie, 238
    Miso Barbecue Sauce, 282
    Mixed Berries with Crème Patisserie (Vanilla Pastry Cream), 227
    Nutty Coconut Delight, 113
    Orange Herb Dressing, 284
    Peach and Blackberry Chutney, 286
    Peach and Pineapple Dipping Sauce, 285
    Peachy Barbecue Sauce, 279
    Pineapple Cherry Delight, 170
    Pumpkin Custard, 162
    raw, 27, 36
    Sweet and Tangy Baked Chicken, 145
    Toasted Coconut Almond Muffins, 173
horseradish, 27, 235
    Chicken Milanese, 249
    Horseradish Mustard Sauce, 289
Horseradish Mustard Sauce, 289
hummus
    Artichoke Hummus, 138
    Red Pepper Hummus, 182
hydrogenated oils, 28
hypersensitivity, 69

I

ice cream
    Berry Frozen Dessert, 111
    Chocolate Banana Ice Cream, 250
    Strawberry Ice Cream, 229

Iced Minted Raspberry Green Tea, 163
imported foods, 46–47
Indian Chickpea and Spinach Fritters, 129
infectious microorganisms, 15
inflammation, chronic, 14–22
ingredients, 49
    buying online, 51
    making your own, 50
insulin resistance, 17
interleukins, 15
irradiation, 46
Italian Breadcrumbs, *257*, 267

J

jalapeño peppers
    Fruit Salsa, 196
    Guacamole, 199
jicama, 26, 166
juices, 26, 28. *See also specific juices*

K

kale, 26
    Crispy Kale, 95
    Green Smoothie, 84
    Kale Chips, *194*, 195
    Lentil Soup, 137
    Veggie Burgers, 201
kefir, 27, 38, 120
    Coconut Chicken Tenders, 150
    Mango Pineapple Smoothie, 238
    unsweetened, 235
kelp, 26, 37, 120
ketchup, 287
kidney beans, 27, 41*t*, 120, 201
kimchi, 58
kiwi, 26, 235
kohlrabi, 26, 120
kombu, 26, 37, 120, 191
kombucha, 57
kvass, 57

L

lakanto, 27, 36
lamb, 27, 28, 120
    Greek Ground Lamb Crumble, 218
    Lamb with Apricots and Prunes Tagine, *146*, 147

Roast Rack of Lamb with Mustard Herb Crust, 143
lard, 28
leeks, 26
  Chicken Bone Broth, 264
  Stir-Fried Bok Choy, Leeks and Pine Nuts, 99
  Vegetable Broth, 259
legumes, 27, 120
lemon grass, 27
lemon juice
  Lime Ice, 228
  Raspberry Lemonade Slushie, 231
lemons, 26, 166
lemon thyme, 182
  Béarnaise Sauce, 273
  Broiled Shrimp with Shallots and Tomatoes and Herbs, 245
  Chicken Milanese, 249
lentils, 27, 40–41, 120
  Lentil Soup, *136*, 137
  Spinach and Lentil Salad with Warm Honey Vinegar Dressing, 131
leptin resistance, 18
lettuce, 26
  Apple and Pear Salad with Honey Mustard Dressing, 133
  Grilled Salmon over Assorted Greens with Fresh Herb Vinaigrette, 94
leukotrines, 15
Lime Ice, 228
lime juice, 228
limes, 26, 166
  Fruit Salsa, 196
  Tomato Salsa, 197
  Watermelon Lime Cooler, 231
locally grown foods, 46–47
lyme disease, 16
Lyme Inflammation Diet, 15, 23–51
  allowable foods, 26–27
  basic principles, 24
  food glossary, 34
  general food guidelines, 28–29
  phases of, 24–27, 64
  preparing for, 54–55

M

macaroons, Chocolate Coconut Macaroons, 251

mackerel, 27
Make-Ahead Brown Rice Porridge with Mixed Berry Compote, *74*, 75
Mango Dressing, 276
mango juice, 285
mangos, 26, 120
  Fruit Salsa, 196
  Mango Dressing, 276
  Mango Pineapple Smoothie, 238
maple syrup, 27, 120
  Chocolate Coconut Macaroons, 251
  Mango Dressing, 276
  Maple Walnut Shortbread Cookies, 232
  Mixed Berries with Crème Patisserie (Vanilla Pastry Cream), 227
  Pumpkin Custard, 162
  Toasted Coconut Almond Muffins, 173
Maple Walnut Shortbread Cookies, 232
margarines, 27, 28, 120
Maryland Crab Cakes, 247
Mashed Cauliflower, 96, 211
mayonnaise, Garlic-Shallot Mayonnaise (Aioli), 271
meal plans, making, 54
measuring, 55
meat, 27. *See also specific meats*
Meatballs and Spaghetti Squash, *220*, 221
meatloaf, Classic Meatloaf, 242
meats, 28. *See also specific meats*
Mediterranean Chicken, *214*, 215
Medjool dates
  Chocolate Banana Ice Cream, 250
  Easy Spicy Ketchup, 287
  Peanut Butter Banana Smoothie, 170
  Strawberry Ice Cream, 229
microorganism, infectious, 15
milk, 27, 166. *See also specific kinds of milk*
millet, 26, 34, 166, 234*t*, 266
Millet Flour, 239, *256*, 266
minerals, 49
mint, 27
  Grilled Chicken Souvlaki, 151
  Iced Minted Raspberry Green Tea, 163
  Mint Tea, 117

Mixed Herb Pesto with Brown Rice Pasta, 153
  Tzatziki Sauce, 278
mint extract, 27
Mint Tea, 117
miso, 27, 37, 166, 282
Miso Barbecue Sauce, 282
Mixed Berries with Crème Patisserie (Vanilla Pastry Cream), 227
Mixed Berry Compote, 75
Mixed Herb Pesto
  Even Oven-Roasted Marina Sauce, 280
  Roasted Vegetables, 187
  Mixed Herb Pesto with Brown Rice Pasta, *152*, 153
mold, 15
money, saving, 50–51
monosodium glutamate (MSG), 29, 31
Moroccan Spice-Rubbed Salmon, *102*
muffins
  Apricot Oat Muffins, 125
  Toasted Coconut Almond Muffins, 173
Multicolored Stuffed Peppers, *216*, 217
multi-vitamins, 29
mushrooms
  baby bella, 109
  Brown and Wild Rice Cauliflower and Mushroom Curry, 104
  Chicken Croquettes, 243
  cremini, 109, 154, 259
  Green Beans with Shiitake Mushrooms and Almonds, 98
  Herb Scrambled Eggs with Shiitake Mushrooms, 81
  Sautéed Salmon Cakes, 107
  shiitake, 26, 98, 107
  Slow Cooked Brown Rice Risotto and Mushrooms, 109
  Stuffed Turkey Burger, 154
  Vegetable Broth, 259
mustard, 27
  Chicken Milanese, 249
  Classic Meatloaf, 242
  Honey Battered Chicken, 222
  Horseradish Mustard Sauce, 289
  Mustard Ranch Dressing, 283
  Roast Rack of Lamb with Mustard Herb Crust, 143

Seared Peppered London Broil, 213
Spicy Rub, 266
Sweet and Tangy Baked Chicken, 145
mustard greens, 26
Mustard Mayonnaise, 270
mustard powder, 27
Mustard Ranch Dressing, 283, *283*
mustard seeds, 27

N

natto, 27, 37, 166
navy beans, 27, 41*t*, 120, 191. *See also* white beans
nectarines, 26, 166
nightshades, 26, 165, 166
nitrates, 29
non-GMO labels, 46
nori, 26, 37, 120, 210
nut butters, 50, 56. *See also specific nut butters*
nutmeg
   Butternut Squash and Apple Soup, 185
   Pumpkin Custard, 162
nutrients, 48–49. *See also specific nutrients*
nutritional yeast, 27, 38, 166
Nutrition Facts labels, 48, *48–49*
nuts, 26, 28, 39, 56, 94, 120, 166, 235. *See also specific nuts*
Nutty Coconut Delight, *112*, 113

O

Oat Crepes, 128
oat flour, 26, 120
oat groats, 166
   Overnight Oatmeal with Dried Fruit and Almonds, 127
oatmeal, 26, 120, 127
oats, 26
   Apricot Oat Muffins, 125
   Banana Raisin Bread, 237
   Blueberry Oatmeal Pancakes, 123
   Classic Meatloaf, 242
   Oatmeal Craisin Cookies, 233, *233*
   Overnight Oatmeal with Dried Fruit and Almonds, 127
obesity, 17

oils, 27, 28, 43. *See also specific oils*
olive oil, 27, 28, 43, 56
olives, 26, 120
   Mediterranean Chicken, 215
   Olive Tapenade Baked Haddock, 142, *142*
omega-3 fatty acids, 18
omega-6 fatty acids, 18
onion powder, 268
onions, 26. *See also* scallions; shallots
   Chicken Bone Broth, 264
   Chicken Croquettes, 243
   Chicken Fajitas, 219
   Classic Meatloaf, 242
   Easy Spicy Ketchup, 287
   Garden Fresh Tomato Sauce, 281
   Guacamole, 199
   Maryland Crab Cakes, 247
   Mediterranean Chicken, 215
   Multicolored Stuffed Peppers, 217
   Roasted Vegetables, 187
   Savory Vegetable and Herb Biscotti, 89
   Shepherd's Pie, 211
   Sloppy Joes, 205
   Slow Cooked Baked Beans, 191
   Slow Cooked Pot Roast with Root Vegetables, 246
   Slow Cooked Vegetarian Tempeh Chili, 223
   Vegetable Broth, 259
   Veggie Burgers, 201
   Zucchini Corn Bake, 193
online shopping, 51
Orange Herb Dressing, 284, *284*
orange juice, 26, 166
   Orange Herb Dressing, 284
   Peach and Blackberry Chutney, 286
   Peach and Pineapple Dipping Sauce, 285
orange peppers
   Chicken Fajitas, 219
   Maryland Crab Cakes, 247
   Multicolored Stuffed Peppers, 217
oranges, 26, 166
oregano, 27
   Almond and Herb Crusted Tilapia, 105
   Even Oven-Roasted Marina Sauce, 280
   Greek Ground Lamb Crumble, 218
   Grilled Chicken Souvlaki, 151

Moroccan Spice-Rubbed Salmon, *102*
Multicolored Stuffed Peppers, 217
Spicy Rub, 266
Organic Farming Association of NH "Why Buy Organic?" brochure, 45–46
organic foods, 28, 45–47
Organic Foods Production Act (OFPA), 45
Organic Trade Association, 47
Overnight Oatmeal with Dried Fruit and Almonds, *126*, 127

P

packaged foods, 28, 57
palm oil, 27, 35, 166
palm shortening, 35
pancakes
   Blueberry Oatmeal Pancakes, 123
   Brown Rice Pancake, 82
   Carrot Almond Pancakes, 73
pantry items, 256–268
   Almond Butter, *257*, 262
   Almond Flour, 260
   Almond Milk, 260
   Beef Broth, 264
   Brown Rice Milk, 261
   Cashew Honey Butter, 263
   Chicken Bone Broth, 264
   Coconut Milk, 261
   Croutons, 268
   Ghee, *257*, 258, *258*
   Homemade Baking Powder, *256*, 262
   Italian Breadcrumbs, *257*, 267
   Millet Flour, *256*, 266
   Spicy Rub, *256*, 266
   stocking, 54
   Tahini, 263
papayas, 26, 207, 235
paprika, 26, 166
   Chicken Fajitas, 219
   Easy Spicy Ketchup, 287
   Greek Ground Lamb Crumble, 218
   Honey Battered Chicken, 222
   Sloppy Joes, 205
parasites, 15
Parmesan cheese
   Chicken Croquettes, 243
   Chicken Milanese, 249

Croutons, 268
Italian Breadcrumbs, 267
Red and Green Pepper Frittata, 225
Spinach and Sun-Dried Tomato Quiche, 209
Zucchini Corn Bake, 193
parsley, 27, 182
  Almond and Herb Crusted Tilapia, 105
  Broiled Shrimp with Shallots and Tomatoes and Herbs, 245
  Chicken Croquettes, 243
  Chicken Milanese, 249
  Cream of Tomato Bisque, 200
  Garden Fresh Tomato Sauce, 281
  Grilled Chicken Souvlaki, 151
  Guacamole, 199
  Mediterranean Chicken, 215
  Mixed Herb Pesto with Brown Rice Pasta, 153
  Multicolored Stuffed Peppers, 217
  Sautéed Filet of Sole with Artichoke Pesto, 110
  Steamed Vegetables and Brown and Wild Rice with Fresh Herb Vinaigrette, 93
  Tomato Salsa, 197
  Vegetable Broth, 259
  Veggie Burgers, 201
  White Bean and Sun-Dried Tomato Spread, 183
  Zucchini Corn Bake, 193
parsnips, 26, 235, 246
pasta
  Homemade Pasta, 226
  Meatballs and Spaghetti Squash, 221
  Mixed Herb Pesto with Brown Rice Pasta, 153
  white, 28
Pavlova, *156*, 157
peaches, 26, 166
  Fruit Salsa, 196
  Peach and Blackberry Chutney, 286
  Peach and Pineapple Dipping Sauce, 285
  Peachy Barbecue Sauce, 279, *279*
Peanut Butter Banana Smoothie, 170
peanut oil, 27, 235
peanuts, 26, 39*t*, 166
pears, 26, 120

Apple and Pear Salad with Honey Mustard Dressing, 133
Berry Pear Sauce, 274
peas, 27, 40–41, 120, 189. *See also* split peas
Pecan Cherry Cookies, 155, *155*
pecans, 26, 39*t*, 120
  Apple and Pear Salad with Honey Mustard Dressing, 133
  Apricot Oat Muffins, 125
  Chocolate Coconut Macaroons, 251
  Date Nut Bread, 171
  Fruit and Nut Bars, 161
  Granola, 121
  Honey Nut Bars, 159
  Pecan Cherry Cookies, 155
  Spinach and Lentil Salad with Warm Honey Vinegar Dressing, 131
pepper, black, 27. *See also* peppercorns
peppercorns, Seared Peppered London Broil, 213
peppers
  hot, 26, 166 (*see also* chilies; *specific varieties of peppers*)
  mild, 26, 166
  sweet, 26, 166 (*see also* green peppers; orange peppers; red peppers; yellow peppers)
pesticides, 45
pesto
  Mixed Herb Pesto with Brown Rice Pasta, 153
  Pesto Mayonnaise, 270
Phase 1: Induction Phase, 67
  foods allowed during, 26–27, 68, 69
  meal suggestions, *70–71*
  Pantry, 258, 259, 260, 261, 262
  recipes, 72–116, 270, 272, 273
Phase 2: The Early Reentry Phase, 118–163
  foods allowed during, 26–27, 120
  Pantry, 263
  preparing for, 120
  recipes, 121–163, 274, 275, 276, 277
Phase 3: The Late Reentry Phase, 164–233
  foods allowed during, 26–27, 166
  Pantry, 264, 265, 266

recipes, 278, 279, 280–288
Phase 4: The Maintenance Phase, 234
  foods allowed during, 26–27, 235
  Pantry, 267, 268
  recipes, 237–255, 289
Pickled Beets, *52*, 88, *88*
pickles, 26, 166, 235
pineapple juice, 276
pineapples, 26, 120
  Fruit Salsa, 196
  Mango Pineapple Smoothie, 238
  Pineapple Cherry Delight, 170
pine nuts, 26
  Autumn Mixed Green and Roasted Butternut Squash Salad, 132
  Mixed Herb Pesto with Brown Rice Pasta, 153
  Stir-Fried Bok Choy, Leeks and Pine Nuts, 99
  Stir-Fried Brown Rice and Vegetables, 101
pinto beans, 27, 41*t*, 120, 201
pistachios, 26, 166
planning, 54–55
plums, 26, 120
plum tomatoes, 264
Poached Eggs Florentine with Béarnaise Sauce, *78*, 79
pollutants, 16, 45
pomegranate juice, 26, 77
pomegranates, 26
popcorn, 27, 56, 166
poppy seeds, 26, 120, 134
pork, 27, 28, 235
porridge, 75
potatoes, 166
  Chicken Croquettes, 243
  Classic Meatloaf, 242
  red, 26, 235
  Red and Green Pepper Frittata, 225
  Slow Cooked Pot Roast with Root Vegetables, 246
  white, 26
potato starch
  Classic Sandwich, 241
  Gluten-Free Baking Mix, 265
  Gluten-Free Italian Loaf, 239
  Homemade Pasta, 226
  Maple Walnut Shortbread Cookies, 232
poultry, 28. *See also* chicken; turkey

preparing for the diet, 54–55
preservatives, 28
prices, 51
probiotics, 57, 58
prostoglandins, 15
protein, 27, 49, 56, 120, 166, 235. *See also specific sources*
prunes, 26, 120, 147
psyllium husk powder, 27, 37, 120, 134
pudding, 253
pumpkin, 26, 120
    Pumpkin Custard, 162
pumpkin seeds, 26, 39*t*, 120, 134
    Fruit and Nut Bars, 161
    Seed Sandwich Thins, 134

Q

quiches, 209
quinoa, 26, 34, 166, 234*t*
    Broccoli, Red Cabbage and Quinoa, 179
    Meatballs and Spaghetti Squash, 221

R

radishes, 26, 235
raisins, 26, 28, 235
    Banana Raisin Bread, 237
    Peach and Blackberry Chutney, 286
    Rice Pudding, 253
raspberries, 26
    Berry Frozen Dessert, 111
    Berry Pear Sauce, 274
    Coconut Berry Smoothie, 77
    Cran-Raspberry Glazed Salmon, 149
    Cran-Raspberry Sauce, 275
    Iced Minted Raspberry Green Tea, 163
    Make-Ahead Brown Rice Porridge with Mixed Berry Compote, 75
    Raspberry Lemonade Slushie, 231
    Raspberry Syrup, 288
    Whole Grain Waffles with Assorted Berries, 169
raspberry juice, 26
raw apple cider vinegar, 27, 38
recipes
    decoding, 64–65, *64–65*

grouping, 55
    as a template, 59
Red and Green Pepper Frittata, *224, 225*
red cabbage, 179, 189
red onions, 187, 199
Red Pepper Hummus, 182
red peppers, 166
    Chicken Fajitas, 219
    Kale Chips, 195
    Maryland Crab Cakes, 247
    Multicolored Stuffed Peppers, 217
    Red and Green Pepper Frittata, 225
    Red Pepper Hummus, 182
    Roasted Vegetables, 187
    Slow Cooked Vegetarian Tempeh Chili, 223
    Stir-Fried Chicken with Red Peppers and Cashews, 203
red potatoes, 26, 235
refined foods, 44
rice, 26, 234*t*
    Brown and Wild Rice Cauliflower and Mushroom Curry, 104
    Chicken Tamaki, 210
    Chicken Wild Rice and Vegetable Soup, 181
    Sautéed Salmon Cakes, 107
    Slow Cooked Brown Rice Risotto and Mushrooms, 109
    Steamed Vegetables and Brown and Wild Rice with Fresh Herb Vinaigrette, 93
    Stir-Fried Brown Rice and Vegetables, 101
    white, 28
rice cakes, 56
Rice Pudding, *252*, 253
risotto, 109
Roasted Vegetables, 187
Roast Rack of Lamb with Mustard Herb Crust, 143
romaine, 94
Roma tomatoes, 197, 199
rosemary, 27, 185

S

safflower oil, 27, 35, 166
sage, 27
salad dressings. *See* dressings

salads, 56
    Apple and Pear Salad with Honey Mustard Dressing, 133
    Autumn Mixed Green and Roasted Butternut Squash Salad, 132
    Calico Slaw, 95
    Chicken Salad, 140
    egg salad, 85
    Grilled Salmon over Assorted Greens with Fresh Herb Vinaigrette, 94
    Pickled Beets, 88
    Shredded Carrot Salad, 97
    Spinach and Lentil Salad with Warm Honey Vinegar Dressing, 131
    Summer Vegetable Medley Salad, 189
sales, 51
salmon, 27
    Cran-Raspberry Glazed Salmon, 149
    Grilled Salmon over Assorted Greens with Fresh Herb Vinaigrette, 94
    Moroccan Spice-Rubbed Salmon, *102*
    Sautéed Salmon Cakes, 107
salsa
    Breakfast Burritos, 176
    Fruit Salsa, 196
    Tomato Salsa, 197
salt, 28, 49
    sea salt, 27, 38, 56
    table salt, 29
Salted Roasted Chickpeas, 135
samples, asking for, 51
sandwiches
    Classic Sandwich, 241
    Seed Sandwich Thins, 134
    Stuffed Turkey Burger, 154
    Veggie Burgers, 201
sardines, 27
sauces, 270–289
    Béarnaise Sauce, 273
    Berry Pear Sauce, 274
    Blueberry Syrup, 277
    Even Oven-Roasted Marina Sauce, 280
    Garden Fresh Tomato Sauce, 281
    Horseradish Mustard Sauce, 289
    Miso Barbecue Sauce, 282
    Peach and Pineapple Dipping

Sauce, 285
Peachy Barbecue Sauce, 279
Tzatziki Sauce, 278
Zabaglione Sauce, 272
sauerkraut, 58
Sautéed Filet of Sole with Artichoke Pesto, 110
Sautéed Salmon Cakes, *106*, 107
Savory Vegetable and Herb Biscotti, *86*, 89
scallions, 26, 235
   Chickpea and Sweet Potato Patties, 139
   Fruit Salsa, 196
   Peach and Blackberry Chutney, 286
   Stir-Fried Brown Rice and Vegetables, 101
   Stir-Fried Chicken with Red Peppers and Cashews, 203
   Tomato Salsa, 197
seafood. *See also* fish; shrimp; *specific kinds of fish*
Seared Peppered London Broil, *212*, 213
sea salt, 27, 38, 56
sea vegetables, 37
seeds, 26, 28, 39, 56, 120, 134, 166, 235. *See also specific kinds of seeds*
sensitivities, 16
servings, 48
Sesame Chicken Tenders, 141
sesame oil, 28, 210
sesame seeds, 26, 120, 239
   Fruit and Nut Bars, 161
   Seed Sandwich Thins, 134
   Sesame Chicken Tenders, 141
   Tahini, 263
   Veggie Burgers, 201
shallots
   Broiled Shrimp with Shallots and Tomatoes and Herbs, 245
   Butternut Squash and Apple Soup, 185
   Cream of Tomato Bisque, 200
   Garlic-Shallot Mayonnaise (Aioli), 271
   Sautéed Filet of Sole with Artichoke Pesto, 110
   Slow Cooked Brown Rice Risotto and Mushrooms, 109
   Spinach and Sun-Dried Tomato Quiche, 209
shellfish, 27, 28, 235. *See also* shrimp
Shepherd's Pie, 211
shopping, 55
Shredded Carrot Salad, *52*, 58, 97, *97*
shrimp, 245
sides
   Broccoli, Red Cabbage and Quinoa, 179
   Calico Slaw, 95
   Chickpea and Sweet Potato Patties, 139
   Cinnamon Applesauce, 96
   Classic Sandwich, 241
   Corn Fritters, 186
   Crispy Kale, 95
   Deviled Eggs, 85
   Gluten-Free Italian Loaf, 239
   Green Beans with Shiitake Mushrooms and Almonds, 98
   Guacamole, 199
   Indian Chickpea and Spinach Fritters, 129
   Mashed Cauliflower, 96
   Pickled Beets, 88
   Red Pepper Hummus, 182
   Roasted Vegetables, 187
   Savory Vegetable and Herb Biscotti, 89
   Slow Cooked Baked Beans, 191
   Soft Flour Tortillas, 177
   Steamed Vegetables and Brown and Wild Rice with Fresh Herb Vinaigrette, 93
   Stir-Fried Bok Choy, Leeks and Pine Nuts, 99
   White Bean and Sun-Dried Tomato Spread, 183
   Zucchini Corn Bake, 193
Singleton, Kenneth B., 16, 234
   Chronic Inflammation Self-Assessment Tool, 19, 20–21
   on food sensitivities and testing, 69
   The Lyme Disease Solution, 19
   Lyme Inflammation Diet, 23–51
slaws, 95
sleep, lack of, 17
Sloppy Joes, *204*, 205
Slow Cooked Baked Beans, *190*, 191
Slow Cooked Brown Rice Risotto and Mushrooms, *108*, 109
Slow Cooked Pot Roast with Root Vegetables, 246
Slow Cooked Pulled Chicken, 207
Slow Cooked Vegetarian Tempeh Chili, 223
sludge, 45–46
smoke point, 43
smoking, 16–17
smoothies
   Coconut Berry Smoothie, 77
   Green Smoothie, 84
   Mango Pineapple Smoothie, 238
   Peanut Butter Banana Smoothie, 170
snacks
   Artichoke Hummus, 138
   Crispy Kale, 95
   Curried Cashews, 135
   Fruit and Nut Bars, 161
   Guacamole, 199
   Indian Chickpea and Spinach Fritters, 129
   Kale Chips, 195
   Salted Roasted Chickpeas, 135
   Savory Vegetable and Herb Biscotti, 89
   Seed Sandwich Thins, 134
   snack ideas, 56
snow peas, Summer Vegetable Medley Salad, 189
sodas, 28
sodium, 49. *See also* salt
Soft Flour Tortillas, 177
   Breakfast Burritos, 176
   Chicken Fajitas, 219
   Greek Ground Lamb Crumble, 218
sole, 27, 110
sorbitol, 27, 120
sorghum, 26, 34, 166, 234*t*
sorghum flour
   Gluten-Free Baking Mix, 265
   Gluten-Free Italian Loaf, 239
   Maple Walnut Shortbread Cookies, 232
soups
   Beef Broth, 264
   Butternut Squash and Apple Soup, 185
   Cauliflower Carrot Soup, 91
   Chicken Bone Broth, 264
   Chicken Wild Rice and Vegetable

Soup, 181
Cream of Tomato Bisque, 200
Creamy Asparagus Soup, 87
Lentil Soup, 137
Vegetable Broth, 259
sour cream, 176
souvlaki, 151
soybean products, 27, 37, 41*t*, 166
spaghetti squash, Meatballs and Spaghetti Squash, 221
specialty stores, 46
spices, 27, 120, 166, 235. *See also specific spices*
Spicy Rub, *256*, 266
spinach, 26, 56
   Indian Chickpea and Spinach Fritters, 129
   Mixed Herb Pesto with Brown Rice Pasta, 153
   Poached Eggs Florentine with Béarnaise Sauce, 79
   Sautéed Filet of Sole with Artichoke Pesto, 110
   Savory Vegetable and Herb Biscotti, 89
   Spinach and Lentil Salad with Warm Honey Vinegar Dressing, *130*, 131
   Spinach and Sun-Dried Tomato Quiche, *208*, 209
   Stuffed Turkey Burger, 154
   Vegetable Broth, 259
split peas, 41*t*
spreads, 183
sprouts, 26
squash, 26, 120
   Autumn Mixed Green and Roasted Butternut Squash Salad, 132
   Butternut Squash and Apple Soup, 185
   Meatballs and Spaghetti Squash, 221
Standard American Diet (SAD), 14
starches, 36–37
Steamed Vegetables and Brown and Wild Rice with Fresh Herb Vinaigrette, *92*, 93
stevia, 27, 36
stews, 147
Stir-Fried Bok Choy, Leeks and Pine Nuts, *53*, 99, *99*
Stir-Fried Brown Rice and Vegetables, *100*, 101
Stir-Fried Chicken with Red Peppers and Cashews, *202*, 203
strawberries, 26, 166
   Berry Frozen Dessert, 111
   Strawberry Ice Cream, 229
string beans, 26, 94
Stuffed Turkey Burger, 154
sugar, 18, 49. *See also* coconut palm sugar; sweeteners
   cravings for, 29
sulfites, 29
Summer Vegetable Medley Salad, *188*, 189
sun-dried tomatoes, 183
sunflower seed oil, 27, 166
sunflower seeds, 26, 120
   Fruit and Nut Bars, 161
   Granola, 121
   Kale Chips, 195
   Seed Sandwich Thins, 134
   Veggie Burgers, 201
supplements, 29. *See also specific supplements*
sushi, 210
Sweet and Tangy Baked Chicken, 145
sweeteners, 27, 28, 31, 35–36, 120. *See also* coconut palm sugar; honey; maple syrup; sugar
sweet potatoes, 26, 56, 120, 139
sweets, 28. *See also* baked goods; desserts
symptoms journal, 32–33

T

tagine, 147
Tahini, 138, 263
tamari, 27, 37, 166
   Chicken Tamaki, 210
   Fruity Glaze, 288
   Honey Battered Chicken, 222
   Miso Barbecue Sauce, 282
tapioca (cassava), 26, 37, 120
tapioca flour
   Homemade Pasta, 226
   Maple Walnut Shortbread Cookies, 232
   Soft Flour Tortillas, 177
tapioca starch
   Classic Sandwich, 241
   Gluten-Free Baking Mix, 265
   Gluten-Free Italian Loaf, 239
tea, 26, 120
   cultured, 57
   Iced Minted Raspberry Green Tea, 163
   Mint Tea, 117
teff, 26, 34, 166, 234*t*
tempeh, 27, 37, 166, 223
testing, 69
thickeners, 37
thyme, 27, 182
   Almond and Herb Crusted Tilapia, 105
   Béarnaise Sauce, 273
   Broiled Shrimp with Shallots and Tomatoes and Herbs, 245
   Chicken Milanese, 249
   Greek Ground Lamb Crumble, 218
   Grilled Chicken Souvlaki, 151
   Multicolored Stuffed Peppers, 217
   Roast Rack of Lamb with Mustard Herb Crust, 143
   Spicy Rub, 266
   Summer Vegetable Medley Salad, 189
   Vegetable Broth, 259
   Zucchini Corn Bake, 193
tilapia, 27, 105
Toasted Coconut Almond Muffins, 173
tofu, 27, 166
tomatoes, 26, 166
   Broiled Shrimp with Shallots and Tomatoes and Herbs, 245
   Chicken Bone Broth, 264
   Chicken Wild Rice and Vegetable Soup, 181
   Cream of Tomato Bisque, 200
   Even Oven-Roasted Marina Sauce, 280
   Garden Fresh Tomato Sauce, 281
   Roasted Vegetables, 187
   Slow Cooked Vegetarian Tempeh Chili, 223
   Tomato Salsa, 197
   White Bean and Sun-Dried Tomato Spread, 183
tomato paste
   Easy Spicy Ketchup, 287
   Even Oven-Roasted Marina Sauce, 280

Mediterranean Chicken, 215
Multicolored Stuffed Peppers, 217
Sloppy Joes, 205
Tomato Salsa, 176, 197
tomato sauce
   Meatballs and Spaghetti Squash, 221
   Multicolored Stuffed Peppers, 217
Tortilla Chips, 177
tortillas
   Breakfast Burritos, 176
   Soft Flour Tortillas, 177
   Traditional Soft Corn Tortilla, 206
toxins, 16, 22, 45
Traditional Soft Corn Tortilla, 206
trail mix, 56
trans-fatty acids, 28
tumeric
   Brown and Wild Rice Cauliflower and Mushroom Curry, 104
   Lamb with Apricots and Prunes Tagine, 147
turkey, 27, 120, 166
   Classic Meatloaf, 242
   Multicolored Stuffed Peppers, 217
   rotisserie, 56
   Shepherd's Pie, 211
   Stuffed Turkey Burger, 154
turnips, 26, 235, 246
tyramine, 31
Tzatziki Sauce, 218, 278

U

USDA
   National Organic Program, 45
   USDA Organic seal, 46

V

vanilla extract, 27
Vegetable Broth, 259
vegetable juice, 26, 120
vegetable oils, 28. *See also specific oils*

vegetables, 26, 28, 56, 166, 235
   Chicken Wild Rice and Vegetable Soup, 181
   cultured, 57
   growing your own, 50
   Roasted Vegetables, 187
   Steamed Vegetables and Brown and Wild Rice with Fresh Herb Vinaigrette, 93
   Stir-Fried Brown Rice and Vegetables, 101
   Summer Vegetable Medley Salad, 189
   Veggie Burgers, 201
Veggie Burgers, 201
venison, 27, 120
vinaigrettes, 93, 94, 95
vinegar, 27, 38, 56, 166, 280
viruses, 15
vitamins, 49

W

waffles, 169
wakame, 26, 37, 120
walnuts, 26, 39*t*
   Apple and Nut Skillet, 83
   Applesauce Walnut Tea Bread, 175
   Autumn Mixed Green and Roasted Butternut Squash Salad, 132
   Banana Raisin Bread, 237
   Date Nut Bread, 171
   Fruit and Nut Bars, 161
   Honey Nut Bars, 159
   Maple Walnut Shortbread Cookies, 232
   Nutty Coconut Delight, 113
   Stir-Fried Brown Rice and Vegetables, 101
wasabi, 26, 120, 210
water, 26, 120
watercress, 26, 235
Watermelon Lime Cooler, *230*, 231
watermelons, 26, 120, 231

White Bean and Sun-Dried Tomato Spread, 183
white beans, 183. *See also* cannellini beans; Great Northern beans; navy beans
whole grains, 28, 42–43
Whole Grain Waffles with Assorted Berries, *168*, 169
wild rice, 26, 234*t*
   Brown and Wild Rice Cauliflower and Mushroom Curry, 104
   Chicken Wild Rice and Vegetable Soup, 181
   Steamed Vegetables and Brown and Wild Rice with Fresh Herb Vinaigrette, 93

X

xanthan gum, 27, 37, 166
xylitol, 27, 35, 36, 120

Y

yams, 26, 235
yeast, 27, 235
   nutritional, 27, 38, 166
yellow peppers
   Chicken Fajitas, 219
   Maryland Crab Cakes, 247
   Multicolored Stuffed Peppers, 217
   Roasted Vegetables, 187
yogurt, 27, 57, 166, 278

Z

Zabaglione Sauce, 157, 272
zucchini
   Chicken Wild Rice and Vegetable Soup, 181
   Lentil Soup, 137
   Roasted Vegetables, 187
   Zucchini Corn Bake, *192*, 193

About the Authors

Gail Piazza has developed and tested recipes and styled food for movies, television commercials, print ads and packaging for many high-profile clients for over forty years. In addition to authoring this cookbook, she wrote *The World of Wok Cookery*, and has also collaborated on a half-dozen other cookbooks. She has developed, adapted or tested recipes for numerous projects and clients; worked with small appliance designers to refine and test their products; and provided props and styled food for print, movies and television commercials. Her extensive list of clients has included All-Clad, Dr. Andrew Weil, Emeril Lagasse, Tony Little, Lennox, Krups, Farberware and Hamilton Beach/Proctor-Silex Inc.

Laura Piazza is an award-winning Certified Professional Photographer and graphic designer and has created thousands of design projects for many employers and clients. She is the graphic designer at University of New Hampshire at Manchester and operates her own freelance graphic design and photography business, Piazza Creative (www.piazzacreative.com). She photographed the recipes featured in this book, designed the book and is the voice behind their website, www.recipesforrepair.com. Still battling chronic Lyme disease, she speaks at events on the topics of Lyme disease prevention and the important role good nutrition plays when battling any illness, in the hope that she can help others facing similar challenges.

The Story Behind the Book

With Gail's culinary talents, years in the industry and nurturing personality, it was natural for Gail to offer to develop delicious, nutritious recipes for her daughter's health and recovery process when Laura first discovered and wanted to try the Lyme Inflammation Diet. Shortly after trying some of her mom's recipes, Laura came up with an idea to combine their unique skills to create collaborative cookbook with recipes and tips specific to the diet. After hearing from readers of the far-reaching benefits of the diet they have made major revisions, updates and additions in this new expanded second edition. Now those with *any* inflammatory condition, and those wishing to discover hidden food sensitivities and combat chronic inflammation with nutrition have a resource that will allow them to do just that. To read their full story and get even more diet tips and recipes, visit their website, **www.recipesforrepair.com.**